To the Midnight Sun

A STORY OF REVOLUTION, EXILE AND RETURN

STEPHEN SALETAN

For my grandmother

Посвящается бабушке

Contents

PREFACE

Why do family stories continue to fascinate us? Because they preserve memories that would otherwise fade and disappear, of course. And because they link us to our legacy, helping us to better understand who we are. But perhaps most of all, it is because they are *our* stories, their characters the people we know and love. They are about *us*.

And yet, family stories are not purely personal. They unfold against a backdrop of history.

To the Midnight Sun is one such story. It recounts the adventures of my paternal grandmother, Eda Grigorievna Bamuner, as a young revolutionary in tsarist Russia at the turn of the twentieth century and the events that take her from her comfortable life in the ancient Russian city of Pskov to an isolated settlement of prisoners and political exiles in Russia's remote far north; from which she manages to escape, but not before beginning a love affair with a fellow young exile destined later to become a hero of the Russian Revolution and Civil War and, eventually, People's Commissar of Military and Naval Affairs, commander of all Soviet armed forces. It tells of how she comes to America; but tethered by family ties and her lingering youthful ideals of freedom and revolution, and by some innate, unbreakable tie to Russia and Russianness, how she returns to Russia during the 1920s and 30s, finally taking me with her in the 1960s to meet my relatives in the crumbling but still darkly imposing city of Leningrad, today's St. Petersburg. And how her ten siblings, who remain behind, survive World War I and the Russian Revolution, eventually settling together in a version of that peculiarly Soviet phenomenon, the communal apartment, in an ornate building dating from 1832, once a grand cosmopolitan dwelling but now a dilapidated relic heated in the winter by wood-burning stoves. And of how her youngest brother, a well-known photographer who works in the avant-garde, heroic-constructivist style of early Soviet art, dies of starvation during the Nazi blockade of Leningrad during World War II. And finally, of how I return to Russia in the 1990s to investigate the deeper layers of the story and reconnect with my cousins, newly freed from communist rule but still living in the same apartment first settled by their grandparents in the 1920s. All of which can be taken to affirm that family stories, indeed, unfold against a backdrop of history.

Revolution, arrest, exile, escape, and return trips to Russia: these were the stories I first heard as a child when my grandmother came to visit us in our quiet suburban home on Long Island. The historical scale and drama of the world that she came from – and with her frequent return trips to Russia, still inhabited – fascinated me. The contrast with my bland suburban world was almost unimaginable. Gradually the stories became part of my worldview, as if they were somehow part of my own past. On summer visits to her country cottage in Westchester County, surrounded by a community of like-minded Russian émigré idealists and artists, it felt as if

I'd already half-made the journey back to her homeland. And then, suddenly, the year I turned thirteen, she announced her intention to bring one of her grandchildren along on her next trip to Russia. I was the one who knew all the stories and the names of the Russian relatives; it soon became clear that I was the one to go. That summer, I traveled with her to Leningrad and met my Russian great-uncles, aunts, and cousins, all still living in the old family communal apartment on the city's Vladimirsky Prospekt. I had been inducted into the family history. Eventually, I came to realize that I would write the story one day, and that to write it I would have to return to Russia.

To the Midnight Sun is an exploration of the ways in which legacy and history help form our identity and shape our lives. It is a story about uncovering the meaning of the past, of how certain places play a crucial role in this process, and what it feels like when we make these discoveries, these connections, when we are in those places. And while my grandmother's story unfolds against the backdrop of Russian history and culture, with their own very specific qualities, her saga of exile, emigration, and the longing to stay connected to cultural identity and family roots is one that resonates across American society for a majority of people of widely varying backgrounds. In that sense, *To the Midnight Sun* is a very American story.

My opportunity to return to Russia arose serendipitously when the Soviet Union collapsed in 1991. Or perhaps not so serendipitously, since by the late 1980s communist Russia was in an obvious state of slow-motion collapse. It felt almost natural when the cousins I had first met as a child in closed-off Leningrad were suddenly able to board an airplane to come visit their American relatives and see how the rest of the world lived. The Iron Curtain that had penned them in seemed an absurd anachronism in the open, interconnected world of the late twentieth century. And just as suddenly, I was able leave New York of an evening and find myself the next day strolling down the Nevsky Prospekt in the timeworn but still majestic, as-if-preserved-in-amber city I remembered from childhood: the newly free and now rechristened St. Petersburg. After an initial visit, I arranged to return for an extended stay to investigate my grandmother's story more deeply. Up to that point I knew only the fragments she had told me when I was a child, along with a tape recording my uncle had suggested we make when she was already in her eighties. He had gone with her to Leningrad in 1932, when he was seven, and lived in the family communal apartment on Vladimirsky Prospekt for a year. He spoke Russian fluently and over the years had returned to Russia many times. But even he felt he didn't know the whole saga and that we should capture what we could for posterity before it was too late. At one point during the taping my grandmother suddenly switched from English into Russian. "Mom," my uncle said, "hearing you speak Russian is wonderful for me, but please switch back to English so everyone else can understand."

Yet even after the taping session, the story was incomplete. By the time I went to St. Petersburg in 1998 to carry out my research, I had learned Russian. It was a pragmatic necessity, but also something I'd longed to do since first hearing my grandmother speak Russian when I was a child. As I worked through the archives that summer and visited the places where the adventures had taken place, I came to understand that the story would never have fully come alive if I hadn't been able to read for myself the documents I discovered and speak personally with the generous Russian historians who kindly agreed to help me. And, as I later realized, if I hadn't been able to go back to the part of the tape where my grandmother switched to Russian and finally understand what she had said.

The new freedom of the 1990s afforded academic and non-professional researchers alike an unprecedented opportunity to access formerly sealed-off government archives; the trove of documents I found confirmed some things I already knew and revealed some fascinating new secrets. The nineties were a time of optimism in Russia, despite the chaos and economic woes of the Yeltsin years. There was relative freedom of the press and media and people were generally unafraid to speak openly, despite a lingering hangover after seventy years of Soviet surveillance, censorship, and violent repression. There was even a lively gay scene in St. Petersburg. I, along with many others, did not anticipate how rapidly the window would slam shut and Russia sink back again into the very worst of its bad old ways.

As much as the beauty of Russian culture captivated me as a child, when I went to Leningrad I quickly realized that my relatives lived in a kind of prison. The menace of the Soviet police state was like a kind of faint soundtrack continuously echoing in the background. Yet somehow they evaded the danger, resisted the monotony, and managed to live meaningful lives. This was part of what fascinated me, what made it seem that the stage was larger and the drama more heroic. One could fairly say that resistance to oppressive, brutal government has long been a hallmark of Russian life and society, from the Decembrists of the early 1800s to the era of my grandmother's youth, and throughout the dark period of Soviet oppression. It was the force that inspired Eda and her fellow revolutionary idealists, persisted through the Soviet period, and ultimately spelled the doom of communist rule in 1991. It is what motivated writers like Turgenev and Tolstoy and, later, any number of Soviet authors, dissidents, artists, and emigres. Whether the Russian people will once again be able to bring down a corrupt, dictatorial regime that treats its citizens as prisoners and seeks to conquer neighboring nations, as they did twice before in 1917 and 1991, is as yet unknown. But the fact that I knew so many people there committed to decency, culture, education, and art gives me hope that one day they will.

PART I

BOLSHEVIKS AND THE PTA

CHAPTER I. MY RUSSIAN GRANDMOTHER

My Russian grandmother was a revolutionary. Or, as she would say in the mild Russian accent she retained to the end of her life, "I was a *ryev uh lyoo shun ery*," with a dramatic pause for emphasis on the drawn-out third syllable.

My Russian grandmother. Never mind that she arrived in America half a century before I was born. Never mind that she spoke English as well as her native Russian—well, almost, and to tell the truth, never with as much passion. Never mind that she raised her firstborn, my father, just like any other American child, speaking English; although she came to her senses a decade later when her second son was born and she brought him up speaking Russian as his first language. To the family she left behind in Russia she became an American. For me she always remained, simply, my Russian grandmother.

Her name, after all, was Eda Grigorievna Bamuner. Even as a child I somehow knew that real Russians had three names, with the middle one coming from the father. I'm not sure how—I just knew. With my grandmother, the emphasis was always on her three full names, including that very Russian middle one.

She grew up in the ancient Russian city of Pskov in the last decade of the nineteenth century and the first decade of the twentieth, the years of epochal change that finally pulled Russia into the modern world and transformed it into the potent shaper of the twentieth century that it became. Her family was Jewish, but unlike most Jews in virulently antisemitic tsarist Russia they were able to live in comfortable, privileged circumstances. My great-grandfather owned an elegant tailor shop on the city's main square that produced uniforms for the local army regiment along with stylish civilian clothing, as his advertisements proudly proclaimed. Because of his success in business, the Bamuner family was allowed to live outside the Pale of Settlement, the part of Russia to which Jews were normally restricted. And so my grandmother grew up in the small but gradually expanding community of assimilated Russian Jews—Jewish by last name and heritage but primarily Russian by language and culture—and received a classical education at Pskov's academic women's high school.

And yet, despite all these advantages, despite the promise of a privileged and secure life, she chose the cause of revolution. As my grandmother was growing up, Russia was still ruled by the tsar as absolute monarch, its social system rigid and hierarchical, and political freedom nonexistent. At the same time, the modern era that had been transforming America and Western Europe since the 1880s—mechanization and industrialization on a colossal, previously unimaginable scale, vastly expanding travel and communication and radically changing the material and social conditions of everyday life—had finally begun to seep into even faraway, conservative

Russia. (When I was a child listening to my grandmother's stories, this part fascinated me especially—the background was storybook, fairytale Russia, horse-drawn carriages and sleighs, forests, frozen rivers, Victorian-era dresses for the women and frock coats and high collars for the men; but the foreground was trains, transatlantic travel, and education, work and social life that sounded not too different from the contemporary world I knew. She was the living link to a bygone time and place; and at the same time to the very beginning of the new, modern world that I lived in, that she and I lived in together.) This spark of modernism and the intense tension it provoked within the backward social and political environment of late imperial Russia was the kindling that ignited my grandmother's revolutionary ardor—and ultimately fed the revolutionary flames that transformed Russia completely.

At the same time, of equal or perhaps even greater importance was her own character. The times, one might say, were necessary but not sufficient. History shapes individuals, and individuals shape their own histories. My grandmother was precocious, headstrong and rebellious, and she grew up in a milieu—Russia's new middle class—in which she was able to get an education, a distinct rarity for women at the time. Her mother died when she was a teenager, thrusting her into the role of surrogate mother to her nine younger siblings and surrogate head of her father's large and elaborate household. Her father was old-fashioned, patriarchal and tyrannical in the way of his time and place, but my grandmother made up her mind to defy him. And she succeeded.

For my grandmother, revolution signified the idealistic struggle for freedom and equality. The bitter truth of Russian revolutionary politics emerged only later, after she had fled her homeland. Only when she returned in the 1930s to rejoin her family and possibly settle in the Soviet Union permanently did she see for herself the harsh reality of what the Russian Revolution had brought.

"I was revolutionary, from the age of sixteen," she used to tell me. "And when I was seventeen, I made a strike in Papa's shop." I always suspected a touch of hyperbole, but when I went to Russia years later to learn more about the stories I'd heard as a child, I came across a newspaper article about a strike in 1906 that halted production in the shop of the Pskov tailor Bamuner. The timing was exactly right.

My grandmother's illegal activities during the years of violent political upheaval that swept over Russia following the outbreak of a war with Japan in 1904—fomenting protests in her school, attending meetings of the outlawed Socialist Revolutionary Party, distributing forbidden revolutionary literature—might well have led to her own arrest; but in a strange twist of fate that perfectly captured the arbitrary application of repressive force in the police state that was tsarist Russia (a police state which paled, in comparison, with the one the Soviet Union was to become), it was her younger sister, Rulia, aged fifteen, who was suddenly arrested along with a group of other students in the spring of 1908. All were innocent of any crime except being the classmates of a student whose brother had attacked a government informer. (The authorities apparently found it easier simply to arrest and deport them all.) Rulia was held in the city jail for a year without a trial or judicial hearing. The following spring, along with fifteen other teenagers, she was sentenced to three years of exile in a remote, isolated village in the far north of Russia.

After Rulia received her sentence, my great-grandfather obtained permission for his teenage daughter to travel to the north on her own, rather than in a convoy with other prisoners, with my grandmother as chaperone and their father as guarantor that the sisters would reach their destination and report to the Governor of Arkhangelsk Province. Such was one of the peculiarities of political exile in tsarist times, where social distinctions were honored even among the convicted. My grandmother was of course prepared to go with her vulnerable younger sister to watch over and protect her, but her willingness was motivated at least as much by her own desire for adventure and the opportunity to meet with a new community of revolutionary exiles; to plot, perhaps, new revolutionary deeds. When my grandmother boarded the train for Arkhangelsk in April 1909, she did not yet know she would never return to Pskov. If she had, she would undoubtedly have gone anyway.

The sisters left Pskov at the beginning of spring, the time of year when the days are getting warmer, but Russia still struggles to shed the last, lingering effects of the long winter. Rulia's sentence stipulated that she travel to a distant outpost of Arkhangelsk Province, to one of the remote settlements that could be reached only by sailing across the White Sea. Until late May, the sea remained icebound. After their arrival in Arkhangelsk, the sisters stayed in the provincial capital for a few days before being sent to the nearby city of Kholmogory, to live there in the colony of exiles until the opening of navigation. Only then would they set off on the final leg of their journey, to the isolated village of Mezen.

Arkhangelsk, Kholmogory, Mezen. Together with Pskov, these were the names that limned my grandmother's Russian universe, names that only she could articulate properly, in the sonorous, orotund tones of the Russian language. Or Mezen', to render it in its accurate transliteration, the apostrophe indicating the Russian soft sign, which transforms the final consonant from a sharp ending that snaps shut into a light, whistling puff that floats softly away on the air.

And just as my grandmother was making her way to Arkhangelsk, in a separate but parallel script written by a different scenarist and shot by a different crew—by the kind of chance event, the unforeseen coincidence that so frequently helps to write history—another political exile arrived in Mezen just a few months earlier. A young revolutionary, about my grandmother's age, from a working-class family in the Lugansk province of Ukraine, who had already been arrested for revolutionary activities several times; this was his third stint in exile. His name was Kliment Efremovich Voroshilov—or Klim, as he was known to his intimates—who in the coming decades was to become one of the most senior leaders, grim-faced and hardened, of the fearsome Soviet Union, but who, in Mezen in the summer of 1909 was still young, dashing, and idealistic. Soon after my grandmother arrived in Mezen, she and Voroshilov met. And shortly after they met, the two young revolutionaries began a love affair.

Their relationship changed profoundly both the fate of my grandmother and that of the numerous siblings she left behind. Two decades later, when she decided to return to the Soviet Union, she was able to do so only under the protection of Voroshilov. If she had not known Voroshilov, her siblings and their families would likely never have survived the Stalin era. When my grandmother rejoined her family in Russia in 1932, she changed the familiar story of emigration and rupture into one of continued connection. In the end, she returned to America, but her relatives continued to depend on the family link to Voroshilov for their very lives.

Following World War II, my grandmother began making return trips to Russia again, eventually bringing me with her to Leningrad in 1963 to meet my cousins and cement the ties of our Russian American family into a new generation. To cement the ties, but also to connect me to the long thread of the story that had begun in the last years of pre-revolutionary tsarist Russia and endured through the turbulent decades of the twentieth century, until the final collapse of the Soviet Union in 1991. With the fall of Communism, my cousins and I were able to start traveling freely in and out of Russia for the first time and to meet again after thirty years, amidst the feeling that Russia might finally be transforming itself into a modern country with freedom of speech, thought, and behavior.

Or that was the hope, at least, during the nineties, chaotic and difficult as those years were—the years before the arrival of Vladimir Putin and a new dictatorship as oppressive and brutal as any Russia has ever known.

CHAPTER 2.

BOLSHEVIKS AND THE PTA

When I was a child growing up in one of the countless suburbs that had sprung up across Long Island during the 1950s, I would look around at my bland surroundings and try to imagine what else might exist beyond the monotonous rows of black asphalt streets, gray concrete sidewalks, and identical little brown shingle houses. Everything was brand new—a place without history.

The answer arrived on Friday afternoons, when my Russian grandmother came to visit.

My parents had left New York City when I was six months old, along with my two-year-old brother and four-year-old sister. Though New Yorkers by birth and temperament, the daunting prospect of raising children in the city had convinced them to follow the tide of America's postwar suburban migration. Our family gradually adapted to the strange, featureless new world of identical little houses, but New York City remained the lodestar, longingly remembered.

And yet, as cut off as our suburban world felt from New York, less than a mile beyond the turnout onto the old main road that bordered the subdivision (and served as a reminder that something older had actually once existed there; in the nearby woods, the remains of long-forgotten Jazz Age estates could just be glimpsed amidst the dense undergrowth) there stood the alluring, mysterious link to the world we had left behind: the train station that sent my father to Manhattan each morning for work and brought my grandmother every Friday to tell us stories of distant, more vivid worlds.

From earliest childhood I loved going to the station. Unimpressive and dilapidated though it was, it represented the magical gateway to places beyond our circumscribed little world.

On Friday afternoons, my grandmother would not so much arrive as sweep in, trailing in her wake the aura of Europe, Russia, and the places whose exotic-sounding names—Pskov, Riga, Leningrad, Arkhangelsk, the White Sea—transfixed me with some irresistibly seductive power. Pskov, the ancient Russian city where she grew up. The very ring of it—unpronounceable really, except by her—conjured some essence of Russianness. A faint trace of Russia and my grandmother's youthful adventures accompanied her every time she stepped off the train. At the first sound of her voice, like the scent of ozone before the lightning, I sensed the presence of her past life.

Shortly before my grandmother's train was due to arrive, my mother would round up her three young children, bundle us into the back seat of the red family Plymouth, and set off for the station. We drove along the tree-lined main road, dappled with shadows from the latticework of branches overhead, turned onto the avenue to the station, and parked in the blacktop parking lot of the new local grocery store, where we waited for the sound of the train whistle. A minute or two after we heard its shrill crescendo moving toward us, a hulking grey diesel engine with two or three dusty cars in tow rumbled over the crossing grade and jerked to a halt. The car doors slid slowly open, letting passengers out onto a little platform from which they descended, gingerly, to the gravelly strip below.

My grandmother appeared on the train platform, gazing about her somewhat unsteadily. She was fairly short and amply built and had a way of carrying herself that seemed to confer a certain authority but that involved a slight swaying motion; her capacious patent leather shoes, usually ivory-colored, were always high-heeled. This all required some concentration. She had a tendency to lean back, as if to ensure that she maintained her modest full height at all times. The postural complexity made descending the metal Long Island Railroad steps a moderately hazardous affair. Unlike the old days in Europe, no attendant stood by to assist.

She was a messenger from a series of magical worlds that fanned out in space and time far beyond the bland, recently plowed-under potato field world in which we now lived, a world which yielded up no more history than the occasional rotting tuber that appeared when one of the suburban homesteaders turned over the soil to plant grass or a new border hedge. That very day she had come from New York, more particularly from Manhattan, and Greenwich Village. Before that, sometime in the last decade or so, she had returned from one of her periodic trips to Europe and Russia. In the early 1930s she had moved to Russia for a year with her young son, my uncle, and lived with her Russian brothers and sisters in the communal family apartment in Leningrad on the street with the fateful-sounding name, Vladimirsky

Prospekt—like Pskov, a name and place that formed as much a part of my childhood universe as the Arbor Lane on which our family actually lived.

All of this, as she descended the steps of the sooty Long Island railroad car onto the asphalt strip of Albertson Station, came along with her.

We waited for the crossing guard with its flashing red signal and clanging bell to lift and ran across the tracks to greet her. Tugging at the cache of packages she had, as always, dangling from her arm, we walked her back to the car. As we climbed into the back, my grandmother arranged herself in the front seat next to my mother.

As if by some unspoken agreement, my mother waited, silently and with slight impatience, as my grandmother clicked open her pocketbook, removed her compact, reapplied her lipstick, and placed a used tissue between her lips, adding yet another crescent-shaped, glossy red imprint to the fluffy white surface. While this ritual proceeded, my mother gradually tightened her grip on the steering wheel, though we were not yet moving. With the tissue finally refolded and replaced in my grandmother's purse, we backed out of the parking lot and set off on the short ride home. As we drove, I strained to hear what was being said in the front seat, where an uneasy truce had taken hold.

My mother tried dutifully to begin a conversation. In answer to her questions about some touring Russian dance troupe coming to the City Center or a finer point of Kremlin politics she had read about in the morning paper, my grandmother merely nodded and muttered an occasional noncommittal answer. With the back of their heads just visible to me above the front seatback, I could see that neither turned to the other as she spoke.

Over time, I came to understand the problem: my mother had never managed to become a member of the family Russian brigade. This little unit came into existence when my grandmother and her younger sister Rulia first arrived in New York. Although they adapted—learning English, finding work, marrying—they remained attached to the old life in Russia, to their brothers and sisters, their friends, their youthful adventures. Until the end of their lives they spoke Russian to one another. And their first experience of New York, admittedly, was unsettling, after the polished surroundings of their life in Pskov, comfortably ensconced in the culture of Europe. When they moved into their first New York apartment, arranged by cousins who had preceded them, the frail and delicate young Rulia looked around and lamented, "How did we ever end up here, with underwear hanging from the pipes?"

My grandfather, whom my grandmother met and married soon after arriving in New York, also grew up in Russia and had only recently immigrated; but he was more interested in adapting to life in his new country than pining for the one he had left. And so, when my father was born, my grandfather insisted that he and my grandmother speak English at home. Improbably, my father never learned Russian.

By the time their second child arrived, ten years later, my grandparents had started to go their separate ways. My grandmother was thus able to speak Russian at home to her new son, my uncle Eugene. Rulia, whose marriage was also failing, happened to give birth to a daughter just a few months after Eugene was born; she also spoke to her new child, Sonia, only in Russian. The two sisters and their children became a little

Russian-speaking family unit. The Russian brigade had added two new members, this time born in the U.S. It was my uncle, of a very different, more bohemian temperament than my father, who became the family's next generation Russophone and Russophile. Partly because he was so much younger than my parents and never had children of his own, as a child I was very close to him. His bilingualism fascinated me, along with the fact that he had lived with my grandmother in Russia for a year when he was seven years old.

My mother also grew up in New York with parents who were born in Europe, but her mother came from a Yiddish-speaking Russian Jewish family for whom the assimilated ways of Eda Grigorievna Bamuner were completely alien. My mother had spent a year in school outside of Paris and spoke perfect French, but when my father brought her home to meet his parents and younger brother and they tried to teach her to say the Russian version of his nickname Lenny—'Lyonchik'—she could not manage the strange, thick syllables. The ordinarily soft and musical name came out sounding like "lunch" and "check." The Russian brigade dissolved in peals of laughter. The cerebral mindset of the French language suited my mother. The extravagant emotions of Russian went right over her head.

Years later, after I had become a member in good standing of the family Russian brigade and linchpin of the connection to the Russian cousins—in succession to my uncle—I realized that all through our childhood my grandmother had been watching her three grandchildren, wondering which one would join the brigade and continue the family Russian connection.

I slowly became aware of the complex generational drama playing out between my parents and my grandmother. For her, English was an adopted means of communication—she wore it easily, but like a cloak she longed to shed so she could return to expressing herself naturally, at full force. Her son spoke to her in his first language, but she answered him in her second. It seemed to create a kind of distance between them. When he called her "Mom" it sounded curt and American; it did not seem to fit this exotic Russian lady.

I wondered how it all fit together and where I fit in. Which world did I belong to? The practical, bland world of suburbia—elementary school, bicycles, the neighbors? Or was I part of a Russian-American family, culturally speaking? It was not a question of whether we were fully assimilated; that had been settled long ago and I was as American as apple pie with my dungarees, my sneakers, my crew cut, and my freckles. The question, rather, was existential.

My mother turned into the development, rounded the corner into our street and parked the car at the top of the driveway. Having discharged her duty by picking up and conversing with my grandmother, she walked briskly into the house and sat down at her desk to finish the memo she was writing for an upcoming meeting of the PTA. I helped my grandmother gather up her packages and overnight case and followed her into the house.

In the late afternoon, my mother left for New York to meet my father for their Friday evening out. Alone now with her grandchildren, my grandmother began to cast her spell.

We sat down in the kitchen as the bright afternoon light softened toward dusk. The house was perfectly quiet. My grandmother began her ritual—taking out her presents, and setting out on the kitchen table the letters and photos she had recently received from our cousins in Russia. We listened as she conjured for us, in her lilting accent, the long line of her life and drew us into her world.

She started to read the letter she had received from her brother Arkady in Leningrad, translating aloud as she moved her finger down the lines of elegant Cyrillic script. He had just retired—or perhaps, I sensed, fallen afoul of some authority and been punished—from his job as a journalist. His grandson, my cousin Sasha, was coming from Moscow to spend the school vacation with his grandparents. Sasha was making good progress in his English-language school; soon he would write to us in English, Arkady promised.

My grandmother showed us the snapshot that her brother Arkady had enclosed of himself, his wife, their daughter and son-in-law in his Red Army uniform, and their two young sons, Sasha and Sergey, all standing together on the balcony of the family apartment on Vladimirsky Prospekt in front of the elaborate carved stone façade of the building—unchanged, except for the traces of a century and a half of wear, since it was built in the early nineteenth century. They were unsmiling. I peered at the thin, angular faces that I had come to know over time, with their always-serious expressions, their modest clothing and spare surroundings. Their lives were impossibly remote; yet my cousin Sasha went to school just as I did; in a few months, he would be going for his vacation to the same Riga seaside where my grandmother and uncle had once spent a summer. We were connected in some way. I wondered if our lives could be anything alike.

Now my grandmother had us in thrall. The stark impressions of the present-day Soviet Union dissolved and mingled imperceptibly with warmer images of old Russia and my grandmother's childhood. By now only the silhouettes of the trees and houses were visible outside the kitchen window in the final moments of twilight. We sat under the cone of light from the kitchen lamp as the rest of the house grew dark. As I listened to my grandmother's stories, our surroundings seemed to transform—or so I imagined. Our house became a cottage; the trees outside were our woods. They were part of nature, not the artificial work of some suburban landscaper. Beyond them lay a forest. Something mysterious might be happening in the shadows outside, something besides commuters coming home from work and the evening walking of dogs.

With my grandmother in charge of the house, my incomprehension at the separate worlds I had inherited abated. The places she told us about made me believe that my bland surroundings might be more alive than I had been able to perceive—maybe our little community concealed marvels like the ones we heard about in her stories of Pskov, with its meadows and lakes and winter ice, and the slow river that coursed below the city's ancient Fortress Hill. Maybe such things could be found anywhere, if only you knew how to look for them.

Eventually, my sister wandered off to her room to read and my brother went to the backyard to practice throwing his ball against the garage. My grandmother gestured to me; I got out of my chair and walked over to her. She looked at me, pulled me toward her, and hugged me with her soft, fleshy arms. We both sensed which of her grandchildren was going to pick up the family Russian standard.

CHAPTER 3. AMERICAN DACHA

My grandmother's weekend visits ended every year in June, when she moved for the summer to her small country house in the eccentric rural enclave known as Mohegan Colony, in northern Westchester County. If ever there was any doubt that my grandmother could never relinquish the part of herself that was essentially Russian, a visit to her summer house in Mohegan Colony was enough to prove otherwise. For me, as a child, every trip to Mohegan was like a visit to a faraway, enchanted land. Each visit instilled in me, ever more deeply, a desire to follow her into that land, into her story.

In English my grandmother never called the house her dacha, though once I found out what a dacha was, I realized she must always have called it that when speaking to her Russian friends.

Mohegan Colony was founded in 1923 by Harry Kelly, an American anarchist who spent his youth in London among exiled radicals like the famous Russian anarchist Peter Kropotkin. The Colony, his second venture in the United States, was a vivid mix of fellow anarchists, Socialists, card-carrying Communists, unaffiliated bohemians, and square dancers. My grandmother was among the original subscribers. Kelly's prior attempt at creating a utopian-style communitarian settlement in rural New Jersey had ended in failure. Mohegan was organized along similar lines but more loosely, without the communal living. The colonists were mainly non-religious Russian Jews like my grandparents, with a few other leftist-anarchist Europeans—French, Italians, and Spaniards—sprinkled in. The majority lived in New York and came to Mohegan only in the summer. When I visited as a child, my grandmother and her friends still spoke, in hushed and doleful tones, of one of the neighbors, a Spaniard, who had gone back to Spain in the 1930s to fight for the Republicans in the Spanish Civil War and never returned. William Foster, one-time head of the Communist Party USA, had once lived in the Colony as well.

In Mohegan, surrounded by the woods and her community of fellow believers, my grandmother seemed each summer to metamorphose gradually back into her true Russian self. After shedding her formal city attire for one of the light, sleeveless summer dresses she always wore there, and her high-heeled shoes for the pair of old leather sandals that looked like they had just come from a market in Samarkand; after speaking to her next-door neighbors exclusively in Russian for a few days, spending afternoons at the lake, picking raspberries in the evening from the prickly bushes tangled in the shrubbery at the edge of her property, and cooking her first batch of summer beet borscht—she was transformed, or so I imagined, into the version of her young self she had been each summer at her family's dacha by the Riga seaside. She became, once again, the ardent young idealist, the revolutionary, who had not yet left for America.

It was only natural, of course, that my grandmother should have gone to Mohegan. Like all Russians, she loved the forest. Like all Russians, she loved rustic wooden houses. And like all Russians, she loved to commune with nature, above all with the thicket of white birch trees that luxuriated across the property, the serendipitous touch that so perfectly recalled the woods of her native Russia. Nature-love was inherent in the Russian temperament, inspired, I eventually came to understand, by the sweetness of the short, luxuriant Russian summers contrasting with the seemingly endless—but still beloved—snowbound winters. Besides, it was something that Leo Tolstoy had advised. And my grandmother, like all educated, liberal, cosmopolitan Russians at the turn of the twentieth century, was a great admirer of Tolstoy. On the bookshelf in her apartment in Manhattan, set against the thick volumes with heavy leather bindings tooled with Cyrillic letters, stood a porcelain plate with a portrait of Tolstoy, his intense blue eyes gazing out severely and his long white beard proclaiming the presence of a prophet.

Though it was just a few hours by car from Long Island and two or three hours by train from Manhattan, traveling to Mohegan was like a journey across continents, as if to some rural backwater of Eastern Europe. Every one of the sagging wooden houses was enshrouded in faded, peeling paint. The yards were overgrown with undernourished shoots of pale, permanently uncut grass and weeds. On more than a few properties a trailer that had once been unhitched for an overnight stay but for some reason had never moved again sat among the underbrush as the only permanent structure.

The year of my tenth birthday, just before my sister turned fourteen, our family was plunged into crisis.

When my sister turned thirteen, her behavior began to change drastically. She withdrew into herself and began to wear a perpetually sad expression. Just before her fourteenth birthday, she smashed a mirror in the locker room at the school gym and began to cut herself on both forearms. Taken for evaluation to a nearby psychiatric hospital where there was a unit specializing in the treatment of adolescents, she was admitted immediately and—suddenly, incomprehensibly— no longer at home. My parents, hesitant to go into detail but too enlightened to hide the basic information from my brother and myself, appeared to be in a state of shock as they explained: "Your sister is very sick, but she is getting the best care available. Everyone hopes she will get better and come home soon." She never came home to live with us again.

Visiting my sister at the hospital and conferring with her doctors began to occupy more and more of my parents' time. As the first summer of her hospitalization approached, the question of what to do with my brother and me arose, since my parents could not look after us at home while at the same time attending to the needs of my sister and her treatment program. For the last few summers my brother and sister had gone to sleepaway camp; I, a shy child, had demurred when the possibility was presented to me the previous summer, at the age of nine. For the coming summer, my brother would go to camp as before; when I again appeared hesitant, my parents—or was it perhaps my grandmother?—proposed an alternative: I would spend the summer in Mohegan. There was a day camp I could attend and, perhaps more decisively, take piano lessons with Frances Chesno, my grandmother's next-door neighbor and closest friend in the Colony. Frances, a professional violinist who had retired after a career in New York, now lived full-time in Mohegan with her retired dentist husband, Jack (both Russian born and raised, of course), in one of the rare houses that had been 'winterized,' teaching violin and piano to the local children while Jack spent his time sculpting in the basement studio below. On the days between my weekly lessons, I could practice on Frances's grand piano in the center of the house's open ground-floor living space, with its latticework of dark brown wooden beams supporting the raised loft ceiling overhead—a place that seemed, to me as a child, half fairy tale cottage and half sanctuary of music and art.

I had started occasional piano lessons with my mother a couple of years earlier; she had once played well and had brought her old Knabe grand piano to the new house on Long Island. I could already read music and play a few small pieces, and as I appeared to have aptitude and had expressed interest in taking lessons, my parents were already looking for a serious teacher for me in the fall. The opportunity to study with Frances over the summer seemed perfectly timed.

On a drowsy summer morning in late June, the family (including my sister, who had been released on a weekend pass) assembled in the driveway to pack up the car up for the journey to Westchester. A few hours later, we turned into the dirt driveway of my grandmother's house. As the summer tenants had not yet arrived, the whole family was to spend the weekend in the main part of the house, upstairs. In another week or two, my grandmother and I would move to the small basement apartment she had built after my grandfather moved out and she began to manage the house and property herself.

The front part of the upstairs house consisted of a small living room bordered by a short hallway leading to two minuscule bedrooms. In the middle of the living room, a boulder too large to have been removed from the ground when the land was cleared for the house to be built protruded through the wooden floor and served as a kind of coffee table. A few simple chairs were grouped around it. A daybed decorated with a multicolored pile of small pillows was pushed up against one wall. At the other end of the room, a large fireplace with a rough hearth made of stones pulled up during construction occupied the entire wall. The rustic décor, combined with the faint smell of earth, rock, and wood that always permeated the house's damp air, made me feel in Mohegan that I was somewhere deep in the country, far away from the neatly ordered world of my parents.

A small passageway led from the living room to a screened porch that ran the full width of the back of the house. The left side of the passage opened into the old-fashioned kitchen, connected to the screened porch by a large pass-through which we used at mealtimes to stack plastic soup bowls and the plates of sour cream, chopped vegetables, boiled eggs, and cold potatoes—known, collectively, as "the improvements"— that we added to the homemade borscht my grandmother served at almost every meal.

It was here, the weekend we arrived, that we enjoyed one of those rare occasions that took place once or twice each summer, when the whole family gathered on the porch— sometimes along with my young uncle and his wife, or my grandmother's sister Rulia, or even my grandfather, since he and my grandmother had never officially divorced and remained on good terms—and sat down together along the picnic-table style benches for a meal. I gazed in wonder at the animated scene of my family laughing, reaching across the table for the plates of improvements, basking in the uncomplicated ease of Mohegan life, so different from the normally somber, now entirely gloomy, atmosphere at home on Long Island. Even my eternally serious parents seemed to relax and lighten their mood. For a few hours, I sensed, they once again became the young couple they had been twenty years earlier, when they first visited Mohegan and my mother, intrigued but not quite comprehending, experienced for the first time the warmth of family life, Russian style.

The next morning, after the rest of the family left for Long Island, my grandmother took me to Mohegan Lake to register for day camp. In the afternoon, we went to visit the Chesnos, where Frances gently coaxed me to sit down at the piano and play a few pieces, so that she could begin to plan my lessons.

After a few weeks, I had learned my first piece of classical music, a sonatina by Beethoven. The gracious shape of its little arpeggios and scales, the way the music of the two hands fit together in an elegant mosaic, floating up to the dark-beamed rafters of the house that smelled of wood, old pipe smoke, Persian carpets, and the glue from Jack's sculpture studio in the basement below, transported me to a place—I could not quite name it, but I sensed it acutely—of culture, of history, evoking a connection to the past that came alive as my fingers moved across the keys of Frances's grand piano, which itself exuded a particular fragrance, equally redolent of layers of time.

According to the original design of the cooperative, each property occupied a full acre, which at first sounded grandiose, but the houses were small and the soil poor, infiltrated with sand and strewn with boulders—the residue of retreating glaciers, as I eventually learned. (And as I discovered when I went to Russia years later, strikingly similar to the sandy landscape of forests and lakes around St. Petersburg and Pskov.) Our acre, narrow and long, sloped gradually and continuously down from the road in front of the house to its boundary, deep in the woods at the lower end. Because of the sloping land, the house was flush with the ground in front but seemed to stand on stilts—in fact the iron poles supporting the screened porch—at the back. Behind the house, as if on a lower level, was a small garden planted with flowers and vegetables that quickly gave way to the thick woods beyond. And somewhere near the—to me as a child, very distant—property boundary stood the remains of a low stone wall, virtually unreachable through the dense underbrush, the ghostly remains of some earlier, unknown habitation.

When the summer tenants arrived, my grandmother and I moved to the basement apartment. Because of the sharp slope of the land, the basement was below-ground at its back but open at the front, with a screen door leading onto a small patio. The back wall was formed by the base of the boulder protruding into the upstairs living room above. With its little living room, minuscule bedroom with two cots, and tiny kitchen wedged up against the boulder in back, this unprepossessing but comfortable abode provided cool shelter during the hottest part of the day and a place to sleep at night; but for the most part we spent our time outdoors on the patio that looked out onto the back garden and the birch woods on the lower part of the acre beyond.

It was in Mohegan, gazing out from the patio behind her summer cottage, that my grandmother took up painting.

Most afternoons, after I finished my piano practice and had crossed back through the mossy patch of woods that divided our property from the Chesnos, I would find my grandmother out on the patio in front of her easel. There, in her sleeveless sundress and straw hat, seated on a folding metal chair, she daubed away at her canvas for a few hours each day, painting scenes—in her strange primitive-expressionist style—that always came out looking like Russia. Probably, for the most part, because of the ubiquitous birch trees, which she always rendered as a series of white stripes delicately overlaid with horizontal black lines; but also because every picture contained some detail that was not a part of the actual landscape in front of us—a wooden hut, a horse-drawn cart, a pair of roughly-rendered figures that my grandmother inevitably referred to by the Russian name for peasant, *muzhiks*. As she painted, she dreamily explained how the scene reminded her of something in the countryside around Pskov, or of northern Russia—beyond the White Sea—where she and Rulia had spent their summer of exile. "This is what Russia looked like when I was young, so beautiful, before a lot of things changed," she told me. And as I sat there alongside her, looking down into the woods, the shiny white bark of the birch trees appearing and disappearing like momentary flashes of summer lightning as the light wind rippled through the mass of green trees surrounding them, with my grandmother's lilting, accented voice floating out over the warm afternoon air, the faint image of a lost Russian world, dimly projected through the pinhole of an invisible camera obscura, took shape before me.

After the woods, the most alluring feature of Mohegan for its displaced, nostalgic-for-home Russian denizens was the lake. Second only to a trip to the woods to pick berries or mushrooms amidst the white birches and silvery aspens, swimming in a woodland lake was—and still is—the most delectable of Russian summer pleasures. On weekends, my grandmother and I usually spent a few hours at the lake in the late afternoon.

An afternoon at the lake was like visiting a foreign country. At home, we went swimming at the so-called country club, in reality just a modest swimming pool with a few tennis courts at the edge of the development. But compared to Mohegan Lake, the club was manicured and luxurious, the young families there like subjects out of a Norman Rockwell illustration. At Mohegan Lake, the people—my grandmother's compatriots— were as if rough-hewn, in their canvas bathing suits and threadbare bathrobes. The ungroomed woods around the lake, glinting with filamentous golden reflections thrown up from the surface of the water by the afternoon sun, crowded down to the water's edge. The unkemptness of this little parcel of nature was interrupted only by a small expanse of mud-brown sand that served as a kind of beachfront, upon which an array of metal chairs upholstered with multicolored plastic strips and the occasional sagging, tent-like structure set up by one of the solar-phobic former inhabitants of the northern European forests were arranged in a kind of anarchist-style version of communal life. When I went to Russia many years later, my cousins took me to the same kind of lakes, in the same kind of woods, in the countryside near St. Petersburg.

My grandmother sat in her folding chair, chatting with some of her relatives and friends, who were probably fellow party members (although my grandmother never acknowledged whether or not she had been a member of the Communist Party USA) or fellow ex-party members, or fellow travelers (though by then, 1960 or so, enthusiasm for the Communist Party and all it had represented was pretty much a spent force), and who answered her back in their variously accented versions of English. Or else she would read a bit. She sat there somewhat grandly, since the people she spoke to always came to her, never the other way around. And yet she was modest—that was my grandmother, grand in principle but modest in practice.

We normally spent a few hours in that almost-foreign country, as I longed to understand, to connect, to what this atmosphere seemed to contain, to what it might reveal. After which, filled with the heat of summer, late in the afternoon—because, just as when we went to one of the ocean beaches near our house on Long Island, spending a few hours by the water on a summer afternoon always induced a sense of time suspended—with the bright orange tiger lilies shimmering amidst the marshy overgrowth of reeds at the water's edge, I helped my grandmother pack up our things as we prepared to go back to the house.

We walked back along the blacktop road, its surface melting slightly in the intense afternoon heat. My grandmother moved forward efficiently, but swayed slightly as she walked, as if in a dimension of her own, tracing a gracefully arcing path, never a straight line, first a bit to the right, then to the left, never quite parallel to the edge of the road, which was lined by the cottages with their sagging screened porches, set back among the pine trees, inside which her friends and cousins and fellow travelers were moving about slowly, getting ready to prepare their summer suppers.

And so we walked and talked about—well, what did we talk about? Whether I had practiced the piano for my lesson with Frances the next week, what I had done at camp on Friday, whether I had read some more of my book. And with all those things, so local, so only in and of our little world of woods and screened porches and old ex-Eastern Europeans who still imagined they were sitting in a country cottage somewhere in Karelia, or Galicia, or by the Riga seaside, the conversation inevitably drifted to our family in Russia, what my cousins were doing, which ones were staying with which grandparent in which summer resting point. Because almost no one in Russia stayed in the city in the summer.

We walked and talked, the ten-year-old child with his seventy-five-year-old grandmother, and we were perfectly attuned to one another, this European lady with her American grandson who was able to listen to her story, and to have her pay attention to his. The grandmother who contained at least two, if not more, distinct worlds and sets of experience within her, so different from anything I had ever encountered, but which compelled me, which I wanted to be able to experience in some way, or at least understand better, and understand what it had to do with my life. We were now a kind of a pair. My grandmother, who had left Russia—and as much as she conjured it along the shore of the lake, amidst the people who were like aging facsimiles of her peers when she was young; as much as the cottages and the road could have been somewhere in the sandy dacha country north of St. Petersburg, or the lake country around Pskov; as much as all of that was conjured, the place she was now in was none of those things, in the end. She had left all that behind. She needed to transmit her story. She was walking with the person she had decided, consciously or unconsciously, to transmit it to.

Finally we returned home and found ourselves sitting on the patio before we began our own evening ritual of supper and cards before bedtime, as the heat of the summer afternoon made us drowsy and cloaked the world in stillness. And because the afternoon sun and heat made me suddenly think of what she had told me about the midnight sun, I asked my grandmother what it was like when she and her sister, my Aunt Rulia, were in that place—what was it called, Mezen, am I saying it right? Did the sun really never set at night, I asked, wondering what it could be like if the intense afternoon sun and heat were to last into the nighttime, how such a thing could even be?

The birch trees glistened, I felt a thousand miles away from Long Island, in another world; perhaps this really is what it was like in Europe, by the Riga seaside. These places were so charged for me, they seemed to provide the setting not only for more dramatic lives, lives full of feeling conferred by different customs, different mindsets, different ways of being in the world, but also by the aura of history at its most fateful.

And so we sat there, with the heat of summer casting its own inimitable spell, when all languid conversation, either hanging in the humid air with a peculiar resonance or drifting slowly away on the light warm breeze, takes on a greater weight.

"Tell me more about Mezen and the midnight sun," I asked my grandmother.

CHAPTER 4. THE ANNOUNCEMENT

The first question was, which grandchild would go?

One Friday afternoon in the fall of 1962, when I was twelve, two years after my summer-long stay in Mohegan, my grandmother came to visit for the weekend as usual, although by then my brother and I didn't really need anyone to babysit us. My mother and I went to meet her at the train station. A few hours later, my father arrived home with my sister, who had been released from the hospital on a weekend pass.

The family's gloom over my sister's illness had gradually been compounded by economic woes, as the expenses of her treatment mounted. My mother went back to school to earn a teaching degree and returned to work. Life for my parents became a joyless series of duties and tasks. My brother plunged into American teenage life—Bandstand style. He was rather slight but handsome, and despite his short stature became a star athlete at school. I retreated into the piano, my relationship with my grandmother, and reveries of New York City and other faraway places, looking for the door to some imagined, enchanted garden where things would be easier, where I could engage with other topics besides the unhappy life of my immediate family.

My mother had told us earlier that after dinner a family meeting would take place. "Your grandmother has some important news."

At six o'clock, we crowded around the little kitchen table—tonight we were six, whereas by now the family had gotten used to being only four for dinner. This evening we were all back together, with my grandmother, just as we had been as a young family a decade earlier. But we were not that young family anymore. Had we once been happy or carefree? Looking back, I could never tell. Sometimes the changes that color the present for a child are so enormous that it seems that things have ever been thus; and in all likelihood—so it seems to the child—will forever be so.

My mother served the meal, standing by the stove and filling our plates directly from the pots in which she had boiled some frozen vegetables and reheated the pot roast she cooked the weekend before. Arriving home from school just in time to gather me up and meet my grandmother at the train station did not leave much time for elaborate dinner preparations. Everyone ate quickly, with little conversation, reaching across the table for dishes, slices of bread, and the bottles of milk, ketchup, and salad dressing. My grandmother, whose idea of family meals had been formed at the turn of the century in her father's rather formal household where she presided alongside him amidst her younger siblings as two or three maids helped with the serving, looked on with a warm but slightly baffled expression.

"Let's all go into the living room," my mother said after we finished. "We're going to talk about your grandmother's news."

We had gotten used to this formal construction from my parents over the past couple of years, as they used such gatherings to impart news about our sister, or about our straitened economic circumstances and how we all had to pitch in and tighten our belts. Accordingly, the idea of a family meeting after dinner did not promise anything pleasant. On the other hand, news from my grandmother traditionally focused on happier things.

We three children sat on the couch at one end of the living room, with my sister, still a head taller than either my brother or me, in the middle. This recaptured fleetingly the time from our early childhood when she seemed very grown up and treated us maternally, the older sister with her two young charges, though those days were now gone. She peered through her thick round glasses as if everything were slightly blurry, trying to bring it all into focus. Rather, it was a kind of reverse blurriness—she preferred to retreat into a fuzzy background space of her own.

My parents sat on the love seat, at a small distance from one another, at the other end of the room. The other two sides of the room consisted of a fireplace on one side and a wall of windows on the other, which gave the modest suburban house its little touch of design sophistication. My grandmother seated herself in the easy chair in front of the windows and looked on with a benevolent expression as she waited for my mother to open the meeting. Even as she aged, she had kept the fine oval line of her face with her hair, now dyed blue gray, still sweeping upwards above her forehead before falling back in two plaits to meet in a knot at the back of her neck. Her cheekbones were still prominent, her nose and mouth soft and round. As always, she wore a fine silk blouse, a long, straight woolen skirt, and patent leather, properly heeled shoes. She filled the room with her air of New York and Europe—still the same elegant Russian lady, carefully put together every time she left the house, who first came to visit us a decade earlier.

My mother, the inevitable chairperson of every meeting—family or otherwise—opened the session. Adopting her best forced smile, she told us: "Your grandmother has offered to take one of you to Europe this coming summer, including a trip to Russia!"

This announcement was met with a sense of bewilderment, since it was clear immediately that my sister couldn't go. But we understood that this was how my parents did things, by the book. Each child was to have equal opportunity, no playing favorites. My sister adopted a look of heightened injury. This was becoming yet another way to torment her, to evade the truth of her situation.

My grandmother continued, with a softer tone than my mother's: "Now, the oldest grandchild has first choice."

My sister said nothing.

"But Susie, dear, I guess you are planning to spend the summer in school, to catch up, right?"

My mother jumped in to provide this detail, soliciting my sister's assent. My sister was already sixteen but still there was something rather strange in the way my mother spoke to her as if she were the sole decider of her own fate, her own activities, as if her parents were simply neutral bystanders. Particularly in light of her situation. My parents had begun treating me the same way, though I was only twelve.

My brother sat there as if struck dumb, seething ever so slightly. What on earth had all this to do with him? Why was he being tortured, when all he wanted to do was play sports, listen to his transistor radio, and go visit the girls he had gotten friendly with in this, his first year of high school? Who, I felt he must be thinking, were all these people, with their weird obsessions—Russia, books, pretensions of every kind? By now he had found a warmer welcome in houses other than his own and happier family atmospheres that he could at least sample for a few hours, before returning to gloomy scenes like the one he was now enduring. His nervous energy was bubbling over, awaiting release on the basketball court or football field.

Again, my mother answered for him: "But you already made plans to take Driver's Education next summer, didn't you, dear?"

"Yes," my brother answered.

Regal in her armchair, my grandmother looked on sympathetically, if a bit uncomprehendingly, as the council proceeded according to my mother's methodical plan. Her primary focus was on her mission to return, yet again, to the homeland. My mother, though trying hard to maintain control and show she could manage the situation, had once again been thrown off balance as the Russian brigade mounted one of its periodic offenses.

And so, the answer was clear: I would go with my grandmother. She fixed her big dark eyes on me expectantly, with a reassuring smile that seemed to beckon me toward her.

My first reaction was a feeling of near panic—too many new people, everything too different, what would I say and do—constrained by the desire to please everyone by projecting enthusiasm and concealing my discomfort. I had turned twelve only a half year earlier and was still a chubby, freckle-faced child. I tried to wear my hair stylishly, in a flat-top like my brother, but try as I might I remained a serious and nerdy preteen. I normally dressed in little chinos with a beaded belt.

But there it was: I had been selected. Things just seemed to keep happening to me. A few years earlier I had casually put my fingers to the piano keys and the next thing I knew I was playing pieces by Beethoven and Mozart. After my summer of lessons with Frances, my parents started looking for an important teacher for me and found one; soon enough I was working on more serious pieces I was supposed to play for visitors at home and with the orchestra at school. And now, I was the one who was to carry the family standard on a trip to meet the Russian relatives, then travel for the rest of the summer imbibing European history and culture. As much as the thought of meeting all my Russian relatives seemed daunting, I understood that of the three siblings only I could make the trip. My parents and grandmother had made a show of deliberating fairly among the three of us, but it was clear that I was the only one who wanted to go—really, the only one who was capable of going—and that the others were indifferent.

My sister used to say to me, a bit enviously, later in life, "You are so lucky you actually enjoy all that culture stuff."

I was going to go to Russia! Amazing as it was, a bolt from the blue, it was a tiny bit expected. Everyone knew my grandmother would be taking another trip back to the Old World one day, and we suspected that she had been harboring the idea of bringing one of her grandchildren along. A trip to Russia followed by a trip around Europe on her modestly-scaled version of the Grand Tour, just as she had been doing since the 1920s. We had heard about all those trips—or at least

I had. Years later, I was talking with my brother one day and reminded him of it all, the backstory of my trip to Russia. He looked at me in bewilderment. He had never heard any of it. He never knew who all the relatives were; all the Russian names sounded the same to him. Whereas before the trip I knew them all and had a very specific mental image of each. Every name—Arkady, Volya, Nina, Lusya, Vasya, Mila, Tanya, Sasha, Seryozha—was like a word picture, each a unique permutation of musical Russian vowels luxuriating within a cocoon of gliding consonants and conjuring a portrait of the individual to whom it belonged.

Yes, the promise of a journey to the mysterious, magical land had probably always been out there. My mother had announced, "One of you will be going with your grandmother on a trip to Europe." Exciting, of course, but lots of people went to Europe, even in those days. It was one of the favored status symbols of the suburban set. But Russia? That was not part of the usual itinerary. There was nothing stylish or pleasurable about going to Russia. Uplifting perhaps, enlightening in some obscure way, the sort of thing intellectuals and serious people did, first in the thirties to see "what the future looked like" and later, by the sixties, mostly to support the "good Russians" as they struggled against their oppressive state. The funny thing was, I didn't know exactly which side of the divide we were on. I understood that my relatives were suffering because they lived there—that had come across quite clearly—indicating that the state of affairs was more Orwellian than Utopian. My grandmother certainly seemed to view contemporary Soviet Russia as dark and forbidding; yet she had once been on the side of the Revolution. But beyond that rather confusing duality, I sensed a more fundamental message: that Russia embodied some sort of special beauty, an exalted culture, a kind of philosophical truth combined with heightened forms of human warmth and intimacy. And that the beauty and truth were accompanied by a suffering that was somehow inevitable, decreed by some implacable fate, and therefore ennobling.

All this I somehow intuited, even if I couldn't articulate it, as we started to plan for the trip. We were to sail to England, then make our way to Russia, just as my grandmother had been doing for almost fifty years. In the early sixties, Russia still seemed very far away. Universally accessible air travel and globalization did not yet exist. Such a trip was both arduous and a great adventure.

And somehow, I also knew that once you made the trip you became part of the story.

I sensed that for me this was a turning point. Even before my grandmother came to visit that weekend, I had begun to understand that my future lay not in Little League or spending Friday nights in the bleachers at the edge of the school athletic fields. I was going to play the piano and go to Russia. My developing adolescent life was setting off on a new trajectory. My Russian grandparents' personalities and style and stories were like great blocky foundations beneath our quiet suburban life, like the ruins of some grand Roman baths; vestiges that were faint but still present. And now I was going to walk down an invisible passageway, across an imperceptible bridge and enter the buildings sketched out by those ruins. I was no longer to be just another kid from Long Island, driving up the old roads with evocative names that I tried to imbue with some romantic past—Hillside Avenue, Roslyn Road, I.U. Willets Road. Now I had a foot in another world. I was going to have a bigger vessel to contain my desire to see what other, more distant places could reveal. It was no longer just the Gatsby-era Old Motor Parkway, just beyond the fence at the edge of the subdivision; the older, half-hidden houses along Roslyn Road; the imagined places along the railroad track after it curved away beyond the horizon. There was now a new place, much larger than all these, and I was connected to it.

No, the bleachers alongside the athletic fields could not contain this. And at the age of twelve, though I could not yet comprehend it – given my age and the times I grew up in I could not even name it – I sensed there was also something else defining my feelings of difference. Though I was not yet fully aware, some part of me already knew that I was gay.

CHAPTER 5. THE RUSSIAN LESSON

After the trip to Russia was announced, my grandmother stopped coming for her regular visits. My parents decided that my brother and I were old enough to stay alone in the evening on the increasingly rare occasions when they went out. My sister's absence had changed the ecology of our household in a profound way. After she left, no one entered the room at the top of the stairs under the eaves of the old attic that my parents had built for her, though I longed to go there and look at the rows of books with their colorful dustjackets neatly arrayed in the little shelves, and the glass case with the collection of elaborate dolls and figurines that my grandmother had brought back from her trips to Russia and the rest of Europe. The room remained permanently shrouded in a silent half-light; gradually, the gloom spread through the rest of the house. Each member of our family seemed to be on a separate trajectory, nobody quite sure anymore how the pieces of the nuclear family fit together, if at all. I was only twelve, but in some incipient manner understood that I now had to find my own way. My childish intuition that life was elsewhere, it seemed, had been affirmed. My grandmother would not be coming anymore to ignite my imagination; I would have to go to her world.

My parents, trying in their own fashion to make life better, to find things that might seem pleasurable, announced a month or two after my thirteenth birthday that I should go to New York by myself to visit my grandmother. Other kids from my school, albeit a year or two older, were already going to New York on Saturdays for their art or music lessons, and it had been decided that I would start to do the same the following year to take my piano lessons with my new teacher, the distinguished pianist Vivian Rivkin, in the Ansonia Hotel—the famous Belle Epoque building on Broadway and 72nd Street where many musicians, including Caruso, had stayed—where she lived and taught her more serious students. I was a bit young to travel to New York alone, but things had reached the point where my parents were relieved to see my brother and me going off to do anything that suggested we were moving forward successfully; with their own heavy set of worries and preoccupations they had no desire to be supervising either one of us too closely. If they could convince themselves we were properly accounted for and had a nominal idea of where we were, they were relieved, at least temporarily, of one additional burden.

My parents drove me to the station. We got out of the car and stood together on the asphalt strip waiting for the city-bound train to arrive from the east. I looked down the track, waiting for the headlight to appear as the train rounded the last curve before the station. The train lumbered to a stop and I climbed the steps, with their little raised pattern embossed into the steel, up onto the platform and looked back at my parents. They smiled at me in their oddly noncommittal way, as if to indicate that nothing unexpected or wonderful was happening, that everything was supposed to be known in advance and never be surprising, as if a lack of foreknowledge suggested some shameful ignorance (an attitude I felt I should emulate and aspire to, until many years later when I realized it was essentially self-annihilating). As the train moved away, they turned and started to walk back to the car, resignedly preparing themselves to return to the house and the duties that awaited them. Family weekends had taken on a strange hue—it seemed nice, in principle, that everyone was at leisure, yet the mood was always one of uncertainty, as if no one knew exactly what to make of the freedom, as if the strictures of our little world were too tight to allow for pleasure and the expansion of the soul. Soul expansion seemed to be an activity for a parallel world they no longer inhabited. I wanted to find that world. I didn't want life to be just a series of tasks, duties, and disappointments. I wanted to go to New York and plan my trip to Russia. I wanted soul expansion.

I watched through the grimy window as the suburban landscape, with its faint echoes of former countryside, gave way to the gritty outskirts of the city; eventually, as the train pulled away from Jamaica, I caught my first glimpse of the Manhattan skyscrapers, before the train plunged into the dark tunnel and pulled up to the platform beneath the great cavern of Penn Station.

I climbed the stairs up to the main hall and walked along amidst the smell of diesel fuel and cigarettes, past the newspaper stands and food concessions, to the entrance to the subway, encrusted with layers of accumulated grime like some abandoned archaeological dig. Neither Penn Station nor the dilapidated subway were remotely beautiful, yet both captivated me with a kind of semiotic alert—that the city was one of the places I was seeking, where time and what had happened in the past were part of the fabric, still hanging in the air, immaterial but perceptible.

I walked up to the toll booth and, amassing all the confidence I could (I had seen my grandmother do this, many times, and had carefully listened to how she addressed the token seller), bought two tokens. I wedged the token disc into the old-fashioned receptacle, whose little sculptural form atop the flat surface of the turnstile provided another signal, a reminder, that I was entering a more charged world where things seemed to carry greater weight and meaning.

I came back up into the daylight at 66th Street and Broadway. The recently constructed Philharmonic Hall, where my grandmother had promised to take me to hear a concert conducted by Leonard Bernstein, loomed in front of me across the wide swath of asphalt where two avenues merged and crossed. A billboard with a life-size picture of Bernstein, young and dashing, beckoning the viewer into his glamorous world of music and culture, stood in front of me on the sidewalk.

I walked down West 66th Street toward West End Avenue, where my grandmother's new building—she had found an apartment in an affordable housing cooperative newly built on land cleared for Lincoln Center, as climbing five flights to her apartment on West 16th Street was no longer feasible—stood on the last stretch of the street before it dead-ended abruptly at the edge of a cliff that fell away to the Hudson River below.

My grandmother opened the door and looked at me with her encouraging expression. She was still wearing her housecoat, though it was already eleven in the morning. I followed her through the narrow galley kitchen to the small dinette. The thin dry wall, the industrial design of her little balcony, the still-perceptible smell of new construction—it all seemed an incongruous setting for my time-traveling Russian grandmother, this bland new apartment with no trace of the past. Until she moved to 66th Street, all the places I associated with her had been old.

She told me that she had prepared lunch and afterwards, she promised, I would have my first Russian lesson. The mellifluous sound of her accented voice, still the same, dispelled the strangeness of her new surroundings.

Alien as the atmosphere of the new apartment was, she had managed to find places for all the things from her past life and apartments—the Russian books, the Tolstoy plate, the old Persian carpets and heavy wooden furniture, the pile of throw pillows, with their same smell of stale perfume and the clothing of innumerable people who had reclined against them, heaped up on the couch where I used to sleep when I visited her overnight in Greenwich Village. Her collection of family photographs from the days before she left Russia were arranged on the shelves of the intricately carved hutch from her old apartment that she had somehow managed to wedge into the little space along the back wall of the dining nook. The elaborately framed picture of her father, in his perfectly pressed wing collar, elegant suit jacket and tie, and jet-black Vandyke beard, looking down at us with his implacably severe expression, stood at the center of the uppermost shelf.

I sat down at the kitchen table. The scraping sound of the trains moving around in the railyards on the riverbank below filtered up through the half-open balcony door. In the distance I could see the industrial landscape on the far shore of the Hudson River. Inside, listening to my grandmother's voice and looking at her familiar possessions, everything she had always been for me was once again the same. We were ready to plan our trip to Russia.

We finished lunch and moved the dishes to the white linoleum counter next to the sink. My grandmother turned over a straw box containing the letters of the Russian alphabet, turned them right-side up, and spread them out on the table in front of me.

There are thirty-three letters, she explained, immediately suggesting a richer and more enigmatic world than the one contained by the twenty-six plain-looking letters of the alphabet I already knew. Since I had first seen their elegant forms on the spines of my grandmother's books, each Cyrillic letter seemed to me like a little sculpture, a hieroglyph conveying a coded message. I could not quite imagine them transforming from mysterious symbols into actual words.

My grandmother produced a chart with the letters in their proper order. Sounding each one aloud in imitation of my grandmother, I sorted them out and arranged them in front of me. There were five kinds of E's, my grandmother warned me. Two of the letters had no sound, she elaborated, but only changed the way another letter is pronounced. And there used to be a few more letters, but they were thrown out after the Revolution, she explained in a serious tone that seemed to indicate approval, such that the alphabet took on the character of having two versions, like my grandmother's Russia itself—the older Russian one, elegant and aesthetic, and the new, more utilitarian Soviet edition.

"When we get to Leningrad, I want you to at least be able to read the signs," my grandmother said.

As we moved through the lesson, I felt something shift in our relationship. Even as a child, I intuited that my grandmother's deepest sense of self existed in another language, in her native Russian. Which sometimes made it seem that she was just a visitor to the present, that her authentic self was the self of the adventures, the great experiences of her past that she had told me about. Now, as she began to teach me—to impart to me—the Russian alphabet and its sounds, I felt I was being invited into that world. She and I were becoming a kind of team, a duo.

"All right, that's enough for today, we made a very good beginning," she said with evident satisfaction as we ended the lesson. "Next time I will teach you a few phrases."

And then, she placed her palms down on the table as if in a gesture of decision. After a few moments, she stood up abruptly and turned toward the hutch standing against the wall behind her.

"Let me find some pictures of the family," she said in a soft voice, as if thinking to herself aloud.

This came as a surprise. When I first arrived, she had said we'd go out after lunch to do some shopping. To her favorite department store, I guessed—as she loved to board the bus that stopped at her corner and ride it all the way across Manhattan to Bloomingdale's, for her the height of chic, at Lexington Avenue and 59th Street, where she would occasionally indulge herself and buy me a brightly striped dress shirt. I assumed she'd decided that I needed one or two new ones for the trip. The plans for the afternoon had apparently changed.

The hutch was like a tabernacle, containing everything essential having to do with Russia—china, books, little boxes of metal with geometric designs in blue and gold enamel, quintessentially Russian in one way but evocative of Turkish or Persian style as well, conjuring for me the mysterious European-Asiatic duality of Russia; or of lacquered wood painted with fairy-tale scenes of princes taming firebirds in enchanted forests. And arranged throughout, on every shelf, the pictures in their silver frames—of her father, presiding over all; of my grandmother as a student with her serious, intellectual-looking friends with whom she talked and dreamed about the Revolution; and the formal portrait photograph of my grandmother with her young sister Rulia—my grandmother seated, looking down at an open folio in her lap, with the young and delicately beautiful Rulia, as if painted by Botticelli save for her dark, luxuriant hair, standing alongside, her left hand resting lightly on my grandmother's shoulder, as she too looks earnestly at the text in the open folio. Both wearing long dark skirts and white blouses trimmed with lace, both with their hair parted in the middle, framing their young faces, there in a well-appointed corner of their home in Pskov, a year or two before they were suddenly swept away to the remote north of Russia and on to America, never to return to the comfortable life, the elegant home, the fine clothes, the books, their idealistic dreams of the future. All of it frozen, there on the shelf of the hutch in my nearly eighty-year-old grandmother's new apartment, in the soft brown and white tones of their adolescent portrait photo.

"Yes, let me find some photos, it will help you understand who everyone is, to get ready before we go," she continued.

She stood in front of the hutch with the slight swaying motion that signified concentration, trying to remember where she had put the box with the family photos and letters. It was there, somewhere, amidst the clutter of saved possessions, gifts, mementoes, photos, documents, and correspondence; all the things she had relating to—representing—Russia, from the moment she arrived in America onwards.

"Aha, here it is," she said with a laugh. She bent forward, carefully withdrew the box from the back of the upper shelf and placed it in the middle of the table.

The box contained the unframed pictures from her youth, the snapshots and photos from her early days in New York, her trips back to Europe and Russia in the twenties, thirties, and fifties, and the pictures her siblings had enclosed in their letters over the years of themselves, their children, and now their grandchildren—the cousins who were around my age, whom I was to meet the following summer. My grandmother had shown me the odd snapshot before, from a letter she had just received before coming to visit on Long Island, or in the weekend mail when I was visiting her in New York. Now we were going to have a look at things in more systematic fashion. She motioned for me to bring my chair closer. For a few minutes she sifted silently through the contents of the box as if reflecting across the decades on the things that had been, and the things that might have been but finally never were.

"They all live in one big apartment; it's called a communal apartment," she explained. "Each family has a room." She arranged the pictures in the shape of a family tree.

"Here are your great-aunts and uncles," she began. Nina, the widow of my grandmother's brother Volya, who had died in the early fifties, lived with her daughter Mila in one room—together with Mila's baby Seryozha, whose father was a visiting French professor of Slavic languages who had promised to marry Mila and take her and Seryozha back to

Paris, but who had disappeared without a trace at the end of the school term. Which somehow sounded familiar and perfectly predictable when it came to our Russian relatives—people were sick, had marital troubles, professional and financial difficulties. My grandmother imparted this sort of information with a sense of calm inevitability; for Russians, it seemed to be the default condition. Only the kids of my own generation seemed to be relatively healthy and carefree. I got the sense that in Russia, it was best to be young.

There were two sisters, Lilya and Lyuba, who lived alone. And last, my grandmother's brother Arkady, whose name for some reason always sounded tremendously refined and cultured to me, who lived with his wife Lyolya. Their grandson, Sasha, spoke English and was to be my main contact when we arrived. He lived with Arkady and Lyolya in their room when he was in Leningrad, although his parents lived in Moscow, so he sometimes lived there as well.

This was another strange aspect of life in Russia that diverged so strikingly from my world—everyone seemed to move around a lot. From Moscow to Leningrad, Leningrad to the Riga seaside in Latvia, Estonia for a time, Tashkent, back to Moscow. Especially the kids in my generation—sometimes they lived with their parents, but often with their grandparents. I was a little envious when I heard about that.

There was one large room that everyone used in common, my grandmother explained, a sort of living room and dining room for special occasions. I sensed from my grandmother's tone that the communal living arrangement had created an element of ongoing strain in the various inter-family relationships, if not outright strife.

I had already known most of the names and family relation-ships of my Russian relatives—my grandmother had told me enough about them over the years—but as we looked at their pictures and I heard more about their lives I began to see them differently. They were no longer just European unfortu-nates. People in Europe in the years after World War II were seen as poor, hungry, ill-clothed, unsmiling, scrounging for daily essentials. Fifteen years later, the Russians were still the same way. Part of the dynamic with the Russian relatives had always been that comfortable Americans like us (we were not overly comfortable but compared with them we were) had an obligation to help, to look on them with pity and indulgence. And yet, I understood that their lives followed the normal trajectories of marriage, family, professions; and that they all sprang from the same privileged, cosmopolitan root stock as my grandmother. This part was particularly strange; I could never reconcile how educated, professional, worldly people could end up living such threadbare lives, spending so much of their time and energy foraging.

As we looked at the pictures and contemplated our trip to Leningrad to meet them, my Russian relatives started to become more real. I was becoming more connected to them. I sensed that we belonged to each other.

This was the mysterious thing—the connection. My grand-mother had once lived in the city and the apartment we were going to visit. The trip we were about to embark on was not a simple touristic excursion, a heritage tour organized by some well-intentioned group to see how our forebears had lived in the Old Country. We were one family. I was as closely related to these people as I was to my Aunt Rulia in New York, to her daughter Sonia, and to Sonia's children—my cousins who lived in the big apartment on Riverside Drive, whom I knew well and considered my close relatives.

As my grandmother talked about Vladimirsky Prospekt and the family, the sonorous Russian sounds, once again, drew me in. Her voice modulated into Russian as she spoke their names; the foreign words and sounds, no longer foreign, came alive in her own tongue, her natural language, conjuring images of specific tonality, opening the door into the world she was describing.

Years later, I realized that our lives had been altered by them as much as theirs had been altered by us, with our letters and packages, our dollars, our promise to bring word from the outside world into their restricted realm. Having relatives in Russia who still lived in the place my grandmother had once lived, continuing the relationships she had begun as a child, was really what kept the Russian part of my grandmother alive her whole life, and the living Russian part of my grandmother was the heart of the story. Without Vladimirsky Prospekt and the people who lived there, whom I was about to go and meet, there would have been no Russian grandmother, no story.

My grandmother rearranged the pictures slightly, moving them around the tabletop as she had rearranged the letters of the alphabet a few minutes earlier. "You know, when your uncle Eugene and I lived there, with Aunt Rulia and Sonia, Arkady and Lyolya gave Rulia and me their room to sleep in, while the kids slept in a little room next to the kitchen, it was just a pantry really," she said reflectively. "Arkady and Lyolya slept in the main room."

Her focus was moving back in time.

"I looked for a room for months, but in those days there was no housing in Russia, you couldn't find anything. And I looked for work because we were planning to stay in Russia for a long time, but I wasn't successful. I found out how hard things were, how you needed connections. I even tried calling Voroshilov a few times, but his secretary wouldn't put me through. Arkady was already having trouble at his job, because he wouldn't join the Party.

"So finally, we had to leave. Life in the Soviet Union didn't turn out to be what I expected."

My grandmother nodded to herself, as if completing a thought. She turned to look at the hutch again, as though she needed something, something she had forgotten. And suddenly, the thing I had always felt, had almost known, became clear. Everything about Russia had to do with time.

I knew from the beginning that our trip, like all my grandmother's previous trips, was about reconnecting with past time. The time in the early thirties when she had lived in the apartment on Vladimirsky Prospekt, when the Revolution and the country that had emerged from it were barely fifteen years old and the future still seemed full of possibility; or so my grandmother believed until she spent a year there and began to comprehend what was really happening. And the time of her youth in Pskov, which still lingered faintly in the apartment on Vladimirsky, the latter-day gathering place of the siblings who had once lived together in a different grand apartment, above their father's elegant shop, before the Revolution. I was more than eager to go to Russia, meet my relatives, see the city of Leningrad with its grand historical sights—the Russia of the present, of course. But what I really wanted was to go with my grandmother to the older Russia, the one she had left and still longed for, the Russia with promise and a future, because it was central to who she was.

I knew that I would never really understand it all, or know her completely, unless I went to Russia myself.

And as I sat there alongside my grandmother, swept up by her magical powers of time travel, I began to feel a kind of longing of my own for the lost Russian time. It was as if going to Russia had everything to do with my own sense as a small child, amidst the blank canvas of suburbia, that the past had been erased, leaving behind some kind of void, that time had been cheated, that I had to look for what had been abandoned and lost. And perhaps, regain it. I suddenly perceived that going to Russia was central to the quest.

I looked at my grandmother, sitting at the kitchen table in her housecoat, and imagined her aging siblings in Leningrad padding around the apartment in their old bathrobes. Soon I would be meeting my teenage cousins—a new generation to take up the Russian American family connection.

I looked out her kitchen window toward the Hudson. At the edge of the water the trains moved slowly along in the railyards. On the far shore I could see the dun-colored cliffs of New Jersey, still bare after the winter. Gray-white clouds scudded over the water, gradually widening out as the river flowed on to the harbor and the ocean beyond. Suddenly, I was struck by the transience and mutability of things, by the strangeness of my grandmother sitting there, speaking English to me in her Russian accent, when part of her was not there at all, but in the place we were about to go.

CHAPTER 6. DEPARTURE

At the end of April, my sister came home from the hospital to visit for the weekend. Though we never spoke in any detail about my trip—my sister said very little when she was at home—I could tell that she understood my uncertainty, from the way she looked around and took everything in as she always did, gazing first at my parents, then at me, with her sad, knowing look. That was my sister's specialty—empathy. She had too much of it.

After breakfast on Sunday morning, as she was preparing for the drive back to Philadelphia with my father, she asked me to come upstairs to her room. She handed me a wrapped package.

"For the trip," she said.

She had gotten me an oversized notebook—oversized in a way that was intended to make it look festive, yet it looked only forlorn, with its brown and purple cover made of heavy cardboard coated with plastic and *'Journal'* written on the front in gold cursive letters. An oversized ball point pen was scotch taped to the back.

"So you can write down everything you see," she explained, gazing at me, once again, with her sad look.

One of my roles in the family, which was never really acknowledged or alluded to, was the confidant of my sister. She and I understood each other in a special way, in a way that no one else in the family knew much about. We shared a sense of loss, with a kind of tacit agreement that it was connected to some general state of cosmic injustice. The question was, where did you go after that? The journal was her effort to tell me: I encourage you, go forth and do the things I can't do. And don't forget to come back and tell me about them. It was a very tender message, from a sibling who was older and wiser, but whose age and wisdom were no longer instrumental. With an undertone—how could it not have communicated such an undertone?—of disappointment, of profound sadness for herself.

At the end of June, a week after I finished the seventh grade, my parents and I packed up the car early one Saturday morning with my suitcase and other belongings for the trip. My mother and father were somber, as if unsure what the right attitude toward the day's events should be. This was not a festive leave-taking; rather, just another methodical packing up of the car for a Saturday morning chore, an outing to bring me, dutifully, to the morning's appointed destination. But the destination this day happened to be a pier on the west side of Manhattan where my grandmother and I were to board an ocean liner bound for Europe; in two weeks' time I would be in Russia. All I could glean from my parents, as we pulled out of the driveway and set off, was the feeling that I was being sent off to accomplish something, that I needed to come back with important information. With a shiver of trepidation, I thought about the journal my sister had given me. Would I be up to the task? Would I be able to discern weighty, revealing things? Would I be able to find the words to record them?

My grandmother and I sailed on a relatively new ship, the SS Statendam, which seemed to me—despite our tiny, bunk-bedded interior cabin—so luxurious that I nearly swooned with delight. My grandmother smiled. Only on our return trip two months later, traveling third class on the aging and soon to be mothballed RMS Queen Mary, did I see the less glamorous side of ocean liner travel. On the evening of the fifth day at sea, it was announced that we would approach Land's End at six the next morning. I got up early and went up onto the deck. The low headland, far in the distance and shrouded in fog, came slowly into view. I ran down to the cabin to tell my grandmother that we were arriving. From afar, the land looked no different than the shorelines I had seen in America; but I watched with fascination, incredulous at the notion that within a few hours we would be stepping off the ship onto the land appearing in front of us—Europe.

At noon we arrived at the pier in Southampton. A huge terminal at least six stories high occupied its entire length. Aboard ship I had learned the intricacies of English currency. My grandmother reached into her pocketbook and took out a few shillings, which she told me to hold onto to give to the porter. I felt a burst of excitement as we shared our first ritual of European life together. As my grandmother smiled at me, I sensed her happiness at once again coming back to the part of the world she knew best, where she felt most at home. We showed our boat train tickets to the porter, who rolled our luggage away on a cart, promising to deliver it to our compartment.

We crossed the gangway into the terminal, passed through the customs booth and made our way downstairs to the boat train to London. We walked along the platform, comparing the numbers painted on the train cars to our tickets, until we located our compartment. Our luggage lay neatly on the overhead rack, undisturbed. The train was old and ornate, with velvet seats and wood paneling. I looked at everything with a sense of amazement. My grandmother smiled indulgently—to her, everything was familiar. We had moved backwards in time. The journey to the mysterious origins of her life had finally begun.

We stayed in London for two nights in the hotel my grandmother had been staying at—or stopping in, as she put it—since her first trip back to Europe in the twenties. For me, it was all stupendously new and exciting. I was in Europe! One can only experience once in a lifetime the delight mixed with incredulity you feel setting foot onto European soil for the first time, moving about among things you have only read about and seen in pictures. Things, as you try to comprehend without fully succeeding, that are so old yet still stand there, as they did hundreds of years ago when the actual events—events so grand, romantic and epic in your imagination (and, likely, in reality)—you have read about unfolded within and around them. Things that are five hundred years old, a thousand years old, even older. Thirteen may be the ideal age to experience all that for the first time.

And Europe, in 1963, was still so close to the war, its atmosphere evocative in ways that would soon disappear. Though I couldn't really know or understand that at the time—when you are thirteen, things that happened fifteen years earlier seem awfully remote. But the ambience of the interwar years was still there, in the heavy draperies, the stuffy rooms, the Edwardian look of things, the very proper English way that people still behaved.

On the third morning we left for the airport for our flight to Helsinki. I watched as the plane drifted out over the North Sea and began to traverse the northern edge of Europe. As we crossed Denmark and flew out over the Baltic Sea, my grandmother leaned over to point out the window. The captain announced that in a few minutes we would see the coast of Latvia and the city of Riga from the right side of the plane. Riga, where my great-grandfather had moved his family and his business just before the Revolution; where my grandmother had gone to visit him for the last time, in 1933.

As we crossed over the shoreline of Finland, I looked down at the great unbroken stretch of dark pine forest spreading out below. We were getting closer. Despite the short flight, taking us across half of Europe in a few hours, I began to realize how far away Russia really was. The whole approach—five days across the sea, three days in London to acclimate to the Old World, a flight across a thousand miles of Europe, the dark pine forest—had shown me the scale of the distance. I could see now that one did not simply enter Russia as we had done in Britain, or were about to do in Finland, where you just showed your passport and walked through the turnstile. No, Russia was walled off; it took effort, arrangement, knowledge, connections. Only my grandmother knew how to get to Russia. I waited with curiosity and apprehension.

The plane descended toward the Helsinki airport, which appeared to be in the middle of the forest. I began to sense the northern edge of Europe, something I later discovered I would always feel in Russia. As if one were truly on the edge, literally as well as metaphorically—a long shelf of land that eventually gave way to the limitless northern sea.

My grandmother had arranged for us to travel to Russia from Helsinki. Through her long experience, she knew all the tricks of travel to the Soviet Union. I had understood, without anyone having to explain it explicitly, that traveling to Russia was complicated, overlaid with bureaucracy and formality, even slightly dangerous. But mostly just onerous, and potentially very expensive, paradoxical as that seemed given the material poverty of the country. Everything was controlled by Intourist, the state travel agency. You couldn't move around on your own; you couldn't stay anywhere unless it had been arranged with Intourist and paid for in advance. I had listened as my grandmother complained about all this. The Soviets wanted American dollars. To add insult to injury, the hotels were threadbare and the food was bad. I tried to understand the disdain my grandmother heaped on the country that I knew, in other ways, she loved. But she would not submit to Intourist—she preferred to spend her limited American money to buy things for her relatives at the hard currency shops once we got there, or to give to them outright, though this was dangerous black-market trafficking and was never discussed in front of me. To simplify the trip and make it cheaper, she had managed to get us a place with a Finnish tour group. The last thing she was going to be was a gullible American tourist. That would never happen. After all, she had lived in Russia in the thirties and almost became a Soviet citizen.

We met the tour leader, a young Finnish woman who spoke Russian, that evening, the night before our departure. My grandmother explained our terms: we would travel with them by bus to Leningrad and stay in the Astoria Hotel but would not eat meals or go touring with them, and at the end of the week we would leave Leningrad on our own. We would be visiting our family. Her behavior was a bit peremptory. Was she an American woman who had come to Finland to join a tour to Russia, or a Russian woman going back home? The tour group leader seemed unsure but nodded in agreement as my grandmother set out the plan. It made practical sense—more resources to share among the rest of the group if we were not going to partake. For my grandmother, experienced and thrifty traveler that she was, entering through Finland was the clever way to get there. For me, it created the sense that we were special, that we were going to Russia not as tourists but as people who knew our way around, who had a purpose, who belonged there.

The next morning, we met in the hotel lobby to board our bus. I felt intense anticipation mixed with slight dread. A few more hours and we would be walking down Soviet streets. Ten days earlier, I had walked into the lobby of my grandmother's building in Manhattan to collect her for our trip. The distance we had traversed was hard to grasp.

CHAPTER 7. ARRIVAL

We drove out of Helsinki and snaked along narrow Finnish roads through the sandy pine forest, catching glimpses of the sea as we neared the border with Russia. After a few hours, we reached the border crossing, where a sign announced (in Finnish, Russian, and English): *You are now leaving Finland!* The exclamation mark seemed to provide a tacit, implied warning—proceed on to the next territory at your own risk: things there work by their own rules; we can't protect you anymore once you enter. In those days the borders between Eastern and Western Europe were tightly guarded. The Berlin Wall had gone up less than two years earlier.

We crossed a thirty-meter strip of no man's land and reached the guardhouse at the entrance to the Soviet Union. A group of guards dressed in black leather uniforms, featuring jackets with epaulettes and ammunition belts and jodhpur breeches tucked into knee-high boots, came out of the guard house and positioned themselves alongside the bus. Motioning with their submachine guns, they directed the driver to open the door and ordered us off, collecting our documents as we filed out. The leader of the tour group leader remained behind with the soldiers, speaking to them quietly and deferentially, as they leafed through the passports. It was all a bit scary—not to mention exciting and dramatic—but the tour leader had obviously done this before and everyone seemed to assume, with only slightly bated breath, that everything would proceed smoothly.

My grandmother looked on disdainfully. This was something I would see again and again during our visit—for her, there were two kinds of Russians: sensitive, educated Russians and vulgar, uncultured Russians. The latter, like the guards, drew her scorn. They were not like the people she had known growing up and were not the kind of people she had expected to emerge from the Revolution. She remained silent. She knew better than to start speaking in her cultivated, old-fashioned Russian at a moment like this. We stood on the side of the road as the guards finished examining our documents, then searched inside and under the bus. Twenty minutes later, they waved us on. A few hundred yards down the road a group of signs written in Cyrillic announced our arrival in Russia.

An hour later, we stopped for lunch in Vyborg, the small city where my grandmother was born and my great-grandfather had been the regimental tailor, before the regiment was transferred and the family moved to Pskov. Vyborg and Pskov had previously existed for me only as names. Now we were driving along in a Finnish bus, in 1963, through the places my grandmother had once lived. Leningrad was less than two hours away.

After Vyborg, the road narrowed as we plunged into the dense birch forest of the Karelian Peninsula. The unpleasant impression of the border crossing had by now worn off and my grandmother looked out at the passing scene with satisfaction, reveling in the pure Russian landscape rolling by outside the bus window. A limitless profusion of white tree trunks, each delicately adorned with black accents, stretched out across the mossy forest floor as far as we could see. At her summer house in Westchester, my grandmother had labored for years to cultivate ten or twenty birches, most of which had by now died off due to a blight that had spread through the community. But here they surrounded us with casual abandon, limitlessly, like an army of sentinels, silent, yet somehow charged with meaning.

In the morning, as we boarded the bus that would take us to Russia, I had already seen my grandmother change. The intensity of our already remarkable journey heightened; the sense of anticipation increased. I was intensely curious to see how she would react to arriving in—returning to—Russia. As I watched her take in the beauty of the forest, with a dreamy look of knowing satisfaction, I sensed that the drama had begun. This was the prologue. The actual play would begin when we got to Leningrad.

Suddenly, the road curved sharply, and we emerged from the forest. The Gulf of Finland opened out in front of us, a glowing expanse of silvery water stretching off to the horizon. The road passed through one last small town, a bleak half-mile strip of weathered wood cottages and sheds, without a shop or human being to be seen, and we approached the outskirts of Leningrad. We crossed some open, flat grassland, which seemed once to have been cultivated but now lay fallow. Massive power lines ran between the fields. My grandmother raised herself up in her seat to look at the passing scene more closely, as if to see what had changed. A few miles on, we began to see red brick factory buildings from the turn of the century. It struck me that little had changed in and around Leningrad for decades. Finally, we saw a modern industrial plant with a tall smokestack spewing dense smoke, the signal, at last, that we had arrived in the new Soviet Russia.

As we drew nearer to the city, the road widened and became clogged with small cars and buses. The view opened again onto the Gulf. Across the water, I caught my first sight of Leningrad—a wide, slightly indistinct expanse of low buildings spread out beneath tall, graceful spires.

The city seemed to be floating on the water—an indecipherable mass of islands and inlets formed by the Neva River and its branches. As we got closer the individual islands, linked by a myriad of bridges, became more distinct. We entered the industrial outskirts where crumbling factories and warehouses stood alongside tiny country cottages with carefully tended kitchen gardens, then crossed a series of small bridges, passing from island to island, as the buildings of the city became denser and we began to see apartment houses, schools, and large factories along the banks of the Neva. We were in Leningrad.

Leningrad. If cities had musical characters, Leningrad sounded—and looked—like a city in a minor key. The cracked asphalt of the highway, the crumbling factory buildings, all of it surrounded by the encroaching sea—I tried to connect my first rather grim impressions to the sense I had always gotten from my grandmother that this city had a special beauty, a special importance that we were about to encounter.

The tour guide picked up her microphone and began explaining the sights to her group in Finnish. As we drove along, my grandmother leaned over and told me the name of each island, each branch of the river, each canal that we passed. Listening to her Russian voice, I heard the same, rich dark sounds that I was used to hearing in America, but now she was naming things that we were passing by inside Russia, right in front of us. It was as if by naming things, she conferred existence on them. They assumed their proper, true Russian essence. Before she spoke the names, I was like any tourist, like our Finnish companions who looked on with mild interest as they listened to the explanations of their guide. When my grandmother named them, these places no longer seemed foreign and distant. I felt as if they had been bestowed on me. I started to own them, and they started to own me, too.

Finally, we crossed a long, arcing bridge onto the mainland and began to drive along the opposite riverbank. We had reached the city's historical center. My grandmother pointed out the window and leaned over to explain things to me in a low voice. Whether English was out of place here or to prevent the Finns from overhearing I didn't know, but I got the sense that there was some force of habit at work, that here in the heart of Soviet territory it was best to communicate discreetly. As we passed the Summer Garden, a lush thicket of trees dotted with white statues, surrounded by a fence of black spikes tipped with golden points, looked at the strollers along the riverbank, dressed in their drab clothes. It seemed we had arrived, truly, in the land of workers.

The massive façade of the Winter Palace appeared on our left, continuing for blocks. Inside was the Hermitage, my grandmother told me, the great museum that was to be one of the centerpieces of our visit. Soon we would be passing by the Nevsky Prospekt, she continued. Something in her voice and bearing communicated her pride and satisfaction at being in command of this knowledge, as if it belonged only to her. Vladimirsky Prospekt and the family apartment were not far, just a short tram ride away, she added.

Leningrad, Nevsky, and Vladimirsky Prospekt. These were the talismanic names that I had heard murmured on Friday evenings in Long Island, on the hot afternoons in Mohegan when my grandmother's sister, Rulia, came to visit, evoking looks of longing, tinged perhaps with a note of ambivalence or regret. Now, we were here. One thing I felt immediately, despite my American outfit and the strange and alien quality of everything around me: this belongs to me, too. We rode along in the bus, sitting in the front. The other passengers were tourists. We were returnees.

I looked with wonderment at the profusion of signs written in Cyrillic. The black, sculptural letters were no longer enigmatic ideographs of something exotic and far away. They spoke to the prosaic facts of what we now saw in front of us. Yet they retained their solemnity. Across the wide expanse of the Neva River the far shore was lined with brightly colored palaces. Everything seemed to have been arranged as if to evoke a sense of ceremony, as if we had entered a precinct of solemn rite and ritual.

The city glowed under the bright, raking sunlight that shined almost as brightly, now at nearly nine in the evening, as it had at noon. I knew from my grandmother that we were arriving during the height of the White Nights—the same White Nights she had so often told me about—and that it would stay light until almost midnight. Now I could see that the sun, though bright, hung low in the sky, carving deep shadows even as it lit the city long into the night. We were arriving in the middle of summer—the weather was warm, the trees full of greenery, the air as languid as it could be with swarms of little Russian cars and hulking tram-buses belching exhaust as they flew by us on the road. Like anyone else, I had imagined Russia in winter as a place of snow—ice on the rivers, sleighs and the steaming breath of horses—yet I had also known that there was a summer in Russia, short and intense. I sensed that the bright, oblique evening light was evanescent. Whatever was being illuminated would have to be grasped quickly, lest it dissipate before I could take hold. The enigmatic facades stood silent and imposing under the raking evening light, in the shimmer of the late day's lingering heat.

We drove along the Palace Embankment past the Winter Canal. On the cobblestone pavement, a woman in an elegant dress and hat was walking with a child. She looked nothing like the rest of the Soviet citizens I had seen until that moment. She was elegant and looked almost properly European, though not dressed in truly expensive clothes—this was still Soviet Russia, after all. She didn't seem to be one of the anonymous mass of people moving with grim intent to or from work, or to go wait in line for some scarce provision. What was she doing, strolling along the embankment? She looked cultured, intellectual. Had we arrived in the proletarian paradise, or a center of European culture? What had been my grandmother's destination, her purpose, when she came here in 1932? What gave people pleasure and fulfillment in this strange place, aside from the dignity of forging ahead under dire necessity?

My grandmother caught sight of the woman and smiled. She looked at me and patted my hand. Don't worry, I felt she was telling me, it will all come clear in time. She wanted me to understand. She believed I could.

She whispered to me to cross to the other side of the bus so I could catch a glimpse of the spire of the Admiralty, once St. Petersburg's (as the city was originally named) and now Leningrad's most famous landmark. As we drove by the Admiralty's façade, unchanged over two hundred years and somehow still intact after three years of German shelling and bombing during the war, the enormous figure of Peter the Great, Pushkin's Bronze Horseman, rose up in front of us on Senate Square (where Dostoevsky had stood in the snow awaiting his mock execution before being reprieved and sent to Siberia for ten years, after which he returned to Petersburg to write *Crime and Punishment* and *The Brothers Karamazov*). The lower end of the square was lined with yet another imposing row of neoclassical buildings, beautiful if slightly ominous in their imperial Russian vainglory. We drove by the Peter statue atop its enormous block of stone, larger even than the huge statue itself, with Peter's horse rearing up on its hind legs. The city of ceremony and rite.

As we passed by, my grandmother once again produced her faint, indulgent smile, as if to indicate she had her own special relationship to this individual as well.

The bus came to a stop in front of the hotel. My grandmother drew herself up and moved forward to descend the short set of stairs to the street, just as I had seen her do so many times, coming down from the train on Long Island when she came to visit, or in Peekskill when we traveled to Mohegan; always the journeyer, stepping down from the platform to begin her next adventure. Now she was elderly, living in her little apartment on the fringe of Manhattan, but here she was, once again, setting foot on the soil of this city in which she had once lived, a place that was as much home, as familiar to her, as West 66th Street or Greenwich Village in Manhattan, or Paulding Lane in Mohegan.

I followed my grandmother off the bus and looked around, trying to reconcile the dissonance between the grandiosity, the historical gravity of what I was seeing and the utter shabbiness of it all, the layer of dust covering everything, the litter strewn across the elegant cobblestones of the imperial-era square in front of the once grand Astoria Hotel. It too looked frayed, its façade in need of cleaning and repair, half the awnings torn or missing, with only our rickety bus and two or three unimposing automobiles parked on the vast parade ground in front.

All worn, perhaps, and neglected—but as I started to take in the unimaginably grand scenes around me, I could barely contain my astonishment. In front of us stood the elegant equestrian statue of Emperor Nicholas I, also on an enormous base (how could this land of the proletariat worship its tsarist past so ardently, I asked myself); beyond the Nicholas statue, another imposing palace beside which flowed a stately canal between granite embankments; behind us, the gilded dome of St. Isaac's cathedral atop its enormous base of polished stone and bronze colonnades (as if, I later thought when I returned as an adult, the Roman Pantheon and St. Peter's basilica had been dismembered, transported to Russia, recast in precious materials, then reassembled together to feed a Russian appetite for autocratic display even greater than the one that had summoned forth the original versions in Rome); and leading away from the square on the far side, a broad street lined with elegant houses, albeit in a state of disrepair— one of which, I eventually learned, was the childhood home of Vladimir Nabokov.

Every block of stone, every surface of bronze and iron, every ripple on the canals as they flowed toward the Neva River glowed yellow and gold with the rays of the still bright nighttime sun. I had left the quiet sidewalks and clipped lawns of Long Island just two weeks earlier.

CHAPTER 8. LENINGRAD, 1963—

HOTEL ASTORIA

The lobby of the Astoria was cavernous and empty. It had obviously been designed for swarms of elegant travelers but now, at the height of the summer "season," aside from ourselves—a group of rather bedraggled, worn-out bus tourists who had been traveling for twelve hours—there were only a few dubious-looking characters loitering in the dark recesses. We huddled together a few feet from the front desk, where the tour guide had gone to negotiate our arrival. My grandmother stood slightly apart, waiting. I could sense her impatience—this was not how hotels, even Soviet hotels, had been run in her day. She watched the proceedings, trying to eavesdrop on what was being said at the desk. She was the vigilant observer, the keeper of rectitude—a role I would see her assume over and over in Russia. She knew the right way of doing things and bridled when they were done badly. Russia was like her ward, her property in a way, though she no longer had any claim on it. She knew what Russia had been, what it had meant to her and why, and she wanted all that to continue. She seemed to be trying to will it back into place.

What was unfolding before us, on the part of the staff at the desk, was simply apathy mixed with a light dose of antipathy for the demanding foreigners (never try to pull rank of foreign standards on a Russian, I came to learn), or perhaps just the tiresome effort of maintaining this disjointed relic of a hotel that had been meant for completely different people in completely different times. I saw, again, what I had sensed immediately, from the moment we crossed the border and were stopped by the guards in their impressive leather uniforms, while all along the road the pavement was rutted, the houses neglected and falling back into the earth—that Russia was out of kilter; it retained an essence of its former self, but was drained of all vitality, while at the same time the past was so indelibly embedded it could never be extirpated. The idea that this was a totally new society, a proletarian paradise with no vestige of its imperial and bourgeois antecedents was, accordingly, negated from the start.

We rode up in the steel-cage elevator, watching the floors with their dusty hallways rise up and fall away in front of us until we reached ours. As we came off the elevator we beheld, sitting in front of us at a bare, modern-style desk that looked like it belonged in the interrogation room of an airport rather than the gracious hallways of the Astoria Hotel, the attendant, as one might say in English, or perhaps concierge. But this ferocious-looking individual was so unlike any concierge in both mien and attitude that you could never call her that. You just had to call her *dezhurnaya*, the Russian word, which translates as duty officer, more or less, as appropriate (linguistically and functionally) on a military base as in the halls of a Soviet hotel. We stayed in the Astoria for a week, passing and exchanging greetings of a sort with this person several times a day, but she never smiled, once. Her imposing heft, her cropped gray hair, and drab-colored smock in no way contradicted the potential image of prison matron. We tried to take it in with humor, but a sinister overtone remained. I knew of no reason for it actually to be sinister for us; but then again, what did I really know of my grandmother's position in Russia? Whom did she know? Was she still in contact with Voroshilov? Were the authorities—"they" as the Russians referred to them—interested in her and in our family? Each time we passed the *dezhurnaya*, my grandmother maintained her lightly smiling demeanor, revealing nothing.

We got our key and went down the hall to the room. As we pushed open the heavy, dark mahogany door, a row of white linen curtains, filled with the raking light of the late evening sun, appeared across the room.

The room was large, with a kind of sitting area in front and a sleeping area with two twin beds at the back, below the room's high windows. The two were separated by a large, old-fashioned folding screen. My grandmother told me to go lie down behind the screen while she began to unpack and prepare for a visit from her sister-in-law Nina and niece Mila, who were due to arrive on some important business, late as it was. I understood that in Russia the ties of family are strong, the urgency of meeting relatives a given, no polite waiting until the next day. They would come that very night, never mind the hour. I also understood that the topic was certain to be Mila's dire situation: alone with a one-year-old child after being abandoned by the father, the visiting professor from France who, after spending a year in Russia, had promised to bring Mila and the baby back to Paris as soon as he got settled, but who had never been heard from again. Stories like

Mila's, I came to learn, were all too common. Many educated Russians dreamed of escaping to Western Europe or America. Only a few succeeded.

I took out the journal my sister had given me and thought about writing down the events of the day, but wasn't sure where to begin. I had no idea how to capture the tremendous intensity of my first impressions of Russia. I thought of hearing my grandmother's voice speaking Russian to the people downstairs in the hotel, and while she was telling me the names of the islands and the branches of the river. That's what I wanted to write down, even if I didn't realize it then. What I heard when she spoke.

I looked at the blank page with its widely spaced, light pink lines running across the white background, thinking I should fill it with upbeat phrases in neat cursive handwriting. But I remained at a loss. The things that had happened—standing in the noonday heat on the side of a cracked asphalt road somewhere in the remote forest along the border between Finland and Russia, watching the unsmiling, leather-clad border guards examine our bus; seeing the forlorn but imposing city of Leningrad slowly materialize outside my grimy bus window as we rode through its swampy outskirts in the orange evening light—didn't seem to fit easily into the tone of light-hearted, clever touristic observation I imagined I should adopt.

"We left Helsinki by bus at eight in the morning," I began. "Later, we stopped in a city called Vyborg and had Russian dumplings, called *pelmeni*, for lunch."

Oh, my goodness, no, I thought.

Years later, I realized that what I was trying to write about was what our journey meant to me; and that its meaning had to do with the past. We had just arrived in my grandmother's remembered world. Surely the place we had come to could not exist solely in the present, when its very essence and the purpose of our trip were predicated on memory. This was the phenomenon confronting me, obscure as it was to me at the age of thirteen. I confronted it again when I went back to Russia thirty-five years later. As I looked at the blank page, I asked myself: Why on earth had my grandmother brought me here? What was I supposed to do, to think, to feel? What was my job? Many years later, I understood. What I wanted to do was start writing myself into the story.

Of course, I was eager to meet my relatives and see the great touristic sights of the city. I felt the vibration of the tram-buses crossing St. Isaac's Square and saw the little bursts of dust released from the ceiling each time one passed, floating down through the rays of sunlight filtering into the room. I had no doubt that we were in Soviet Russia, 1963.

But still I sensed that behind it all, separated by a screen like the one that separated me from my grandmother as she bustled about in the main part of the room, was the history, the aftermath of all that had happened—the source of what made my grandmother the cynosure she was for me and so many others, including our relatives here in Russia, throughout her life. Without the years in Pskov before the Revolution, her escapades in exile, her travels, the Soviet Union of the thirties where she came back to live, the war, the histories of her twelve siblings and their trials through the turbulent half-century since she left them—without all that, it was impossible to make full sense of the present or why we had come. I could never quite efface the images, as I moved about the city then and years later when I returned as an adult, of all the things I had heard about: the wood-burning stoves that used to heat the apartment houses in the impossibly cold winters; the horse-drawn carts and streetcars that went up and down Nevsky Prospekt during the thirties when my grandmother lived there (my uncle loved to tell the story of how the other passengers would always shout down the crowded tram: "Comrades, make way, there is a child coming aboard," whenever he and my grandmother got on); the apparently quiet and personal but actually epic drama of the nice, educated, sensitive (and bourgeois) people my grand-mother's siblings had been and their life-long adjustment to becoming Soviet citizens, adapting to the new rituals of life and the harsh material deprivation, matched by a spiritual deprivation; but never total spiritual deprivation since the books and the culture that formed them always remained.

The legacy and grandeur of Russian culture—that was the real keystone in the arch that spanned my grandmother's life. Here, I already had the strong feeling, things played out on the scale of grand opera, Greek drama—no light Viennese operetta or drawing room farce. I had understood something about it from my grandmother long before we came to Leningrad, but now I was suddenly surrounded by it, here in the very place, unalloyed.

The impulse to daydream the past was intensified by my strange surroundings, heightened perhaps by my first experience of the abrupt, intense shifts brought on by jet travel. How on earth had I ended up in this sweltering, dusty room, when a few days earlier I had been in the relatively normal—by home standards—surroundings of London and Finland? And a week before that, in the den of my suburban house, watching American television, with its forced humor and canned laughter? I had landed on the stage for a play set at the turn of the century—no television, no push-button phones, no air conditioning; just ancient furniture, antique plumbing fixtures and lace curtains that seemed to have been there since the hotel opened in 1912. And everywhere, dust.

I listened as my grandmother bustled about in the main part of the room, beyond the screen that closed off the area of our two beds. From the moment we entered the room she had seemed content, moving about in what to her were familiar surroundings, arranging things, putting things away. What was she feeling, I wondered, what was she thinking? I slid down to the edge of the bed to see if I could peek around the screen. She was arranging a set of framed pictures on the large round table in the middle of the sitting area. I could not quite see them—the next morning, I saw there was the picture of her father, the one she always kept on her bookshelf in New York; one of the whole family together in the twenties, when my grandmother had come to visit them in Latvia with my father, who was seven years old; a picture of my own family, my parents with their three children; and one of my grand-mother's summer house in Mohegan. She was preparing the room to receive her niece and sister-in-law. Preparing to make sure they all remembered the past, and to appreciate what the present had brought as well. Amidst these surroundings that had not changed since she left Russia a half century earlier, she was the same person who had always made this trip, so many times, in the twenties, the thirties, the fifties. Those times were as distant to me as lost empires, but to her they were just a slightly altered version of the present, a continuum, all blending together over the long span of her life.

She draped a clean pair of stockings over the high back of a chair and laid out a clean dress, then went inside the large bathroom to run her bath and prepare for the visit. I thought I heard her humming as she went back and forth between the main room and the bathroom; the sound of the bathwater crashing into the giant porcelain basin made it difficult to tell whether it was real. After she went into the bathroom and turned off the faucet, she came back out into the room one more time, went over to the window, and looked down on St. Isaac's Square. I couldn't see her face as she scanned the cobbled pavement; I wasn't sure if she was looking for something in particular or just savoring the pleasure of drinking in the scene.

And as I watched her move about her room at the Astoria Hotel, like a time traveler returning home, I thought of how I had seen her moving about in her housecoat in her apartment in New York, in her summer cottage in Mohegan, in our suburban house in Long Island; and moving about, well-coiffed and carefully attired, through the public spaces in America, getting on and off the train in Roslyn and Peekskill, moving through Penn Station and down the streets of New York. She had adapted to all those places, as slightly foreign as they remained to her for her entire life. She always carried herself with assurance and perhaps an even slightly inflated sense of self—that is who she was—but there was the hint of something tentative always lurking beneath. She had carried on dutifully with her life in America, without protest; she adapted, married, raised two sons, set up house in a series of strange apartments including the peculiar dry-wall box she now inhabited on the edge of the city. She did what people did; she followed the paths the twentieth century laid out for her, like the millions of other Russians—Russian Jews, in particular—who emigrated to America. She had been content with her life, but here I sensed that she felt a sense of completion that always eluded her ever so slightly at home. As she turned around to go to her bath, I saw her smiling. She was back home, and nothing had really changed in the fifty years since she had left, which is partly what made her smile, I imagined. The same Victorian furniture, the same view onto the square, the same turn-of-the-century chandelier. This and the family apartment on Vladimirsky Prospekt, where her siblings, the young siblings she had grown up with before she left them for a distant new life, were waiting for her—a place that was as close as she could come to her childhood household in Pskov, the gracious world of her youth, full of culture and material comfort at a time of amazing change and promise. That is what she was seeking, and what made her smile, as she looked down onto St. Isaac's Square at the incarnation of the Russian culture that she still breathed, that had made her.

The phone rang. My grandmother picked it up and began speaking in Russian, softly at first, then with increasing urgency. I had heard her take similar calls many times in her apartment in New York; there, it always felt like she was switching into the language of some secret society—a wonderful curiosity, an excursion into a special realm that only she occupied, walled-off and hidden from the everyday culture and atmosphere around her. Now she was speaking Russian in the place where everyone spoke Russian, where our English was the language of isolation. I marveled at how easily she slipped back into her milieu. Of course, she was not quite like everyone else, she was better dressed than any

Russian woman I had seen and carried herself with a certain hauteur that seemed a bit out of place in the land of workers. Years later, my cousin Sasha confided to me that her Russian sounded a bit old-fashioned. But suddenly, hearing her speak her natural language, expressing her feelings in its melodious cadences, she seemed to me a slightly different person than the one who spoke to me in her mildly off-kilter, if perfectly fluent, English.

She hung up the phone and told me that Nina and Mila were on their way. Go to sleep, she said, we'll talk softly so as not to wake you. During the White Nights, the sense of time, of early versus late, became fluid; there was no consideration that once it got very late it was time to go home, to end the day's activities. Arriving close to midnight was not unusual.

I stared at the still blank page of my journal. When I first lay down, the filtered sunlight had fallen on the open page; as I pondered my writing assignment an hour later, the light of the White Night still entered through the curtain but no longer illuminated the whole room. The rays of the sun now came in horizontally, skipping over me and the bed, and settled on the upper half of the wall behind me, lighting the soiled wallpaper with a fiery orange glow. The space on the bed now lay in half-light. There was something about the White Nights that evoked the essence of Russia, though I didn't really know that yet; I hadn't read the Pushkin poems or Dostoevsky novels that made it so. But one thing I could tell was that the White Nights belonged to Russia and not to the USSR. My grandmother had told me about the White Nights in the far north, during her summer of exile, her time of freedom and adventure. She had spoken to me about the village of Mezen in the time of the White Nights, where she carried on her love affair with Voroshilov, her intrigues with the notables of the town, and of her flight with her sister into another life, another world. These were the moments lit into incandescent permanence by the never-setting sun.

And gradually, without my fully realizing it then, our memory streams started flowing together. I had come to Russia to enter my grandmother's world, to capture and imbibe it, so that I could understand and keep what she had given me, keep it for myself and pass it on, in turn, to the next generation of the family. I felt the memories of her life here in Leningrad in the nineteen-thirties start to become part of my memory; I felt that they needed to, or they would dissipate and float away with the slowly gathering darkness.

Just as you go back to a place you once knew in your own life and try to see it as it was in the past, to recapture the memory of it, you can go to a place with a past that is not your own, and still imagine, recapture a little, that past. That is what tourists in Rome, in Athens, in Paris, in London do, all the time. My grandmother and I had traveled together to Leningrad; now we would go out to tour the city together, to meet our family in the home they had lived in for generations. She would be looking at her memories, and I, through my young eyes, with no real memories of my own, would be looking at the same ones. We had come to the place where the stories, the aura that she brought to me every weekend as a child, became real. She and I were on the quest together. I had come, with her, to recapture what I was starting to perceive to be part of my own past, though it had taken place two generations before I was born.

For a shy, sensitive, inquisitive child from a place where none of what I was thinking about or feeling was valued very much, this was a somewhat terrifying task. Fortunately, I had my ally, my grandmother, who was an expert at it, who had long ago inducted me into the cult of past-within-the-present. She was next to me, behind the screen in the sitting area of our room.

It was just starting to get dark—those few hours of deep twilight that occur during the White Nights—when Nina and Mila called to say they were leaving Vladimirsky Prospekt. I already knew they were coming to discuss Mila's situation; as I later found out, they gave my grandmother several addresses for us to try and track down the child's father when we got to Paris later in the summer. Yes, it was very late, but Mila's problem was pressing, and as I also came to understand, such a conversation could never take place in the apartment on Vladimirsky Prospekt, where the communal living arrangements made privacy impossible and anything that anyone discussed was known to everyone else.

As I glanced out the window onto St. Isaac's Square, I saw that it had grown steadily more crowded with evening strollers as the heat of the day abated and the evening light spread its inviting glow. Indeed, as I saw many times when I returned to visit St. Petersburg, this was the time when the city became most magical, when the neglect and dilapidation became unnoticeable; when precisely the fact that the city was a relic of the past was what allowed it to be transformed into a magical place of intensified, glowing colors, a strange world of constructed perspectives, as if designed to be a stage on which to enact who knew what lavish dramas.

I was still awake when my grandmother received the call from the lobby that Nina and Mila were on the way upstairs. I looked around the screen and saw her peering down the hall. As she opened the creaking door, I heard the mingling sound of Russian voices, women's voices. The sound of men's and women's voices are no doubt different and distinct in every language; in Russian men's voices are melodic in the tenor and baritone range but generally even and declarative, while women's voices seem to carry the sound of all human experience, running up and down the scale like flutes, they sing and sigh. And the three voices drifting over the screen to me were sighing, it was unmistakable, and somehow, inevitable.

I fell asleep to the sound of the three voices, interrupted at intervals by soft crying. Sometime after midnight, I awoke to the faint afterglow of the sunset. When I woke up again at 4 am, the white lace curtains were filled with the translucent light of dawn. My grandmother was asleep in the bed next to me.

CHAPTER 9. LENINGRAD, 1963—

VLADIMIRSKY PROSPEKT

The next morning, my cousin Sasha came to pick us up at the hotel. Social protocol dictated that my grandmother be accorded this gesture of generational respect, and that the visiting American relatives be escorted back to Vladimirsky Prospekt.

Earlier, we had gone down for breakfast in a basement room that appeared to be a kitchen in former times, with unpainted walls and a black and white linoleum floor. Food was no longer served upstairs in the lobby, now reserved as a place for tour groups to form up and for the desks of attendants who arranged excursions—and kept a careful eye on the comings and goings. The idea of uniformed staff serving well-heeled customers drinks or breakfast in the lobby had ended up in the dustbin of history, as the Bolsheviks would say. The basement room seemed a perfectly adequate replacement by Soviet standards. Women in white smock uniforms did not so much serve as supervise the meal, which consisted of some bland biscuits, black bread, a piece of dark-colored sausage, and bitter tea or watery coffee, with milk of a suspiciously yellow tinge. My grandmother leaned over to whisper to me not to worry, that we would soon be eating with the family on Vladimirsky Prospekt, this was the last meal we would eat with the group.

Sasha was seventeen years old, tall, slim, and blond—perfectly Russian-looking, really. He was courtly—perhaps because he was so tall, he always seemed to be bowing slightly—and spoke entirely fluent, if somewhat formal English. My grandmother told me that he had been sent to a special English school in Moscow, without further explanation. Later, as I thought about it, I assumed this was all part of a bigger story—my grandmother's political intrigues, her connection to Voroshilov, Sasha's father being an officer in the army. But Sasha, when I met him again as an adult, explained that when he was growing up there was interest in developing English speakers for various official jobs and he had simply competed in the usual exams. I'm not sure I quite believed him, but by then it didn't really matter—by that time the USSR was no more, and he was scraping by teaching English privately. In the early post-Soviet days, people didn't talk much about what they had done before. It was easier to forget, to just accept that people did what they had to and that now things were different.

My grandmother caught sight of him waiting for us in the lobby, and we walked over to greet him. He stood in place, as if unsure whether he had permission to move. She laughed when she saw how tall he had become (my grandmother retained her weakness for good-looking men well into old age) and waited for him to bend down and kiss her. He and

I solemnly shook hands, then leaned forward tentatively and embraced one another.

We left the hotel and set out down the street of elegant houses I'd seen the night before—Great Maritime Street, as I later learned when I was able to read the Russian signs. Before the street became a fashionable commercial and residential thoroughfare in the nineteenth century, it had housed sailors and workers from the nearby Admiralty. The area had long since shed its character as a rough dockside district, but the memory of the city's early days after its foundation by Peter the Great in 1703 still echoed in the local street names.

We walked past baroque palaces of the former aristocracy ("former" became a key word after the Russian Revolution, for people whose social status was abolished—former count, former tsar, former merchant of the first guild—in imitation of the practice that arose during the French Revolution. One anecdote relates that Nicholas II, shortly after he was deposed, sat down to dinner one afternoon with his family; he had just read an article in the newspaper describing how "the former tsar, with his former wife, and former children is securely confined in his former palace." Looking at the shriveled cut of meat before him, he announced, "I am about to carve the former ham") and a row of imposing commercial buildings constructed in Art Deco style at the turn of the century. In Leningrad, I could already perceive, the Russian time machine operated at maximum intensity. The general state of disrepair, like a drab scrim covering everything, created a kind of leveling, unified look which—together with the omnipresent hammer and sickle emblem set into the pediments of buildings that once housed aristocrats or great commercial enterprises but were now occupied by government offices, in their endless bureaucratic profusion—proclaimed quite clearly that we were in the Soviet Union. And yet, almost nothing in the city had changed since the time of the Revolution in 1917; and to a great extent long before that. Everywhere I looked, long lines of buildings of equal height, no taller than four stories, stretched continuously along, their facades undulating in an unbroken succession of columns, arches and niches; the sensation of being translocated to the nineteenth century was interrupted only by the occasional baroque palace, even older, painted in shimmering green or overly bright orange. Near the Nevsky Prospekt, the newer Art Deco buildings evoked the last great era of the city before time (I couldn't help feeling as we walked along) stopped. Their simplified, powerful design, contrasting with the city's dominant neoclassical style, proclaimed the achievements of Russia's early twentieth century avant-garde, when St. Petersburg was commercially vibrant and awash in sophistication and internationalism—the so-called Silver Age, Russia's last great, history-changing eruption of art and literature. Somehow, it had all been subsumed into the new Soviet world; and yet, despite the scrim of dust, neglect, and official denial, there it all remained, palpably present.

Multiple layers of time notwithstanding, on this particular summer morning in Leningrad in 1963, I walked along with my grandmother and newfound cousin, Sasha, on Great Maritime Street, under the intense glare of the sunlight reflecting from the golden dome of St. Isaac's Cathedral. We turned onto the Nevsky Prospekt. The Nevsky is one of those streets whose name alone is so redolent with allusion and association that just by setting foot on it your experience is heightened and your state of sensation altered. I felt it the moment we turned the corner, even without having yet read the classics of Russian literature that help make it so. There must have been something in the way my grandmother said its name that inculcated me early on. As well as the way it sounds in Russian—two sharp and perfectly concise syllables, the 'v' transformed to a hissing 'f' because it precedes the letter 's,' followed by the most quintessential (for Americans) of all Russian terminal syllables: 'ski.' So much of what my grandmother transmitted to me about Russia came in the form of sound.

Nevsky is uncommonly wide, evoking to this day the grandeur its creators intended. Lined with churches, palaces, monuments, historic public edifices, and a sprinkling of Art Deco buildings, it is one of the world's famous streets that rightly merits a block-by-block, building-by-building Baedeker of its own. From its origin at the Admiralty to its intersection with Vladimirsky Prospekt, it passes over the city's pictur-esque rivers and canals, affording the stroller three graceful bridge crossings and making an excursion along Nevsky Prospekt the city's most famous, and reliable, pleasure.

Sasha began dutifully explaining the sights to me, inter-rupting from time to time to exchange a few words in Russian with my grandmother. She walked a bit ahead with a slightly imperious air, turned out as she was in her high-heeled shoes and printed silk dress, with her shiny leather purse draped over her wrist, smiling pleasantly at the modestly dressed passersby who looked back with startled expressions. Foreigners were still a rarity in those days, immediately recognizable by their clothing and demeanor.

Despite a light breeze and the crystalline morning air, the street and sidewalk were still covered in the same fine layer of dust I had noticed the night before. Alongside opulently carved doorways of elegant buildings, low archways opened into networks of dark interior passageways. The morning sunshine and my first grand impressions of Nevsky Prospekt had summoned forth an effervescent soundtrack in a major key—C major, most likely. But along with it, I discerned the counter theme I had heard as we drove into the city the day before—Leningrad's ever-present, inescapable minor key. And what, exactly, was the minor key? The material poverty? The inevitable sense of Russian existential gloom? The insecurity of life in a police state? Or simply the accumulated suffering— the social strife of the nineteenth century, the inconceivable violence of the Revolution and its aftermath, the even greater cataclysm of the war and Siege of Leningrad—that had become so deeply embedded in the fabric of memory that it seemed to pervade the present in almost undiluted form?

Sasha smiled and chatted nonchalantly as we walked, but I sensed that he and my grandmother remained watchful—just as my grandmother had been when we stood in the lobby of the Astoria, or when we first encountered the *dezhurnaya* upstairs. The ominous political atmosphere, like the residue of a toxic fog, permeated the crisp morning air. Ungainly trolley buses, tethered to a dense tangle of wires overhead by long black rods resembling giant insect antennae, plodded down the broad avenue, swooping in at intervals to disgorge one group of unsmiling Soviet citizens, as another waited silently to board.

What, I wondered, did my grandmother make of this enigmatic world? I never asked her directly. She had watched the whole story unfold, from the time of her youthful revolutionary idealism to this, her latest return to the place she remained so attached to; a place that now seemed, at once, the inspiration for everything of value in her life, and the remorseless instrument of all her disappointed dreams.

The character of every great city can be distilled in a few words—New York is energy and vitality; Paris sophistication and elegance; London bustle and clamor. Leningrad was the fateful weight of the past, suffusing the present.

We continued along, passing the great monuments of the street—parks, statues, squares, enormous neoclassical buildings with bronze quadrigas surmounting pediments of orange-yellow stucco. Finally we approached the last milestone before Vladimirsky Prospekt—the Anichkov bridge over the Fontanka River. Amidst Leningrad's air of neglect and disrepair, here was an emanation of pure classical beauty, sparkling with the shifting reflections of the morning sun on the river. Four rearing bronze horses restrained by youthful tamers—the height of nineteenth century classicism affirming a world of wealth, possibility, power, and control by man. One would have thought it violated class consciousness, but it was one of the city's most beloved monuments. Perhaps because youths taming horses was a kind of Soviet motif in its own right, if one normally realized in blocky neo-constructivist style.

A few streets beyond the bridge, we reached Vladimirsky Prospekt. We turned the corner and walked down the short, wide avenue, lined with buildings from the early nineteenth century. As in the rest of the city, there was almost no sign of commercial life. A few modest shops were evident on the ground floors (which you entered by stepping down a foot or two from the sidewalk, because ever since its founding the city had been sinking gradually into the marsh below) but without any signage or other feature that might entice a customer inside. Vladimirsky Prospekt—another Leningrad stage set. The tram rails running down the middle of the street and the odd passing car were the only definitive evidence of the twentieth century.

We stopped in front of no. 8. This was the house my grandmother had lived in, with my seven-year-old uncle, in the winter of 1932-33. Her siblings had begun moving into the sprawling apartment on the third floor, family by family, in 1917. The building was fashioned from blocks of purplish-brown stone, its facade an elaborate composition of columns, arches, and carved window frames; adorned by a line of narrow balconies along the upper floors and a decorative pediment at the top with the numerals 1827 set into it. The rusted metal front door—the original carved wooden door had obviously disappeared long ago—hung on uneven hinges, slightly ajar. Sasha pushed the door forward and stepped across the metal threshold. My grandmother followed.

I peered uncertainly into the dimly lit entryway. A strong odor of urine, eliciting an exchange of rueful, knowing looks between Sasha and my grandmother, came wafting toward me. The floor inside was unpaved. Seeing my hesitation, my grandmother leaned over to whisper a few words of encouragement—"Don't worry, everyone is going to like you, they're very pleased you came all the way here to meet them"—and took me by the hand to draw me across the threshold.

I walked into the dimly lit space. It felt like a place that had been ravaged by war, or poverty, or perhaps simply social despair. And yet directly ahead of us, a grand stone staircase swept upwards, interrupted between each floor by a windowed landing giving out onto the building's back courtyard, before the broad steps resumed their climb along the opposite wall. The stairs were worn and had seemingly not been swept in years, but the elegant brass railing and creamy surface of the stone suggested that Vladimirksy Prospekt, no. 8 had once been an elegant residence for some of St. Petersburg's more prosperous citizens.

We climbed the steps to the third floor and Sasha opened the door with his key; unlike the building's front door, the door to the apartment actually had a lock. Beyond the entryway, adorned with a plank of coat hooks nailed to the wall and a low bench with shelving for outdoor footwear and house slippers, a long hallway led to the main sitting and dining room, which now served also as a bedroom for Sasha, his grandfather Arkady, and grandmother Lyolya. The apartment's unpolished but elegant wooden parquet floor flowed along in a continuous geometric pattern from room to room.

As we entered the main room, we caught sight of Arkady standing with a dustpan and broom in his hand—he had apparently not quite finished tidying up in preparation for our arrival—with his worn woolen pants held up around his thin waist by a narrow belt, shirtless, as it was summertime, but sporting nonetheless a beige woolen beret. He smiled at us with a combination of apology and knowing recognition as if to say: this is the way it is, we do our best to preserve a scrap of dignity in this degraded world of ours.

Pulling on his shirt as he crossed the room, he came over to embrace my grandmother. They hugged each other tightly for a few moments, exchanging a few quiet words. Then Arkady took a step back, looked down at me warmly, and introduced himself. He knew enough English to say "Hello" and "Welcome" in his heavy Russian accent.

As with every Russian arrival or departure, the first order of business was a meal. There were at least sixteen people at the table—the eight or so who lived on Vladimirsky Prospekt, my grandmother's sister, Aunt Fredi, who came with her granddaughter Gina from Riga, and a few cousins from other parts of Leningrad. The table was set with china, silverware, and crystal salvaged from the old family apartments in Pskov and Riga before the Revolution. I looked around in slight bewilderment—the scene was at once festive, solemn, and nostalgic. It was a ritual that my grandmother and her siblings had enacted many times before; but for me, it was overwhelming to meet so many new people whose language, appearance, and social behavior were so unfamiliar. And yet, I felt a current of mutual affinity flowing between us. Everyone wanted me to feel welcome, as my grandmother had promised. Sasha laughed as he watched me try to navigate the seemingly endless profusion of small dishes that make up a Russian celebratory meal. Make sure you try a little of each, he advised.

For the next week, we ate almost every meal at home on Vladimirsky, except for the days when I was out touring. Sasha, Gina, and I quickly became a trio, teenagers on summer holiday out on the town, happy to be free of adults. They were a few years older than me and took me in tow; Sasha in his role as interpreter, Gina as a kind of older sister watching over her vulnerable young charge. They were more serious than the kids I knew at home, as if attuned to the gravity of life around them. They had, after all, been raised in the Soviet world; they had attended Pioneer camps where they wore red scarves and were obliged to chant patriotic, Socialist slogans. (When I came to Russia as an adult, whenever

I would casually ask my cousin Lyena whether she was ready for whatever it was we were about to do, she would jokingly reply, "Always ready!" with a stiff salute. "As I learned in the Pioneers!" she would add, laughing.) But both were whimsical and humorous and seemed to have a sophisticated sense of the absurd side of life. As with so much else I had seen and sensed in Leningrad, their Russian sensibility, passed down from their grandparents just as mine had been, seemed largely to have won out over their Soviet one. Amidst the turmoil of their strange world, with all its perils, restrictions, and hypocrisies, they radiated a kind of hearty, dauntless optimism. They reminded me of the teenage counselors I'd had at camp in Mohegan—who, as the second-generation offspring of Russian immigrant grandparents, came from essentially the same stock, the same sensibility.

They took me to the Hermitage, proudly expounding on its history and collection. The grand entry staircase of the Winter Palace, the first in the enormous museum's complex of buildings, gave me my first real lesson in Russian aesthetics— the love of lavish materials, ostentatious display (the colossal bright green malachite columns were the most sumptuous things I had ever seen), and massive scale. At the top of the stairs, in the first gallery, two exquisite paintings of the Madonna and Child by Leonardo da Vinci hung on the dark, polished wooden walls. Though I was too young to realize their extreme rarity and the pleasure of seeing them up so close, without throngs of other visitors, I was enchanted by their ethereal beauty and aura of perfect serenity. When I came back to Russia many years later, Sasha proudly showed me an article that Arkady had written about them in the early fifties—a small, erudite paean celebrating their presence in the city. It fit with the gentle, elegant man I remembered from childhood; the man who would never agree to join the Communist Party.

One radiantly sunny afternoon we set out by hydrofoil across the Gulf of Finland for Peterhof, the summer palace built by Peter the Great to imitate—or, in predictable Russian style, outdo—Versailles. On this outing, the centerpiece of any visit to the city during the warm months, my grandmother, Arkady, Lyolya, and Aunt Fredi came along; spurred as much by the lure of the pleasure trip as the sense that such a canonical cultural experience required the supervisory wisdom of adults. Peterhof had been nearly destroyed during the Siege of Leningrad, partly as a result of Russian bombardment of the German siege lines, partly as an act of pure, senseless vandalism by the Nazis. After the Germans finally withdrew, the Soviets began restoring the ruin almost immediately. Much of what we saw that bright afternoon— the gleaming baroque facades, the golden statues lining the Grand Cascade fountain as it descended from the parterre of the palace to the waters of the Gulf below, the pleasure gardens and pavilions scattered through the surrounding woods—though meticulously faithful to the lost originals, was brand new.

As we strolled the grounds, Arkady lectured on the palace's history and architecture, with Sasha diligently translating. Inside, he discoursed on the paintings and furniture; when they had been made, in which European country, what had been saved during the war and returned to the reconstructed palace and what had been destroyed. The visit had the feeling of a ritual, performed according to the same formula each time, as we moved slowly through the park to the accompaniment of Arkady's gentle tutoring. Throngs of visitors, mostly Russian families, were out enjoying the summer school break and fine weather. The golden statues of the Cascade fountain glistened in the cloud of mist thrown up by the playful spray fountains alongside.

And yet, as we strolled about, I heard a faint strain of the Leningrad minor key, echoing in the background—the ubiquitous groups of Red Army soldiers; the severe looks of the docents; an intangible air of watchfulness. I had the sense that all these people out enjoying the apparent freedom of a summer day's leisure did not, finally, feel free at all.

On our last evening, we gathered again on Vladimirsky Prospekt for the farewell meal. The table was set with the same vintage china and glassware, and an array of dishes—but crowned this time with a *kulebiaka,* a long, rectangular puff pastry filled with salmon, sturgeon, mushrooms, kasha, eggs, and spinach wrapped together in swirling layers. A difficult to prepare, fittingly rare treat, appropriate to the occasion.

After the meal, we hugged one another and said our goodbyes. My grandmother cried—just a few tears, the ones she couldn't hold back. And then she and Arkady exchanged a glance and we all found chairs to perform the Russian ritual of departure: everyone sits down at the same time, exchanges looks, slaps palms on top of the thighs, and stands up in unison. Now we were ready to go.

Sasha walked us back to the Astoria. I was not to see him again for twenty-five years, until the time of Gorbachev, when my uncle and I were able finally to arrange the visits to the

U.S. that our Russian relatives had been dreaming about for so long.

The next morning, we met the tour group in the lobby of the Astoria to say goodbye. My grandmother and the guide stood aside and exchanged a few words with smiles and nods. Apparently things had worked out to everyone's satisfaction. In the afternoon, we boarded a small steamship for the overnight sail to Stockholm. That evening, I became suddenly giddy—with the release of the visit's tension and excitement, my grandmother suggested; and a little later, violently seasick. My grandmother gave me a quarter of one of her phenobarbital tablets and I slept until we docked the next day.

The apartment on Vladimirsky Prospekt remained fixed in my memory indelibly. For the rest of the summer, we toured Western Europe. Stockholm, Copenhagen, Amsterdam, Brussels, Paris, Bern, Lucerne, Vienna, Venice, Milan, and back to London. It was marvelous. But brooding, stage-set, magnetic and enigmatic Leningrad stood apart. No other city could ever evoke its aura of time and fate, beneath the glowing sky with the sun just below the horizon at midnight; elegant yet forlorn, as if living in its own afterlife, in the penumbra of memory. As it had somehow existed for me, in memory, even before I got there.

CHAPTER 10. RECORDED MEMORY

Ten years or so after my grandmother and I returned from Russia, it suddenly occurred to me that I had no permanent record of her stories beyond the ones I carried around in my head. I'm not sure how I failed to notice this earlier—though it tends to be the universal regret of all family chroniclers. Luckily, I came to my senses while there was still some time.

The catalyst, finally, was that my grandmother was getting very old. She had developed an abdominal infection the year before and been hospitalized for two weeks with a high fever, barely avoiding surgery. Afterwards, her memory began to decline. I realized that if I was ever going to do it, now was the time.

One spring afternoon when I was home on break from medical school, I drove to the city to see her. Medicine was a relatively late development in my career plans, since when I first arrived at college I studied music, art, and history, thinking I might become a teacher or even a professor. But the political battles of the sixties sent me off in another direction. I felt I needed to be on the front lines of social change and progress and that becoming a doctor would be a good way to do it. I had evidently inherited some of my grandmother's revolutionary idealism.

As a student, I was good at math and science as well as the liberal arts; a bit like my mother, good at everything. Even though my connection to the Russian side of things and to history, music, and art was perhaps deeper, I could not conceive of them as things to pursue professionally. They contained mysteries. Medicine was concrete, and in that sense, for me, easier—you studied facts, learned them, applied them, and saw results. I didn't quite know how to pursue the Russia story when I was twenty years old. You can't really study the late sonatas of Beethoven until you're older, they say.

My grandmother still lived on West 66th Street, in the same small apartment, with the same dinette, the same hutch, the same books and pictures. I went inside and kissed her hello.

"Go sit down in the living room, I'll be there in a moment," she said. She fussed around the kitchen for a few minutes and put the kettle on for tea.

I took out my tape recorder and set it up on the side table. My grandmother sat down on the couch and eyed the machine suspiciously, as if it were some modern contraption one could not really trust (fear of microphones was an ingrained feature of life in the Soviet Union), but also with a hint of hauteur and anticipatory pleasure. She was more than delighted to assume the role of raconteur.

Rulia's grandson Sven, who lived nearby on Riverside Drive, had recently brought my grandmother a picture of the sisters with their fellow exiles in Mezen, the summer before they fled Russia. Rulia had died a few years earlier, and the family was still going through her things.

"Tell me about the picture," I asked my grandmother, as a way to get her started.

"Oh, when I saw that picture, I could kiss that picture!" she said with delight, pronouncing "that" as "dot," in her usual way.

"That was right after I met Voroshilov," she added.

I let her follow her instincts, and we managed to get to almost everything—Pskov, her girlhood, her father, the family, how she and her best friend Estia Borkhova got their start in revolutionary politics, what she remembered about Rulia's arrest, the trip into exile, and the escape.

We taped over the course of three days. I still listen to the tape from time to time, and revel in the sound of her voice, dreamily, happily, reflectively, sometimes wistfully but mostly with pleasure, reminiscing about her youthful life and adventures in Russia.

When I left, late on third afternoon, I stopped in front of the building and looked up to my grandmother's balcony, where she was standing to wave goodbye, as she always did. I knew that one day I would write the story. And that to write it, I would have to go back to Russia.

PART II

RUSSIA REVISITED

CHAPTER 11. RETURN TO

ST. PETERSBURG

Three years after the taping session, my grandmother died. Just shy of her ninetieth year, she had lived through exile, escape, emigration, the advent of the Russian Revolution that she dreamed about in her youth, two world wars, and perhaps the most astonishing century in human history, starting in the era of the horse-drawn carriage and ending in the age of jet travel and nuclear weapons.

When her memory loss finally became severe, my parents reluctantly concluded that she could not manage alone in her small apartment, even with full-time help. The only option was to move her to a nursing home near their house on Long Island. After the move, to a remote corner of Suffolk County, she died within a few months. She was simply done. She had lived through overwhelming changes, adapted, lived through some more and adapted again, but this last stop was, finally, too alien. She was bereft of anything familiar, of anything that could connect her by even the slimmest thread to the long arc of her life.

The family gathered at my parents' house for an informal memorial service. We sat on the back patio, looking out onto the same yard I had gazed at as a child wondering whether more exciting worlds could exist beyond the hedge; the place where I had sat with my grandmother when she came to visit and ignited my imagination with the belief that, indeed, there were.

My uncle, who had acquired left-leaning views of his own under his mother's influence, praised her revolutionary idealism. "The ugly history of Russia in the twentieth century betrayed the ideals of Mom and her friends, but we should remember and honor them," he said. My father said almost nothing. I sensed that he wanted to express how deeply his mother had influenced his life but was overwhelmed by the regret he felt at moving so far away from her as an adult. My mother leaned over to comfort him. She too seemed stunned by the realization that her husband's Russian parents were finally gone (my grandfather had died a decade earlier). As much as she had failed to plumb the mysteries of the family Russian brigade, both her mother- and father-in-law had loved and supported her with a warmth she never experienced from her own parents. My sister, who had recovered enough to go to college and had gotten involved in left-wing politics and feminism, praised her as a role model.

I said a few words about the time I spent with her in Mohegan and Europe; but my life had changed so vastly since then—I was now a third-year medical student, twenty-seven years old, preoccupied with adjusting to my new professional and young adult life. I wanted to express the richness she had brought to all our lives and how much she had changed mine. I wasn't quite ready.

When I finished medical school, I moved back to New York for my graduate training and stayed on to begin my career. I had no time during those years to return to the theme of my grandmother and Russia, central as it remained to my consciousness. But I knew that I was the keeper of her story—our story, really.

And then, in 1991, the Soviet Union collapsed. Poof. Well, not completely poof, but almost. It had been fairly decrepit for years, and from the beginning of Gorbachev's tenure it was apparent that some form of drastic change was imminent.

Once the Soviet Union ceased to exist, the problem of travel between Russia and the United States evaporated overnight. The restrictions that had kept my relatives locked behind the Iron Curtain disappeared, and travel into Russia for Americans became equally uncomplicated. Several of my cousins, including Sasha, came for their first visits to the West, something that been inconceivable just a year or two before. I realized that traveling to Russia was no longer the arduous undertaking it had been when I was a child.

In 1996, I took my first trip back. When I traveled with my grandmother, crossing the border had been a forbidding experience; now one could just jump on a plane and find oneself walking down the streets of St. Petersburg the next day. Yes, St. Petersburg—shortly after the demise of the Soviet Union the dark-hued city of Leningrad had changed its name back to the somewhat brighter-sounding original.

I arrived in early April. The city looked almost exactly as I remembered it from 1963—as if nothing had been cleaned, repainted, or repaired since 1917. Great rows of ornate nineteenth-century apartment buildings still lined the dusty boulevards, with almost no shops, signs, or cars. The same mottled facades of imperial-era palaces, painted in improbable hues of red, violet, orange, and green, ran along the placid canals, their cobbled embankments lined with linden trees and spanned by small arched bridges. The streets and parks were still covered with the winter snow and ice, but the sun was warm and all across the city dripping icicles sparkled in the sunshine and plumes of vapor rose from the rooftops and spires, as if the city were awakening from its winter hibernation. I had arrived in time to see the metamorphosis that is Russia in the spring.

One afternoon, I was driving with my cousin Volodya along the Hermitage Embankment. (Volodya was one of my younger second cousins, too small for me to have met in Leningrad in 1963, though he grew up in the family apartment on Vladimirsky. The clan of Russian American second cousins—the grandchildren of my grandmother and her siblings—turned out to be a surprisingly small group considering the grandparents had numbered thirteen. Besides myself and my siblings, there was Sasha and his younger brother Sergey in Moscow; my cousin Lyena, also younger, whom I first met when she came to the U.S. on one of the Russian cousin visits in 1991; and my Aunt Rulia's three grandchildren in America. Not counting Gina, that is, whom I met in 1963 but lost track of; and my cousin Sergey—Mila's infant child, when I first saw him, who had been abandoned by his French father and eventually emigrated to America, where he became a well-known pianist.) Across the road, we could see great chunks of ice flowing swiftly along in the current of the Neva River. A gritty mix of sand, melted slush, and automobile exhaust pelted the windshield as the sparkling green façade of the Winter Palace flashed by on our right. Suddenly I saw a policeman in the middle of the wide roadway, directing traffic. I wasn't wearing my seatbelt and reached across to attach it. The policeman—tall and strikingly handsome in his military uniform and round fur hat—looked directly at me and broke into a radiant smile. Volodya let out a soft, approving laugh. The three of us enjoyed a pleasurable moment of shared understanding: we are not in the Soviet Union anymore. A cascade of images crystallized—the splendor of the palace, the sparkling river, the spring sunlight, the dashing militiaman laughing amidst the onrush of mud-spattered cars. Could Russia really contain such beauty, amidst all its squalor and disrepair? Yes, I thought. It was all part of the complicated Russia my grandmother had bequeathed to me.

I told my cousins about my ambitions to come back to Russia for an extended stay to do some serious research into the family history and write a book about it. Everyone was pleased with the idea and seemed almost to take it for granted that someone should do it; I, bright, academically accomplished, single and therefore relatively free, seemed a good candidate. I realized that my grandmother's adventures, especially her connection to Voroshilov, were as big a part of family lore for the Russian cousins as they were for me.

When I got home, I arranged to take some time off from my medical work and decided to enroll in the one-year degree program at the Columbia School of Journalism to prepare for the research and writing that lay ahead. The summer after journalism school, I went to Middlebury College in Vermont for an eight-week intensive Russian course. By the end I hadn't fully mastered the language, but I was well on my way. I got used to reading the letters of the Cyrillic alphabet, no longer simply mysterious symbols, and learned the basics of Russian's complex grammar. The clusters of sound that had been so alluring to me as a child, as my grandmother spoke Russian, evoking sensations of synesthesia, began to acquire clarity, like a developing photograph.

I wanted to go back to Russia to look for sources, to talk to my cousins, to probe into the historical archives to see what more I could learn about what my grandmother had done and why. But there was something else motivating me. I felt I owed it to my grandmother; I owed it to her to take up the mantle of the family tie to the Russian relatives—of the family Russian brigade. The tie had survived over three generations, for almost a century. Now, at the moment of the Soviet Union's long-awaited demise, it felt like it might all drift away into unrecoverable memory; the places where it all happened, the atmosphere, might simply disappear.

I talked over my plans with my professors at Middlebury and the people I had gotten to know in the Russian Department at Columbia. With their help, I made arrangements to affiliate myself with the Herzen State University in St. Petersburg and acquired a list of historians and archivists to contact. And through the Herzen—pronounced with a G in Russian at the beginning, since the Cyrillic alphabet has no letter H—I secured the assistance of a young Russian graduate student to act as my interpreter and translator. This was a stroke of good fortune, because in the nineties English translators were in great demand in St. Petersburg, as celebrities from England and the United States flooded into the newly open lands of the former Soviet Union. Like the sudden ability to walk across the no-man's land from West to East Berlin after the Wall came down, people seemed fascinated by the novel chance to travel in and out of Russia freely. Newly entrepreneurial linguists stopped translating Jack London and Ernest Hemingway and waited for a call from Sting, Bono, or Paul McCartney.

I left in late June of 1998. My flight took off at nine o'clock. The thin line of Long Island, glowing like a jeweled appendage of New York City, fell away below me as the plane climbed into the black night sky and set out over the Atlantic. The next morning, I changed planes in Helsinki and arrived in a small jet at Pulkovo, the St. Petersburg airport, at four o'clock in the afternoon. I walked down the stairs that had been rolled up to the plane, crossed the tarmac and boarded an old shuttle bus for the short ride to the terminal. This time, there were no formalities. A few airport maintenance workers looked on indifferently, lounging on empty luggage trolleys. I was on my way to the new Russia, whatever that was to turn out to be, but one thing was for sure. This was no longer the fearsome Soviet Union.

The other passengers and I formed a line in the arrivals hall and waited for the passport control agents to break off their conversations, before begrudgingly turning their attention to us. The immigration officer looked briefly at my visa, stamped my passport, and nodded me onwards. I walked through the customs checkpoint, where Volodya—his pleasant face with its usual expression of slight skepticism and irony, framed by his reddish-blond hair and cocked slightly to one side—stood waiting for me. We greeted each other in Russian and kissed on both cheeks.

The provincial quality and rundown state of the airport were somehow laughable and appealing at the same time—no unnecessary pretensions here. We walked outdoors. The open asphalt parking lot contained a smattering of small, battered cars—the Land Rovers and Mercedes of the post-Soviet future had for the most part not yet arrived. No parking ticket, no tollhouse, no gate. We simply drove off down the airport's potholed access road and turned onto the main road into town, the Moskovsky Prospekt.

The flat, scrubby landscape stretched away to a low horizon on either side. It was close to six in the evening, but the sun still blazed brightly. I was arriving at the height of the White Nights, just as I had when I came to Leningrad with my grandmother. Slowly, buildings began to appear along the roadway. We passed the Stalin Houses, the imposing apartment blocks built by German prisoners of war after World War II. The best apartments in St. Petersburg, Volodya commented, with a curious touch of nostalgia for some imaginary good old days preceding the Soviet Union's demise. A gigantic statue of Lenin with his arm thrust out, his body surging forward into the so-called bright future of Soviet mythography, appeared on our right. "The dancing Illitch," Volodya said, with a mixture of affection and derision, using the informal version of Lenin's patronymic name by which everyone facetiously referred to this relic of the recently defunct past.

We drove around the traffic circle surrounding the huge Narva Triumphal Arch, clad in bright green copper, that was erected in the nineteenth century to commemorate the Napoleonic War of 1812, and entered the city proper. We crossed the broad Obvodny canal, the official perimeter of central St. Petersburg, and drove toward the city center. After a few blocks, we turned onto Nevsky Prospekt. The famous boulevard was clogged with heavy evening traffic—somewhat disorienting, I thought to myself, just as it always was on the Champs Elysees, to see a swarm of buzzing machines charging heedlessly up the historic, processional way. A line of elegant facades ran the length of the avenue to the high spire of the Admiralty building at the end.

At last, Volodya turned onto Vladimirsky Prospekt. Everything looked the same as it had when I first visited as a child—the baroque buildings, the golden domes of the church of St. Vladimir, the worn stairwell at the entrance to the Dostoevsky metro station.

Except for the fact that a deep trench now ran down the middle of the street. The tram tracks, under repair, had been ripped out, replaced by a muddy cleft with water bubbling up from the marsh below. The transformation is underway, I thought to myself. I've arrived just in time.

Because of the construction, Volodya had to turn onto a side street that ran into Vladimirsky a few doors down from our building. We parked the car and dragged my luggage around the corner to the house.

Volodya, always the precise engineer, silently mouthed the syllables as he rehearsed the sequence of numbers he needed to punch into the newly installed keypad lock. He glanced at me with a faint smile, as if to say: this is the new order of things. When he was growing up nobody had owned much of anything—there wasn't any "private property"—and there certainly weren't any locks. He pressed the numbers carefully and smiled again when the door clicked open. Even more amusing than the presence of the lock was the fact that it had worked. He pushed open the rusted metal door that I remembered from childhood.

CHAPTER 12. VLADIMIRSKY

PROSPEKT, NO. 8

We walked into the dilapidated entryway, also unchanged since my first visit—the acrid smell, the decay; which were now depressing, but in equal measure affirmative of the enduring power of place and time. The musty smell of my grandmother's basement apartment in Mohegan surged up from the neurons of my sensory cortex, which by the magical algorithmic computing power of the brain immediately activated my memory neurons. Both fired off intensely, simultaneously.

I looked around the entryway, adjusting my eyes to the dim light filtering in through the cloudy glass of the transom above the steel door. The same somber atmosphere I remembered from my visit with my grandmother—when she had leaned over to whisper, "Don't worry, everyone is going to like you" and taken my hand to draw me across the threshold—still suffused the half-lit space.

I held the door as Volodya pushed my bags across the portal and set them at the bottom of the stairwell. We paused for a moment to prepare ourselves for the long climb to

Sasha's apartment. With the demise of the Soviet Union—and even before, since the horse-trading of space in existing apartments, their generational passage, and the continuous wheeling-and-dealing to get a new place were constants of Soviet life—the question of who owned which apartment, or room inside a communal apartment, and who was entitled to live where became a perplexing conundrum, eased only slightly by its resemblance to the byzantine bureaucracy that had assigned housing in the days of Communist rule. Sasha had inherited a room in the old family communal apartment on the third floor that his grandparents had lived in, and ultimately traded it for a new flat on the top floor. The old family apartment—the one I had visited in 1963—now belonged to someone else.

The entryway was like the bottom of a well, with its damp unfinished concrete floor and string of cobwebs hanging down from the underside of the stairs. The plaster walls, in theory grey but pockmarked with white spots where the plaster had chipped off, were streaked with water stains. A row of rusty mailboxes without doors was nailed to the wall opposite the stairs.

We began the trek to Sasha's apartment—eight flights altogether, counting the landing with the small, mullioned window looking out onto the back courtyard between each floor. Volodya, laughing, noted that the need to perform this kind of antediluvian labor was one of the reasons he had left Vladimirsky, trading his old room for a new apartment in one of the city's recently developed, peripheral regions. With his practical engineer's temperament, he was not overly nostalgic for the historic city center; he preferred new construction where he could decorate in modern, utilitarian style. Sasha, on the other hand, could never leave the old part of the city and the history that it embodied—his childhood, his grandparents whose presence he still felt, the schools that he and his parents before him had attended. He needed his daily walks past the pre-revolutionary palaces that he had played in growing up—long ago stripped of their interior finery and turned into Soviet houses of culture and sport—and where his own children had played. But though Volodya had left Vladimirsky, its atmosphere and character remained familiar to him. He evinced a sense of coming home, as we made our way up the eight flights, resting at each landing along the way.

Sasha stood waiting for us at the top of the stairs. A bit thicker about the face and the middle than when I first got to know him, but now the host of his own apartment in the building at Vladimirsky Prospekt, no. 8—the family nest through four generations.

Changed though he was, I would always remember Sasha as the blond, willowy teenager standing in the entryway as my grandmother beckoned me forward the first time I came to Vladimirsky Prospekt. The connection that Sasha and I made as teenagers had endured. Somehow, as if by instinct, we understood each other. We shared a reverence for our grandparents and a fascination with our common history. Sasha, his wife, and two children had landed, almost by accident, in a beautiful apartment—by St. Petersburg standards—but their material circumstances were otherwise modest. It was part of his character: he simply did not aspire to acquire great sums of money. His country dacha, which I had lent him a small sum to purchase (and which he promptly repaid), had no indoor plumbing and was simply a refuge from the city where the family could go in summer to rest, grow what they proudly called ecologically pure vegetables, and enjoy their meals outdoors in the cool of the early mornings and late evenings. It always reminded me of the setting of Turgenev's "First Love"—the modest dacha of the impoverished "noble" family who lived next door to the wealthy family of the narrator. Spiritually rich, materially poor. Another facet of Russia.

Sasha was also known for his unpredictable digressions on eccentric topics. "We are still waiting to find out what happened to the three days Stalin took from us in the thirties," he might suddenly exclaim as he rooted around the kitchen late at night preparing tea. His conversation was sprinkled with British-style expressions he had picked up from his old-fashioned English textbooks—"To be perfectly candid," or "Your humble servant." The thirty volumes of his Soviet Encyclopedia were well thumbed. Over the entire course of our lives we had spent no more than three weeks together, but we both felt the ties of ancient kinship.

Inside the foyer I exchanged my shoes for the pair of worn-out house slippers, the so-called *tapochki*—carefully chosen after examining the six or eight pairs lined up against the shoe rack—that were to be mine for the remainder of my stay. This little ritual of Russian household life always made me smile—the sense of refuge from the outside world associated with coming home and exchanging one's outdoor footwear for a pair of worn, soft, comfy indoor slippers. On my first visit with my grandmother I had been given a pair that Sasha had recently outgrown.

From the foyer a long hallway lined with sagging, overstuffed bookcases ran the length of the apartment to a large room at the back that served as a combined living space, dining room, and bedroom. It also housed the spinet piano from the old family apartment downstairs, the same piano on which I played my first Chopin nocturnes from the Russian edition of the score that my grandmother's beloved niece Mila, who also played the piano, gave me on my childhood visit.

In the middle of the hallway, a short corridor led to a second bedroom with two sleeping areas—from the days of communal apartments, Russians had become adept at positioning armoires, bookcases, high-backed desks, any piece of furniture that could double as a wall—to create the illusion of a separate room. As Sasha's wife Marina and young son Sasha had already gone to the country for the summer, Sasha proudly informed me that I was to have the front half of this second bedroom, overlooking the street, as my living and working space for the summer. (Sasha and his wife Marina had two children, also named Marina and Sasha; at one time, when Sasha's mother-in-law, Galina Ivanovna, was living with the family, a visitor observed that the only thing lacking was a second Galina Ivanovna.) Next to a small desk at the back of the room, a pair of French windows opened onto a narrow balcony, with just enough room for one or two people to stand behind the row of metal planters sprouting a tangle of flowers and vegetables and gaze out over the city. From the balcony I could look across to the rococo turrets of a similarly ancient apartment building across the street, catch a glimpse of the golden dome of St. Vladimir to the side, and watch the ever-changing St. Petersburg sky, with its eternal hint of the sea, overhead.

Craning over the edge of the railing I could look down into the cleft of the streetcar excavation, directly below.

A bit later, my cousin Lyena arrived and started cooking the welcome meal. We all gathered in the kitchen. Dishtowels and drying laundry hung from clotheslines crisscrossing above us in the vaulted space below the high ceiling. A spontaneous kitchen celebration—a regular feature of life on Vladimirsky, as in almost any Russian home—took shape. We caught up on family news and gossip as the table filled with loaves of bread and bowls of cucumbers, tomatoes, boiled potatoes, sliced sausage, smoked fish, preserved mushrooms, sour cream, dill and six or eight kinds of parsley and herbs which Sasha, in his willfully eccentric English, liked to refer to as "the grass." This was a Russian family gathering, just like the ones my grandmother used to create in Mohegan.

As the evening wore on, other friends arrived. Everyone seemed to enjoy joking about politics now that fears of reprisal had lifted. On the other hand, thinking about the bad old days seemed to make everyone just a bit uncomfortable. "You were the biggest kitchen dissident of them all," one of Sasha's friends teased him. Which meant: like everyone else, you had no problem complaining about the regime in the privacy of your kitchen, with no one to overhear. Sasha muttered something good-naturedly in response. I knew that this theme was central to a lot of things; I, certainly, couldn't judge anyone, coming as I did from relative luxury and ease. It reminded me of the paradox of my grandmother. She had loved Russia and missed her family and the life there, but when she returned and came right up against the dark politics—in the 1930s, when they were an order of magnitude worse than the sixties or seventies—she had turned around and gone back to America, though she never said precisely why.

Around eleven, Sasha flipped on the television. His favorite program, Kukli—or puppets—had come on. Outrageous papier-mache caricatures of Yeltsin and all the other famous politicians, with even more outrageous caricatures of their voices and thoughts, punched and insulted one other and disclaimed all knowledge of the foolish and corrupt things everyone knew they were doing. This was like nectar to Sasha and his friends—completely unknown to them until a few years earlier. They had been politically isolated their entire adult lives, and now they were free to read a gaggle of new newspapers and watch political satire on television. It was a banquet. But there was an element of reserve in Sasha's laughter. He was still watching and laughing only in his own kitchen, with his voice slightly lowered. It was hard to just spread one's wings and fly.

Gradually, over the course of my stay, I came to realize that people were not quite sure how to adjust to the new order of things on many levels. Of course, everyone I knew celebrated the end of Soviet rule; that was easy to understand. But no one seemed quite sure how to live in the new conditions where their energies were no longer focused simply on surviving; on reconciling the normal ambitions of life—education, romance, work, children, summer cottages— with the daily need to accommodate the unending barrage of half-truths and threats beating down like sheets of cold rain that they had learned to endure. It was clear what had been gained, but had something—paradoxical and uncomfortable as the thought might have been—also been lost?*

Afterwards, despite my exhaustion from twenty-four hours of travel, Sasha suggested we go out for a walk. After all, no one considered going to bed during the White Nights until two or three am.

* The answer to the question of how the Russian people might ultimately adapt to post-Soviet life after the transitional decade of the nineties has become tragically clear: they have chosen to accept a new dictatorship and new set of lies in exchange for a modest improvement in economic status and an illusory sense of stability. Whether Russia will ever be able to create a functioning civil society remains unknown.

CHAPTER 13. JOURNEY INTO THE WHITE NIGHT

This was an irresistible offer under almost any circumstances. A walk down Nevsky Prospekt was an essential part of the ritual of arrival, and during the White Nights eleven-thirty was the perfect time to go out. Dusk was just beginning to settle over the city.

Because really, there is no St. Petersburg without the Nevsky Prospekt. "There is nothing finer than Nevsky Prospekt," Gogol begins his eponymous story. Before I understood a word of Russian, my grandmother taught me to repeat the rhyming syllables—in Russian—of the beloved, most famous of Soviet children's poems:

> *Once there lived a crocodile*
> *Who used to stroll down the Nevsky Prospekt,*
> *Speaking Turkish and smoking cigarettes.*
> *Crocodile! Crocodile! Crocodile Crocodilovich!*

So yes, by all means, I was more than eager to go out with Sasha for a walk in that soft half-light, with the sky, darkening but still blue, hovering overhead like a protective, sheltering dome. The spectral atmosphere of the White Nights never failed—on a balmy, clear and calm night—to evoke the most intense sensation in me; the sense of almost going back in time, or entering some point in which time was suspended, containing both the present and the past; which ignited the sense that whatever I was looking for was now closer to becoming manifest and would be easier to reach out and grasp. The half-light, paradoxically, was clarifying, distilling. Because equally, there is no St. Petersburg without the White Nights.

Pushkin immortalized them in his epic poem of the city, *The Bronze Horseman:* "The transparent dusk, the moonless gleam of the restless night, the Admiralty spire piercing the gold-flecked sky; / As one twilight hurries to replace another, granting the night but one half-hour."

Of the many wonderful things my grandmother told me about Russia, the White Nights always seemed to me, as a child, the most fantastical of all. It was during the White Nights that she accompanied her young sister to the far north of Russia, had her love affair with Voroshilov, and organized their audacious escape—the time when she reached the apogee of her youthful daring. When I asked her, during our taping session, to describe their arrival in the north, she paused for a moment, then told me: "When we got to Arkhangelsk it was just the beginning of the White Nights, and one really has to go up north to know what White Nights are. We would stay out all night and sleep until one or two o'clock in the afternoon. We had picnics, and bonfires, with singing, people playing harmonicas, someone else playing the guitar. One of the boys—Vasya, I remember—played the balalaika."

Sasha was bubbling with energy and a sense of fun.

Watching the television program sending up the country's leaders had made him slightly giddy. Of course, people had gone out for walks during Soviet times—people did all the normal things, even then; but with a sense of foreboding always hovering in the background. Such was the strange duality of everyday existence in those days, which I remembered so well from my childhood visit, from the way my grandmother talked about Russia and our family, and from the family pictures she had shown me. At the bottom of the stairs the entryway was illuminated by soft rays of twilight coming through the etched glass of the transom. We pushed open the heavy metal front door and walked out into the eerie stillness.

We made our way along the wooden planks that had been set up above the excavation on Vladimirsky and turned onto Nevsky Prospekt. The sidewalks were crowded with late night strollers. We joined the bubbling stream and were swept along.

We began to retrace in reverse the walk I had taken with Sasha and my grandmother years before. Sasha pointed out the office building where his grandfather, the elegant and refined Arkady, had worked, writing his evocative descriptions of Leningrad city life. Perceiving the note of pride in his voice, I realized how deeply Sasha and I shared wellsprings of experience, connection, and heritage. Grandparent veneration was our shared, semi-secret cult—not everyone knew that it even existed. Certainly none of the children I knew in the U.S. growing up, nor did any of them understand when I talked about it.

The bronze horses of the Anichkov Bridge came into view. Crossing the short but elegantly proportioned bridge spanning the Fontanka River provided a moment of ceremony every time one walked into town. The beautifully cast, rearing horses, each held in place by a heroic figure of gleaming bronze, set the tone for the historical mile to come. This perfectly graceful bridge, atop three stone arches, caught my heart when I first came to Leningrad. The city was simply a museum—a total museum outdoors.

From the middle of the Anichkov Bridge, a few hundred feet down the river, I glimpsed the façade of the Fountain House, another palace of the old aristocracy that had been turned into the headquarters of a drab Soviet bureau of some sort, now mostly abandoned but transformed partly into shoddily arranged private apartments and cave-like shops. Yet behind the dilapidated façade and muddy front yard which, with its rutted tire tracks and upturned tufts of dead brown grass, was either being repaired or had long ago fallen into ruin and simply been left that way, one could still discern— or at least imagine—the former Sheremetov palace, with its orange stucco walls festooned with lunettes and garlands and its ornate baroque window frames painted in gleaming white. Here Anna Akhmatova, the keening muse, as Joseph Brodsky called her, of twentieth-century Russian poetry, had lived in her squalid room, cooking on a hotplate, writing the epic poems that subsumed the entire Soviet age. Here she had sat talking with Isaiah Berlin, as the KGB listened in, uncomprehending, through an entire night in the autumn of 1945. Here, before that, the wealthiest aristocrats of Russia had given balls of fantastic splendor and excess.

St. Petersburg in the 1990s had the magical quality of a Lost Estate where you could turn any corner and find yourself in another time, walk through the wall of the fourth dimension, follow your imagination where you would. All of the city's history, everything that had happened, stood there in front of you humbly, meekly announcing itself, beckoning you to look, to see, to feel it. Oh yes, there were other cities where great swaths of buildings from the past had been preserved—Paris, for example. But in Paris they were all spic and span, had been continuously restored and polished, the worn stones replaced with shiny brass plaques announcing their new functions—a business, a government agency—set into the creamy limestone. In St. Petersburg at that time everything seemed to be in its natural and original state of slow-motion decay, like a beautiful old forest with lichen covering every tree, mushrooms pushing up through the decaying layer of brown, half-consumed leaves; nothing curated, nothing adapted to the present day, just a continuous accretion, a preservation over the ages. To love St. Petersburg, you had to believe in the past. You had to believe it mattered, that these buildings contained the past, that it emanated from them like delicate, gossamer threads whose thinning, worn ends could still be discovered, as if they were reaching out, begging to be tugged at gently, whispering: remember everything that existed here, remember us, understand that we are connected. When I first came to Leningrad in 1963, I sensed that mysterious things had taken place here that in some obscure way affected even my life; now, thirty-five years later, I felt it again.

The sensation returned over the rest of the summer as I walked through the city, day by day, suddenly arriving at a corner with a finely wrought iron fence surrounding a weed-infested yard in front of yet another neoclassical palace that nobody seemed to care about or even notice. Was it a cadet school? Some other educational institute? The building, the cobblestoned street in front of it—except for the beat-up cars passing by, which gave the whole thing a wild quality of the old and new colliding brashly—all seemed to be exactly as they might have been fifty years ago, a hundred years ago, or some time even more remote.

In Petersburg there was no conscious effort to preserve the atmosphere of the past. Here you could take almost literal journeys back in time, into places that were just as they had been in the 1950s, the Soviet thirties, the early twentieth century Silver Age of avant-garde art, poetry, and the Ballets Russes. Everywhere, the same grand but crumbling buildings, the same threadbare carpets, the same unpolished parquet wooden floors, the same shabby elegance that proclaimed Imperial and Proletariat at the same time. I had seen it in 1963—at that point, Leningrad contained St. Petersburg, which even I could understand was very strange; that the imperial past of Russia had been so carefully preserved and honored. Now St. Petersburg contained Leningrad, which was equally disorienting, equally compelling.

A few blocks further on, we passed the Eliseevsky Food Emporium, a confection of Art Nouveau elegance that had somehow survived intact since its opening in 1903, purveying delicacies to the fortunate few even during Soviet times, though the name was changed to Gastronomy Shop Number 1; but which, since the end of Communism, had been transformed back into a reasonable facsimile of a luxurious gourmet shop, if not yet quite London's Fortnum & Mason or Paris's Fauchon.

Two blocks further on we came to the Garden Road, the broad cross-street whose intersection with Nevsky marks the beginning of the most important stretch of the avenue, lined with great ceremonial buildings and squares, continuing until its culmination at the bank of the majestic Neva River. Nevsky, in Russian, means "of the Neva."

We stopped at the intersection to look at the imposing arcaded façade of the Gostiny Dvor, St. Petersburg's elegant, neoclassical version of the traditional indoor market—"Guest Court" or "Merchant Yard"—of old Russian cities. The immense building stretched a full city block along the Nevsky on one side, and the Garden Road on the other; two tiers of orange stucco arches supported by white pilaster columns ran the length of each façade, enclosing sheltered outdoor walkways above and below with a grand, two-story entryway framed by free-standing white columns and a soaring classical pediment interrupting each rhythmic succession of archways at its midpoint. Gostiny Dvor had always been, in its way, just as much a landmark, an essential evocation of Leningrad— during whose time it housed a melancholy imitation of a Western European-style department store—and St. Petersburg, at the time of city's creation in the eighteenth century and now again, as the statue of Peter the Great, the Hermitage, or St. Isaac's Cathedral. I remembered it vividly from my childhood visit, with its grand neoclassical façade slowly crumbling from neglect, like almost everything else in the city. Now the first stirrings of rebuilding were afoot. Most of the Gostiny Dvor remained ragged but a single section had been shored up and covered with shiny new stucco painted in bright yellow and outfitted with expensive brand name fashion shops. Like the McDonald's that had recently opened on Nevsky Prospekt a few blocks away, this gentrification at first seemed jarring but eventually struck me as salutary in its own way, a reminder that the world does not always operate to feed one's personal time machine, which on the other hand does not mean the time machine cannot continue to operate.

We decided to cross the street and continue our walk along the broad promenade in front of the Gostiny Dvor. To cross the broad intersection of Nevsky Prospekt and the Garden Road, pedestrians were obliged to use an underpass, which also gave access to the metro station below. We resisted the urge to dart across the street, now almost free of vehicles, as the Russian love of bureaucracy and authority that had both preceded and outlived the Soviet Union guaranteed that anyone crossing above ground would be stopped by a policeman and given a ticket. As Sasha and I trudged dutifully down the stairs, I smelled the same odor of diesel fuel and wet concrete that I recognized from my childhood.

The passageway underneath was no longer simply a pedestrian crossing connected to the entryway to the metro. Now it was crowded with kiosks selling newspapers, magazines, cigarettes, toys, cheap jewelry, alcohol, and snacks. Loud rock music blared from shops selling CDs. At the far end, in front of the entrance to the subway, I saw a row of windows for the cashiers selling metro tickets. This was the station from which I had taken my first trip in the Russian metro with my grandmother. She had gone up to the window to buy our zhetons, as the tokens that we inserted into the brass slots of the turnstile were called. The hard plastic discs, in their pastel colors of purple, orange, and red, had fascinated me. I watched as she walked up to the window and conversed with the ticket vendor, just as if we had entered the subway in New York. Suddenly she had seemed to me no longer an American woman on tour in the Soviet Union; rather, just another citizen of the forbidding Russian realm.

The long stretch of sidewalk in front of the Gostiny Dvor was lined with vendors offering Soviet souvenirs—commemorative medals like the ones I had been given in 1963, Red Army hats and jackets, posters extolling the goals and accomplishments of the old regime. Between the stalls, stalwart adherents of the recently deceased Soviet empire distributed pamphlets calling for the restoration of the Communist Party, looking on with sour disapproval at the crowd of hedonistic strollers. We continued down the avenue, as the twilight continued to fade and a hint of night infused the air. When we came to the great plaza of the Kazan Cathedral, Sasha suggested we take a stroll through its enormous colonnade—patterned after St. Peter's Basilica in Rome—to have a look at the posters. Informal, hastily pasted-up posters, some announcing performances, others discoursing on politics, had started to appear all over the city; a kind of exuberant, anarchist-inspired response to the city's newfound freedom of speech after seventy years during which people were unceasingly bombarded with huge propaganda posters bearing slogans that most understood to be ridiculous. Such was the daily cognitive dissonance of life under the Soviet regime, relieved only slightly by a robust underground body of satirical versions, merrily passed along by word of mouth.

Suddenly I saw a poster with the image of Kliment Voroshilov. I knew that Voroshilov on horseback was one of the staples of early Soviet propaganda, since he had been the Commander of the Red Cavalry during the Russian Civil War. But now the image from the 1920s had been overlaid with a lurid red hue. "Come to the Red Cavalry Ball!" the poster proclaimed. The avant-garde imagery of the early Soviet period had been turned upside down. Voroshilov, the stolid figure of grudging respect who toward the end of his life in the 1960s had become something of a symbol of the hollowness of Communist hero-worship, was the perfect foil for a Mad Hatter, out-with-the-old and in-with-the-new happening.

I looked at Sasha, wondering how we were to take this in. He emitted a brief, uncertain laugh. Here was Kliment Voroshilov, who had figured so largely in the life of the family. The connection to someone so prominent and important, the former People's Commissar of Military and Naval Affairs for all of the enormous, powerful Soviet Union, was of course a source of pride, an only too human reaction; but tempered at the same time by the knowledge that Voroshilov had been—or became—one of Stalin's key henchmen, the person who had signed orders of execution during the Great Terror of the 1930s. At the same time, my grandmother's relationship with Voroshilov was likely the critical factor that kept my relatives from perishing in the Terror themselves. There seemed to be little other explanation, when one of the standard reasons for getting arrested and sent to the Gulag was having contacts with Americans—or even just American relatives—which immediately marked someone as a conspirator in the eternally-touted imperialist plot to overthrow the Soviet state. And to add a final note of ambiguity, my grandmother had become intimate with Voroshilov during the relatively innocent times, a decade before the actual Revolution, when revolutionaries could still be seen as idealistic and self-sacrificing fighters, striving toward a better world, rather than primarily agents of repression and murder, as so many of them tragically and monstrously turned out to be.

In the face of the irresolvable contradictions of the family's Voroshilov connection, Sasha appeared unsure how to respond. His cautious laughter seemed a variation on the old response—the kitchen dissident.

Later that summer, I attended parties where people dressed in velvet clothes guzzled champagne and added aristocratic prefixes like "von" to their names—more punk-inspired satire, just like the invitation to "The Red Cavalry Ball." The city was drunk on its new freedom, on the ability to thumb one's nose at the state and the fallen apparatchiks, on nostalgia for the time of aestheticism and decadence. Ridiculous as some of this seemed, I understood that one reason it was happening was because the era just before the Revolution was so compelling and had never been forgotten despite two generations of Soviet life. The transition back to St. Petersburg, which nobody really talked about and which everyone appeared to take casually, was really not casual at all. The craze to return to the old city of splendor and success brought me back to the time that launched my grandmother, and to the place where the Revolution—her Revolution, at least the one she thought she believed in and wanted—actually began. There was an allure to that time at the turn of the century that was hard to resist—the Silver Age, the time of revolutionary ferment not only in politics, but also in avant-garde literary and artistic movements. That period brought forth so much of what made Russia significant, of what redeemed it in the face of its many failings—the country's culture, its creativity and originality. This was the crucible my grandmother grew up in and came out of. It was a time when Russia was giving the world something essential, helping to make it modern. This was part of what made my grandmother's saga compelling—what she was involved in, politically, culturally, and historically, was like a giant comet that hit the earth, resetting its orbit forever.

The palpable sense that this was part of the living heritage of St. Petersburg, that it had been revivified by the return of the city to its original identity, gave out a somewhat intoxicating air in those heady days of the 1990s, when it was still not clear what the political and cultural future of Russia was to be.

We continued down the last stretch of Nevsky Prospekt to the corner of Great Maritime Street, on the left, and the narrow street leading into Palace Square on the right. The Astoria Hotel stood at the far end of Great Maritime Street a short distance away. My grandmother, Sasha, and I had turned the same corner onto Nevsky Prospekt that first morning in Leningrad, thirty-five years earlier. The same smell of diesel from the passing trucks and trolley buses, mixed with a faint scent of the sea, still permeated the fine layer of dust suspended in the air. Looking down Great Maritime Street toward the Astoria, I saw the same scene I had first seen as a child, the scene whose imagery had compelled me in some inexplicable way, telling me that this place was as much a part of me as New York City, or my grandmother's summer colony of Mohegan—it was another one of the places that defined her world, places which by some strange osmosis, some fated law of transmission, had become essential elements of my own. When I first followed her out of the Astoria Hotel as a child and peered out at the utterly foreign yet strangely familiar image of Leningrad, I felt that I was meant to be there too. Inevitably, on our first night out together, Sasha and I arrived at the same corner.

We walked down Great Maritime Street toward the hotel. I looked at the sequence of arched windows that ran the length of the Astoria's block-long façade, each covered with a red oyster-shell awning. The line of ornate window frames, repeating one another in rhythmic succession, grew smaller as the cornice line of the building receded toward the end of the street. The grandiose façade of roughly hewn stone had made a great impression on me as a child; it seemed to hide mysteries. Now the rhythmic repetition of the old-fashioned, arched windows, each sheltered under its heavy awning, reverberated down the street like an echo of receding time. The Astoria Hotel had been refurbished and become quite fancy after the end of the Soviet era; I certainly could not afford to stay there anymore. Another message from the present, another place where the past had been partially obliterated. Yet the memory of the moment of walking out the front door with my grandmother—I had been so impressed with its elegance, perhaps the more so because of its age and worn quality—into a world that I knew contained her secrets, remained indelible. I would always experience that walking onto the square in front of the Astoria.

We made our way back to the short street leading to Palace Square and crossed under the two high archways towering overhead that framed the entrance to the enormous ceremonial space behind the Winter Palace—the square from which the famous Storming of the Winter Palace, marking the end of tsarist Russia and the birth of the Soviet Union, was launched. This small part of the walk, underneath the great arches, felt like entering an indoor gallery, or a stage set framed by a gigantic proscenium, although we were still outdoors. Sasha chattered on merrily, yielding to his associations with each of the places we passed. His girlfriend from the days before he married, Vika, was now a curator at the Hermitage, he informed me. "I'll call her; she'll arrange to take us on a private visit to see the secret collection of Scythian gold," he half-whispered, proud of his connections and access to a high-level, restricted sphere, a mentality that flourished during the secretive, conspiracy-dominated decades of Soviet life. His thoughts shifted abruptly to his boss, whose uncultured nature was symbolic of the erosion of values in new, capitalist-style Russia. "Just last week he told me that important visitors were expected from Moscow, and I should arrange for them to visit the "Her—mi—*a*—tage," Sasha reported, drawing out the mispronounced extra syllable in delighted mock horror. "Imagine, he has never been there, doesn't know where it is, and thinks it's called the Her—mi *–a* –tage!" That any Leningrader, or St. Petersburger, did not know the city's great treasure-house of a museum was beyond his comprehension.

We joined the crowds milling about in Palace Square, moving slowly toward the far corner where the square gave out onto the Neva. The sky had finally grown dark, except for a lingering red stain in the clouds low on the horizon beyond the river. The embankment was thronged with revelers.

After strolling along the Neva for another hour or two, we eventually realized it was time to return home. Crossing back over the Moika, we turned onto the Griboyedova Canal to have a look at the short bridge guarded by four bronze griffins with golden wings, each tethering the end of a suspension cable in its mouth. We followed a series of smaller canals into the quiet side streets and crossed the footbridge of the four stone lions, also holding the bridge's suspension cables in their open jaws. We were by now the only strollers still out. The sound of our footsteps echoed from the stone buildings and the still water of the canal. The forbidding city that had consumed so many lives had suddenly become exquisitely beautiful and serene in the near darkness of the White Night. We reached Vladimirsky Prospekt at three am.

Perhaps, I thought, I can finally get some sleep. The constant clatter of the streetcar passing below had ceased for the time being with the renovation work on the tracks. Not that proper sleep was really on anyone's agenda during the weeks of the White Nights. Twenty hours of daylight put everyone into a state of mild agitation and elation. But soon I fell asleep to soft white light filtering through the lace curtains, the same light that had awakened me on my first night in the Astoria Hotel.

CHAPTER 14. INTO THE ARCHIVES:

FAMILY SECRETS

The next afternoon, after we woke up and had a late breakfast, I asked Sasha what he knew about my grandmother's adventure in the north and her relationship with Voroshilov. Did he perhaps have some documents or photographs that his grandfather had saved and given him from that time, or from the time of my grandmother's return to the Soviet Union in 1932?

"Aside from the paper, no," he replied.

"What paper?" I asked.

"The letter from my grandfather to Voroshilov," he answered. "I told you about it when I was in New York, don't you remember?"

I followed him down the bookcase-crammed hallway to the large room at the back of the apartment. He rummaged around for a few minutes in a large armoire full of dusty boxes overflowing with papers and old photographs, then proudly produced his copy of the letter.

Yes, it was true that I'd heard about the letter to Voroshilov, or "the paper" as my Russian cousins called it, which seemed to carry a greater connotation of official and possibly semi-magical powers—but I had never seen it. Now, as I gazed at the copy that Sasha had produced, nothing could quite have prepared me for the reaction it evoked.

A letter typed by Arkady, with its unmistakably old-fashioned Cyrillic typeface, dated at the bottom 2 /11/1931, with the address underneath: Leningrad, Nakhimson Prospekt (the name given to Vladimirsky Prospekt by the Soviet regime, in honor of some long-forgotten revolutionary hero, eventually changed back to its pre-revolutionary name, Vladimirsky), no. 8, apartment 5.

Vladimirsky Prospekt, no. 8. Sasha and I were sitting in the top-floor apartment in the very same building, the building that the Bamuner family had lived in since 1917.

"Most honored Kliment Efremovich!" Arkady wrote. "I, the brother of Eda and Rulia Bamuner, who were together with you in exile in the city of Mezen in 1907 and fled from there to America, address you with a request. The sisters now express in their correspondence a fervent desire to come to the USSR. I shall need to engage in efforts to obtain visas for them.

"Kliment Efremovich, you are the only living witness who knew the sisters in exile. It is quite possible that in our efforts to petition for their visas, we will need a reference from someone who knew them in Mezen. Would you not object if we referred to you, should such a condition arise?

"I would be very obliged, if you could personally devote 2-3 minutes to specify what answer I might obtain from your secretary. By profession, I am a Soviet journalist. Most recently, I have worked in the Leningrad section of Izvestia."

Signed,
"Arkady Bamuner (newspaper pseudonym, Almazov)"

Across the upper left, the dictated answer by Voroshilov—that certainly you may use me as a reference, but I have no time to receive you personally—was typed out and attested to with a handwritten signature by the Secretary, People's Commissar of Military and Naval Affairs. On the upper right, the word "Copy" appeared. Along the bottom margin, an official stamp of the Commissariat attested to the document's legitimacy.

Slowly, I took in this amazing apparition from the past. In order to get permission to come live in the USSR in 1932, it was necessary to confirm my grandmother's revolutionary bona fides! And the source to vouch for her was, well, the second or third in command of the entire realm, the head of all Soviet armed forces, a man who sat in his office in the Kremlin, wearing his uniform of Marshal of the Soviet Union, a few feet away from Stalin.

Looking at the letter, I had the sensation of suddenly time-traveling back to the year my grandmother pulled up stakes in New York and moved, with her sister Rulia and their two seven-year-old children, Sonia and Eugene—the latter of whom went on to grow up and become my bohemian Boston-based physics professor (and Russian-speaking) Uncle Gene—to Russia. All of which was astonishing enough, but now was added the flavor, the actuality, that my grandmother had entered Stalin's Soviet Union under the protection of the People's Commissar of Military and Naval Affairs, Kliment Voroshilov. It seemed that my grandmother's stories about her intimate relationship with Voroshilov—"he had such a cute little upturned peasant's nose," she had reminisced fondly on the tape—were true!

And now I had a date around which to focus my initial research. Somehow the exact year my grandmother left Pskov and the year she arrived in America had never come up in our conversations.

That was all that Sasha had, but I felt like I had struck gold.

Sasha, in turn, asked me how I was planning to go about my work. I explained that I had met people in the U.S. who had advised me how to penetrate various archives and had given me lists of people to contact. He seemed pleased. Russians always approved of connections. They were really the only way to get things done and possessing them conferred a badge of prestige. As we chatted, it occurred to Sasha that he also knew some people who might be able to help. It slowly dawned on me that Sasha was invested in my project; as the summer progressed, I realized that all my cousins were. Everyone was proud of our common forebear, the prosperous Pskov businessman Grigorii Bamuner, and his cosmopolitan success under the old regime. Equally, the whole family shared a sense of ownership of my grandmother's adventure, which carried with it the connection to the famous Voroshilov. "The paper" was a kind of talisman for the family; it had apparently served as a form of protection during Soviet times, though nobody could—or would—ever provide me details of any specific incident. The level of discomfort people felt in talking about such things—a reflexive response during Soviet times—did not seem to have diminished very much, despite the putative improvement of the political situation following the Soviet Union's demise. Perhaps putative was the operational word.

I telephoned my research assistant, Ekaterina Nikolaeva, and we agreed to meet the following day at the Herzen University.

I met Sasha in the kitchen around nine. As usual, he was frying an egg in the grease of a pungent sausage. I gently suggested that it might not be a very healthy breakfast, at least not on a daily basis; as a doctor I felt it was my duty. "But we like it so much," he said half-defiantly, half-apologetically. I let that small piece of culture clash go, ate a piece of black bread with butter and jam, and drank some bitter instant coffee.

I trotted down the shiny, polished stairs. A hint of morning sunlight brightened the usually dark stairway. It came as a bracing shock to reach the bottom of the musty stairwell, throw open the rusted metal front door, and smell the cool morning air. The bright light of the yellow morning sun, still lying low on the horizon, raked across the cobbled street. A summer morning in St. Petersburg when the weather was fine, with a fresh breeze blowing in off the Gulf—nothing could be more delightful.

I reached Nevsky Prospekt and crossed the Anichkov Bridge. Above the sparkling water of the Fontanka River the great bronze horses, each restrained by its youthful tamer, shimmered in the morning sunlight. The long line of windows in the white façade of the Anichkov Palace glowed with the reflection of the silvery leaves, vibrating in the morning breeze, from the chestnut trees along the embankment. The low rooflines of the palaces, the scrim of tram wires over the Nevsky, the morning traffic and belching trolley buses hurrying by—I imagined with a sense of pleasure joining the city's rhythm of daily life for the next few months.

Katya was waiting for me on the steps of the university. Although we had not yet met in person, we recognized each other immediately—in Russia, it's always easy to pick out an American by their dress and manner; for my part, I could just tell that the serious young woman standing on the steps, attentively scanning the oncoming crowd, was the Russian graduate student I had come to meet.

The moment I laid eyes on her, I knew that Katya was going to be efficient and diligent. Fairly tall with light chestnut hair and high Russian cheekbones, she always wore modest cotton summer dresses and serious-looking open-toe shoes with low heels and discreet buckles. As I got to know her, I noted that she normally carried a hint of humor in her face, which I knew was going help us get along as we were planning to spend a lot of time together over the next eight weeks. She was modest and serious, conservative in her dress and behavior by western European standards, but Russian style always had a quirky way of lagging a few decades behind the West.

Katya—Ekaterina Nikolaeva—was a graduate student studying for her advanced degree as a teacher of English. She was preparing for her general exams in late September but had agreed to work with me part-time over the summer. The professor who directed the American wing of her program had recommended her and introduced us. That she required a PhD and had to pass rigorous general examinations covering all of Russian cultural and literary history in order simply to teach English seemed both unusual—in the U.S. the requirements would be less stringent—and on the other hand, natural, as I well understood the Russian respect for learning, for the icons of cultural history and authority, and for the books any educated person would be assumed to have read. This had been made clear to me from my grandmother's conversations, from the authors and books she would refer to. "Ah, Schiller, he was such a great poet," she would tell me. "Listen to these lines he wrote in praise of women," which she would then recite in the perfect German she had learned in her academic high school—the Gymnasium—in Pskov. And it was clear from my interactions with Sasha, who sprinkled his stream-of-consciousness chatter with historical and literary references. The overstuffed bookcases of the family apartment on Vladimirsky Prospekt, which I remembered from my childhood visit, and the ones now in Sasha's apartment, proclaimed the same devotion.

As Katya and I got to know each other, it seemed natural for us to fall into discussion of historical events, what each of the tsars had done, the Revolution, the personalities of the Bolshevik era, any of the myriad Russian writers; even Russian music and famous performers past and present. I found it captivating. It was not that far removed from the milieu I imagined my grandmother growing up in; still preserved, despite generations of Soviet proletarian propaganda, almost a hundred years later. For me, it was lovely that this reverence for cultural knowledge—for knowledge in general—had remained a deep aspect of the Russian cultural cast. Katya's father was, as she described him, a fine machinist or lathe operator, but was well-read and had strong opinions, which Katya depended on, as she solemnly informed me, to develop her own opinions about politics and history. Katya and I, despite our disparate backgrounds and ages, shared a system of values.

Katya had arranged for us to meet Elena Varustina, a junior historian at the Academy of Sciences who was an expert on the history of late Imperial Russia. She also held an appointment at the Herzen University. We walked through a series of modest corridors—public buildings like this one remained, in the new Russia, thoroughly Soviet-utilitarian in their construction and interior finishes, somewhat reminiscent of an aging mid-century public high school in the U.S.—until we reached Varustina's office.

"He must have been a Merchant of the First Guild, if they lived in Pskov, because any Jew living there needed a special permit or status," Varustina opined about my great-grand-father. "There were books listing people, businesses, and so on for each city—Pskov, Riga, St. Petersburg—for each year. They are called 'Address-Calendars.' Go look through those, you will be able to figure out when he lived in Pskov and where. They're in the main public library, on Nevsky Prospekt."

We stopped at the Registrar's office to pick up the letter establishing my credentials and walked over to the "Publichka," as the main library was affectionately known. We stopped at the registration booth near the entrance; after a brief wait, I received a library pass with my picture. My subject was listed as "Gynecology" in Russian, which apparently sounded even closer to "Genealogy" in Russian than in English. Close enough, it seemed. We agreed to meet in the Catherine Garden in front of the library the following day to begin our work.

As I came down the Nevsky the next morning, I spotted Katya sitting on a bench beneath the enormous statue of Catherine the Great, surrounded at her feet by her numerous statesmen-lovers. The Catherine monument stood opposite the grand staircase leading up to the columned entrance of the Publichka. The library's vast ground floor lobby was of the same Belle Epoque vintage as the New York Public

Library—all polished marble and bronze torchieres—but without any frills or touches of high-style decoration. We climbed a broad staircase rising from the far end of the lobby and found our way to the card catalogue room. The walls were made of dark unpolished wood and the floors of cracked white marble. The catalogue system, unchanged from Soviet times, consisted of large oak cabinets containing boxes with rows of hand-written, dog-eared index cards covered with swirling Cyrillic letters. We started with "A" for Address-Calendar.

Around eleven the smell of cabbage came floating up the stairwell and began to permeate the air around us as the cafeteria in the basement prepared to serve lunch. We ordered the Address-Calendars for Pskov for the years 1900-1908 and went to pick them up in the main reading room. A red runner with green-striped piping ran along a large central aisle between the rows of tables. The floor was of the same unpolished oak laid in herringbone pattern that I saw that summer in every official building. A row of crystal chandeliers hung from the high ceiling. Though the tables were full of people intently reading and studying, the room was completely silent, enveloped in an atmosphere of seriousness. The long wooden tables had an inset of green leather at each workspace; behind them stood dark wooden armchairs with red velvet seats. Just below the high ceiling a gallery with a decorative iron balustrade ran around the room—the reference balcony. We looked through the books for 1905 and 1906, but concentrated mainly on 1907, following the date provided by the Voroshilov letter. There were lists of ministries, churches, and commercial enterprises, but no entry for Bamuner. Deflated, I concluded that a Jewish tailor, even the owner of a large business, was not going to be listed here.

Katya kept muttering, under her breath, "There should be a list of Merchants of the First Guild."

We put the books for 1905, 1906, and 1907 aside. Katya—diligent and persistent as I had predicted—picked up the books for the following years, continuing to mumble about Merchants of the First Guild. We were about to go on to other catalogues, other lists—Riga, St. Petersburg, other years. But at the last moment I decided to look again at the book for 1905, thinking that the family might have left for Riga—where my great-grandfather eventually moved, though I could never find out exactly when—by 1907. I had noticed that there was an alphabetical list at the back when we looked the first time. There had been no headings for merchants—of any guild—or businesses of any kind. I assumed the alphabetical list included only names of titled individuals, government officials, and important institutions. Certainly my great-grand-father's name would not be there. On an idle whim, I opened the page to the letter B. And there it was: Sh. G. Bamuner.

The image seemed to float up, as if from a sheet of photo-graphic paper lying in the developing pan, into sharp view for the first time. The name, the very existence of Grigorii Bamuner had been like a hazy image; perhaps only imagined, the stories somehow all made up. Suddenly, emerging from the murk, the sharp clear image stared back at me. "Sh. G. Bamuner." I turned to the page number listed in the index. An announcement for "Sh. G. Bamuner, Civil and Military Tailoring," outlined with a decorative border, appeared on the page.

For the second time in only the first few days of my visit, I came face to face with my family's past. The ornate design and heavy decorative Cyrillic type of the announcement of my great-grandfather's shop nearly shouted: "1905!" And just as I had been when I sat looking in amazement at the letter written by my great-uncle Arkady to Kliment Voroshilov, I was suddenly transported in time. Just as Arkady's letter had made real and concrete the things that my grandmother had told me—not that I doubted them, but why had I come to Russia, really, if not to see it all for myself, to make it more believable—about Voroshilov and Mezen, I now experienced the same shock of recognition, of affirmation, of what she had told me about her father, his shop, and their life in Pskov. It all existed, just as she had described. Here was the proof. I could touch it.

And with it came the fascinating revelation that my great-grandfather Grigorii's real, or original, name had been Shmuil Gershovich. It came not so much as a shock, since I knew of course that he was Jewish; rather a fascinating twist that at some point he—or perhaps it was only his children, all of whom took the patronymic Grigorievich or Grigorievna— had changed his name. Not that many assimilated Russian Jews in those years hadn't done the same.

That afternoon, when I returned home, I told Sasha about my discovery. He was astonished, of course, and at first perhaps a bit perturbed—but as the product of three genera- tions of inter-marriage, he hardly maintained any connection to the family's Jewish past. With his Gogolesque love of irony and paradox, he quickly warmed to the new revelation, muttering "Sha Gay" "Sha Gay"—as the initials sounded in Russian—as he bustled about the apartment.

My cousin Volodya had invited me to dinner that evening. As his wife, a professional tour guide (which also required a higher university degree in Russia) was off leading a group in Scandinavia, and both of his teenage children were busy, he was alone. I told him about my discovery. Interesting, he said, somewhat noncommittally. He started to play some of his beloved American rock music on the stereo, breaking in occasionally to ask me to translate a word he could not quite make out. He offered me a shot glass of vodka with our hors d'oeuvres—the so-called *zakuski* beloved of Russians—and then another. Skewers of *shashlik* sizzled on the little gas-powered grill in the kitchen.

Volodya was the only cousin in my generation to still carry the last name Bamuner, though it had been changed slightly at some point to soften its Jewish overtone. After the third or fourth vodka, he mournfully announced, "I am sad I have to learn the truth this way."

I wasn't sure if he meant he was sad because something had been kept from him, or because he now realized the family had been more Jewish than he had grown accustomed to thinking. And I sensed in his slightly inebriate announcement an ambivalence that I imagined Volodya himself did not fully understand.

None of my Russian cousins had ever talked much about the family's Jewish past. Mostly I let this go because they had intermarried through the generations—starting with my grandmother's siblings, who all married non-Jews except for her—and were nominally "Russian" rather than "Jewish." For centuries, Russia has been a sprawling country and sometime empire of multiple ethnicities and nationalities. Officially there are something like 186 recognized nationalities, sometimes further characterized through designations like "national republic" or "autonomous region," both within the old USSR and the current Russian Federation. "Jewish" has been one of the nationalities since the early eighteen-hundreds. That may sound antisemitic to American ears, and to some large extent may well be so, but for Russians the distinction lines up with the idea that a person is either "Russian" or something else—"Kalmuk," "Tatar," "Bashkir," "Belarusian," "Jewish," and so on.

Most of my cousins were the grandchildren of one of my grandmother's sisters, and thus had lost the Jewish last name Bamuner. Volodya, though only one-quarter Jewish by heritage, was the only one to have kept it.

I sensed that his sadness hovered on a knife-edge of ambivalence: on the one side, he had been brought up "Russian;" his Jewish last name had been diluted by changes in spelling and pronunciation that had been snuck in somewhere along the way; nobody had encouraged him to think of himself as Jewish in any way; and his grandfather's patronymic (as far as he knew) had been the Russian-sounding Grigorievich. Now he suddenly finds out: Perhaps something has been hidden from me all this time after all! My own grandfather was really Vladimir Shmuilovich, not Vladimir Grigorievich! More evidence of the rampant antisemitism and general obscurantism practiced in this rotten country!

Withal, I could not help wondering whether the sudden augmentation of his linkage to the mainstream heritage of Russian Jewry had activated some sort of—presumably unconscious—internalized antisemitism. Such was the still-thorny nature of Jewishness in Russia, the hangover of two centuries of strife, cruelty, suffering, and tragedy.

CHAPTER 15. INTO THE ARCHIVES: THE RUSSIAN ACADEMY OF SCIENCES

The next day, we reported our initial success to Varustina, who was delighted. "Now," she told us, "I will take you to meet the Academician Rafael Ganelin. He is the expert on the history of the late nineteenth century."

We crossed the Neva River to visit Professor Ganelin in the Institute of Russian History of the Russian Academy of Sciences, in one of the palaces on Vasilyevsky Island that had housed the first Academicians in the time of Peter the Great. The quiet university district of the Vasilyevsky had a rarefied aura all its own. "The combination of water and stone creates a special, majestic atmosphere," the eminent Soviet writer Sergei Dovlatov—who was hounded by the KGB and eventually forced to emigrate, like so many other writers during the Soviet period—observed about his student days there.

We walked up to the Academy, an imposing but neglected, almost crumbling and thinly adorned neoclassical building. As we walked into the foyer I had the sense of entering a restricted, special, possibly magical world. The world of the past I was seeking.

We walked down a dim corridor that led to an interior metal stairwell, descended several flights, and came out into a large room with a low ceiling—a combination of stacks for the books and office space for the distinguished professor, his underground kingdom. The back and sidewalls were lined with the rows of bookcases. In front, in an open space at the center of the room, stood a metal desk piled with papers behind which Ganelin was sitting. Several smaller desks sat behind, nearer the bookshelves. There were no offices, not even cubicles. Just a large, dusty room where knowledge was being pursued, mostly for its own sake, accompanied by the constant brewing and drinking of tea.

A light layer of dust lay over the bookshelves, the professor's desk, and the metal lamps hanging from the ceiling above. Two acolytes stood on either side, leaning over to speak to Ganelin softly in each ear from time to time. These, I later realized, were junior faculty members hoping to solidify their positions, to gain full-time appointments here or at some other university. The three of them looked up at us. Varustina led us forward to meet the great man.

His graduate students and post-docs were dressed in corduroy pants and thick, shawl-collared sweaters for the men; corduroy jumpers over heavy blouses and woolen tights for the women. Everyone, including the Academician, wore open-toe slippers over thick woolen socks.

Ganelin looked at Varustina and broke into a broad smile. "Lyenochka," he cooed. His appearance made me think immediately of Nikita Khrushchev, one of the classic types of Russian men—round, short, and bald with a toothy grin. He was dressed rather shabbily, but in his own elegant, dignified fashion. His white shirt, suit jacket, and pants were shiny from wear and pressing; the jacket and pants did not match. His narrow tie lay askew.

Varustina introduced us. I began to explain how I had found him, citing the professors I knew at Columbia University, the various experts in Russian history, in particular Mark von Hagen, the well-known authority on the period of the late Empire, the Revolution and the Civil War. He brushed all of it aside (although he acknowledged that he knew them all, naturally; all of this was only to be expected) with a casual wave of his hand. All he really needed to know was that his trusted and beloved Varustina had brought him some interesting people who needed help. He was ready to plunge in.

Katya and I outlined the story.

"His name, again?" the eminent academician asked. "Ah, Bamuner—not so much Russian as Jewish," he opined, nodding affirmatively. Ganelin, in fact, was of Jewish extraction himself.

"A merchant of the First Guild? Yes, there were Jews who lived in Pskov and St. Petersburg then, you had to have permission, and being a merchant of the First Guild was one of the ways. Indeed."

"And your grandmother was arrested before the Revolution, and knew Voroshilov in exile? The two sisters escaped from exile in Mezen, then fled to America but came back to the Soviet Union in 1932 with Voroshilov's help?" he repeated, somewhat incredulously. "And you have a letter Voroshilov wrote on their behalf?

"Yes, that's right," I replied.

"Amazing story, remarkable," he affirmed.

"You should go to Pskov," he advised. "I can help you

meet the director of the archive. You can find out what your grandmother was doing and how she got arrested."

I mentioned that my grandmother and Rulia had tried to come back again for another extended stay, in the fall of 1936, but that time they could not get entry visas.

"So, they left the Soviet Union in 1933, and tried to come back in 1936 but weren't successful? Oh, that was lucky, the first departure was timely, indeed," he added, the word for "timely" sounding more ominous, more fateful in Russian.

Naturally, I understood his implication. The majority of people who naively came to Russia in 1936—before the world understood what Stalin's Great Terror was, or even that it had begun—to explore the bright Soviet future never left again. Most of them just disappeared.

"And how long are you staying?"

"Until November," I answered.

"Oh, that's plenty of time. By then we might even find you some more Russian grandmas," he concluded, glancing at Varustina, unable to resist the impulse to try and make her smile.

He immediately started giving instructions to various members of the team, calling out names of people to contact, advice for getting into various archives and sources. Every few moments he turned his attention to Varustina and smiled. "Lyenochka, what an interesting story, we shall have to see what we can do," he said, continuing his mild flirtation and good-naturedly displaying the reach of his command.

He gave Katya his phone number and told her to call him that evening. He would firm up instructions for contacting a certain Professor Kelner, an authority on the Jewish community in Pskov, and advised us to send a letter to the Pskov Archive to see if there was any information on my grandmother's gymnasium and Rulia's arrest. "I can't promise anything," he added. "Remember that two wars have gone through there."

Suddenly there was a great deal to do. Perhaps I might not even finish in four months, I speculated. "Then you will have to take Katya with you," he suggested slyly.

As we were about to leave, Ganelin gave us one more piece of advice.

"You'll have to go to Arkhangelsk, to the White Sea, where they sent your grandmother. The great expert on the life of the exiles from late tsarist times is Mikhail Suprun, my student. He lives in Arkhangelsk and teaches at the University. I'll put you in touch with him."

We thanked him and set off for the climb back up into the daylight. There had been no filters, no formalities, no assistants or administrators to get past to see the important man or to tell us there was no time. We had simply climbed down to the basement of the Russian Academy of Sciences and showed up on his doorstep. He couldn't have been more delighted. Ganelin's enthusiasm for research, for the drama of the past, for academic conquest was infectious. He was a marvelous man, a true academician; one of the intensely intellectual but irrepressibly warm Russian types that I knew from my grandmother's circle of friends during childhood.

From a window in the stairwell, I saw the back courtyard of the old palace, littered with debris and trash. On the roof of a shed an entire small forest was growing—spongy moss, ferns, small trees, various unidentifiable plants, lush, green, and thick. Absurd, grotesque in one way—the Russian Academy of Sciences, no better tended than a trailer lot at Mohegan! And charming—and somehow inevitable—in another. Russia:

everything going to seed, combined with an insatiable love of nature.

We emerged into the deserted front courtyard. Having a spare half hour or so, we decided to take a stroll along the Neva embankment. On the far shore, the spire of the Admiralty glimmered in the afternoon sun. Slowly we walked past the facades of the three-hundred-year-old colleges, first built as palaces for the nobility, but now the haunt of wistful academics in threadbare sweaters and open-toed sandals toiling away in dusty underground lairs that were more like metal cages than rooms, completely disconnected from the elegant facades outside. A squall blew in off the Gulf of Finland. Heavy raindrops pelted the gravel for a few minutes until the squall blew on, leaving glistening gray stones in its wake.

When I returned to Vladimirsky that evening, I found a note from Sasha saying that he had left the city to go black-berry picking, which I found a bit puzzling, as he had never mentioned anything about it before nor did he say when he might return; then again, it seemed consistent with his generally nonlinear approach to things. He also wrote that I should call Katya, who had phoned earlier with an urgent message. I called her back.

"I heard from one of Ganelin's assistants," Katya told me excitedly. "They contacted a colleague of theirs at the State Historical Archive. And guess what? She found a file on the arrest of your Aunt Rulia!"

CHAPTER 16. INTO THE ARCHIVES: THE RUSSIAN STATE HISTORICAL SOCIETY

I asked Katya for more details about the new discovery. The colleague that Ganelin's assistant had contacted at the State Historical Archive—a certain Svetlana—reported that she had found an entry relating to Rulia somewhere in the records of the old tsarist Ministry of Justice. Svetlana had not seen the actual file, but Rulia's name was clearly there on some sort of list. The details were a bit murky, but this was Great News! Even the ever calm and low-key Katya sounded excited. It occurred to me, with pleasure, that she was becoming an ardent, truly committed teammate in our slowly unfolding, labyrinthine journey through the world of Russian memory, deriving as much satisfaction from our cross-cultural collaboration as I was.

The next morning, Katya and I met at the Kutuzov statue—Mikhail Kutuzov, the great hero of the War of 1812, beloved of all readers of *War and Peace*—alongside the Kazan Cathedral and set off down the Griboyedova Canal toward St. Isaac's

Square. We stopped at a kiosk to buy a box of chocolates for Svetlana.

We reached Senate Square, another of the city's majestic ceremonial spaces, second in its grandeur perhaps only to Palace Square behind the Hermitage and dominated by the iconic statue of Peter the Great rearing up on his horse, with the dedication "To Peter I from Catherine II, 1782"—Catherine II being the German princess better known as Catherine the Great—carved into its massive purple granite base. The Russian State Historical Archive stood opposite, in an eighteenth-century former palace of the nobility.

We climbed the stairs to the main reception hall and asked the way to the General Director's office. Following the somewhat confusing directions, we walked through a series of rooms with rows of open offices, mostly unoccupied. Tall windows gave out onto the broad expanse of the Neva alongside. Finally, we reached the Director's office. After twenty minutes, an aide summoned us forward to one of the cubicles.

Before us sat a stern looking woman. She never told us her name. Bone thin, she looked us over with an expression of unrelenting severity. She seemed to be made of a series of ovals—oval face, over-sized oval black glasses framing oval eyes, oval earrings hanging from her earlobes, elongated oval torso. Thick black bangs covered her forehead. She wore a blouse of green, red, and violet paisley.

We explained why we had come. "Well, do you have details?" she asked. "Which party did she belong to? What year was she arrested?" We mentioned Ganelin. She was unimpressed.

This was another side of Russian officialdom, the only too well-known overbearing and bureaucratic side. It had been invented by Peter the Great, satirized at least from the time of Gogol, if not earlier, survived in transmuted but ultimately similar form under the Soviets, and obviously still existed now, at the end of the 1990s.

Once, when I complained about it to my cousin Volodya, he replied, "Well, have you read *The Castle*, by Kafka?"

Everything around her was made of dark wood—the walls, the floor, her desk, and the cabinets—except for her old-fashioned desk phone, which was bright red.

"So, you believe there are records in the Ministry of Justice files?" she continued. "I doubt it, but you can check with your Svetlana yourselves, the building is just around the corner, between the Synod and the Senate. On second thought, I'll call her."

A brief conversation ensued. "Just as I thought, probably nothing there. But here are your passes, go ahead and see for yourselves."

We retraced our steps through the maze of file rooms and came out onto the square. It was raining lightly, though the sky had been a brilliant blue flecked with towering white clouds when we entered the building an hour earlier. Katya and I exchanged a knowing look—nothing too surprising here, everyone was used to this sort of official obstructionism. With Ganelin and his associates, everything had been wonderfully easy. Now we found ourselves once again in the Russian-Soviet world of suspicion and bureaucracy. Another instance of the two faces, the eternal set of paradoxes that is Russia. A sort of tacit acknowledgment passed between us. We would keep moving forward.

We went around the corner to the building housing the Ministry of Justice and walked up the cobbled carriage ramp that led to the entrance on the first floor. The entry hall was almost dark, illuminated only by the thin afternoon daylight filtering in through the high windows. A young man sat in a booth near the front door, thumbing through a ledger. He inspected our passes, written out by hand on the rough, friable Soviet-style paper I remembered from my childhood, and tore them in half by placing a ruler on top and sharply ripping down along the edge.

We went upstairs and passed through yet another series of rooms with enormously high ceilings, with great crystal chandeliers hanging down, all unlit. The walls were lined with card catalogues made of light-colored oak, so tall they required a ladder to reach the top rows. Plaster vaulting frescoed with scenes of trees and flowers swept upward into the high ceiling. There did not seem to be anyone working there—we saw almost no one and the rooms were cloaked in silence. Eventually someone passed by and we asked if he could direct us to Svetlana and her department. He motioned us forward with a vague indication of direction, advising us to ask "them" as we progressed. Finally, we found the Archival Department of the Ministry of Justice and Svetlana. We introduced ourselves and presented her with the box of chocolates.

We reviewed the details of the story. Svetlana had found Rulia's name in the card catalogue; but now we had to find the actual dossier. Svetlana led us back to the main catalogue room with the high ceilings, unlit chandeliers, and frescoed vaulting. She started to look for cross-references, asking us again for names and dates.

"Well, we'll have to write to Moscow to the State Archive of the Russian Federation, to see if they have an entry—that would make it easier," she remarked. "Did your grandmother have exit documents?" I said I wasn't sure. "If you don't know, what is the point of looking? I can't find anything if I don't know what information is there."

Eventually she produced a dossier and looked through it, but Rulia's name wasn't there. She closed the ledger and declared the meeting at an end. But at the last moment, as she prepared to leave, she gave us the number of another file which might—although she doubted it—contain some useful information. We filed a request form and returned the next day to see if the dossier had been delivered. The clerk went to the storeroom and returned with a thick folder filled with ancient-looking papers with tattered edges, all precariously held together by brown construction paper of the folder with "Dossier 497" stamped on the front. Inside was a thick sheaf of documents entitled, "Alphabetical List of Persons Sought by the Police, 16 March 1907—1 January 1910." Some were lists of criminals; others, lists of those to be exiled abroad without the right to return to Russia; others, people subject to search and unspecified but sinister sounding "other measures," all organized according to a complicated system of classification by letter and numerical subscript. We flipped through the pages until the letter B, and suddenly the name of my great-aunt Rulia appeared before us. There, at the bottom of one of the columns, was number 15884: Bamuner, Samuilovna.

Rulia's arrest suddenly became tangible. It sent a jolt through me, looking at her name from the time when she was only fifteen or sixteen years old, among the hundreds of other people arrested and jailed, to realize that she had passed through the hands of the police, through interrogations and prison cells, with her identity recorded in this blandly bureaucratic, but chilling document. Most of her information—photograph, fingerprints, arrest and trial information—was missing. But under the entry—if subject to exile, where, how long, and under which conditions—appeared the text: "Mezen, three years, from February 1909."

The writing was faded, the orthography cluttered with decorative letters that had been declared superfluous after the Russian Revolution and banished from the alphabet. We were working under the assumption, proudly gleaned from Arkady's letter to Voroshilov, that Rulia had been arrested in 1907. My grandmother had never mentioned the specific date, and it never occurred to me that Arkady might have gotten the year wrong.

Katya and I understood the entry to say where Rulia *would* or *should* be sent if found. Assuming she had escaped in 1907, this seemed to be an instruction about what to do if she were recaptured. It appeared to be a kind of future or conditional verb tense, but Russian verb tenses were notoriously complicated. Deciphering the usage—not to mention the handwriting—from a hundred years earlier made it only the more difficult. It was wonderful that we had found a file about Rulia, but it seemed like a ghostly after-image, written two years after the actual events of her arrest and escape with my grandmother—tantalizing but insubstantial. I wanted to know what had actually happened when the sisters arrived in Arkhangelsk and proceeded on to Kholmogory and Mezen.

Katya and I agreed to meet the next day to pick up railroad tickets at the central booking office then spend the afternoon working in the library. Having concluded that we'd accomplished everything we could in the archives in St. Petersburg, we decided it was time to follow Ganelin's advice and travel to the north.

That evening, I caught up on my email. My cousin Sven, my Aunt Rulia's eldest grandson, had sent me an attachment with the picture he had showing our grandmothers, Voroshilov, and the rest of the group of exiles in Mezen—the one I had shown to my grandmother when I recorded her recollections. On the back someone had written the names of the people in the picture and the year, 1909. I looked at the image on the computer and dismissed the date of 1909. See how mistakes get made that just throw everyone off the track, I thought to myself.

Then I started to think again about the circular in the Ministry of Justice. Why did it say she *was to be* sentenced to three years in Mezen, starting in February 1909? The notice was published in September 1909; suddenly it seemed strange to record a theoretical sentence, starting at a specific date earlier than the notice itself, if Rulia were to have been caught again. What if Arkady had gotten it wrong in 1931, so many years after the original events? He was only a boy, living in Riga, when his older sisters experienced their remarkable adventures, beyond the White Sea. Better for us to check the document again the next day, I decided. We had arranged to have the folder left on the will-call shelf for a month, just in case.

The next morning, I explained my suspicions about 1909 to Katya, who seemed perplexed and remained noncommittal. Ever the careful scholar, she wanted concrete evidence and was not easily persuaded to change an existing conclusion. Eventually I convinced her that we better check again, since by the time we returned from our trip to the north the file would be gone.

And so after buying our train tickets, instead of going to the library as planned, we went back to Senate Square. I surreptitiously rejoiced—as if let out of school unexpectedly—at the opportunity to delight in the brisk summer light, to bask in the imperial splendor of this city of split personality. Any excuse to have a walk through the most classical part of St. Petersburg, along the sparkling canals and on toward the Neva River, was always welcome.

We handed the request slip for our dossier to the clerk. It will be ready next Tuesday, she informed us. But by then we will be in Arkhangelsk, we explained. Katya froze with indecision, uncertain what to do next. Here our cross-cultural meeting-of-the-minds foundered a bit; she by instinct was ready to obey the bureaucratic edict and was disinclined to fight back. But I, with a hint of impatience, insisted:

"Tell her the dossier was supposed to be kept onsite for a month; ask her to please go have a look."

(The moment reminded me of Sasha's story about one of my grandmother's visits in the 1950s. He was trying to bring her to the apartment on Vladimirsky Prospekt, but they could not cross Nevsky Prospekt because of some parade in celebration of Socialist Progress. When the militiaman put his arm up and told her to step back, she drew herself up to her full five feet five inches and informed him, I am an American, don't you tell me I cannot cross to meet my family on Vladimirsky Prospekt, I have come here all the way from New York. The militiaman shrank back, and my grandmother, with Sasha in tow, grandly made her way across the boulevard.)

Katya complied and the clerk returned to the file room in back. A few seconds later, she returned with the folder and placed it on the counter in front of us.

We examined the document. Previously we had read the entry as "to be sent"—like some kind of infinitive verb form. Now I pressed Katya: Read it carefully, see if perhaps it has a different meaning. We re-examined the lettering and suddenly realized: it did not say, "to be sent" but rather, "sent," in the past tense. Sent to Mezen, for three years, from February 1909. This was where Rulia *was* sent, and the year she was sent there. The date on Sven's photograph was correct after all.

At the end of the summer Rulia had escaped. We were reading the notification from September 1909 to seek her— as a fugitive—and, no doubt, my grandmother, who had engineered the escapade, as well.

The confusion had hung on a single small letter that we had misread, forgetting that Russian orthography called for so-called hard signs at the end of most words before the Revolution, a sort of decorative affectation in the opinion of the practical-minded Bolsheviks, and thus expunged by them. We had assumed it was a soft sign—they look practically alike—which would make the verb an infinitive. Like so much of the mystery I associated with my grandmother herself, the key lay within the Russian language.

That evening, I went online and checked the Ellis Island Records. They showed that my grandmother had sailed into New York Harbor on the steamship Pennsylvania in 1910. That was one detail she had never mentioned.

CHAPTER 17. JOURNEY TO THE WHITE SEA

At last, I was going to make the trip to where it had all happened. Of course, I wanted to delve into the archive in Arkhangelsk and see what more I could find. My grandmother never told me too many details about her revolutionary exploits, what party she had belonged to, or—irresistibly—her relationship with Voroshilov.

Yes, I had thought when I planned my trip to Russia, I will pull together material from primary and secondary sources and reconstruct the whole adventure like some sort of historical novel—I wanted details and authenticity. I had probably been reading too many biographies of famous Russians, from Catherine the Great to Trotsky, Pasternak, and Akhmatova. I thought my grandmother's story might fit into the mold of a Russian historical epic, if only a minor one.

But the real reason I was going was because I felt my grandmother's guiding hand on my shoulder, gently pushing me forward. How else could I have been there, without her pushing me just as she had taken me to Russia in the first place and beckoned me across the threshold of the family home the first time we came? My grandmother was a shaper of lives. Because of her passion and adventurousness and her uncanny ability to inspire the same aspirations in me, I was now about to embark on a long train journey into the wilds of northern Russia, in the middle of August, a century after she had taken the same voyage.

Marina and Sasha had prepared food for me for the trip—cucumbers, sausage, cheese, black bread, blackberry jam, and a jar of preserved mushrooms. They accompanied me on the short walk to the Moscow Station to see me off.

As we walked up Vladimirsky Prospekt, workers were laying the steel latticework over the center of the street where the trolley rail bed and the rails were to be laid. Soon it would all be filled in with concrete, the exposed trench of the street smoothly covered with the new track and decorative paving stones. Strollers were out enjoying the freedom to wander down the middle of the street with their children and dogs while the avenue remained closed to cars. Innocent scenes of everyday enjoyment like this one still struck me as slightly incongruous in the complicated land of Russia, where nothing was ever quite what it seemed, and a vague sense of menace seemed to lurk below the surface—as I well recalled from my childhood visit. But did it still now, I wondered?

The train departed at midnight, arriving in Arkhangelsk just over a day later, at three in the morning. Katya and I shared the compartment with two women who had the seat opposite. They looked on with a mixture of curiosity and suspicion as we chatted in English. Later we exchanged a few words with them in Russian and they warmed up. As we rolled away from St. Petersburg, an attendant came and turned the two seats into beds of a sort and let down the bunks from the wall above. People went to the toilets at the end of the car, changed into sleeping outfits consisting mainly of sweatpants or tracksuits, and we settled into our modest sleeping arrangements for the night.

By six o'clock the sun had come up and I went into the corridor to watch the landscape roll by. I was looking for the signs that signaled, "We are going north." And I wanted to see what my grandmother had seen.

The low land looked somehow waterlogged, trailing off slowly across grass and forestland to a murky horizon. Small huts intended for people working in the fields occasionally broke the empty expanse. No reason to believe this was much different than it had been almost a hundred years earlier, I imagined. Yes, I was on a very different train from the one my grandmother would have taken, but it was old and worn enough to buttress my meditations backward through time.

According to one of the books Katya and I had read during our research in the Publichka, the police questionnaires prepared for the departing prisoners were precise enough to allow the authorities to group the exiles as "privileged" and "unprivileged," and to treat them accordingly. Those who were privileged were allowed to pay their own expenses and to live in moderate comfort along the way. From what my grandmother had told me, she and Rulia were certainly among the privileged. The unprivileged suffered much harsher conditions.

As I watched the landscape grow ever flatter and emptier, I sensed that we were moving away from civilization. We crossed a wide river with nobody on it and nothing built up on the empty shores. The surroundings grew bleaker, wilder, more threatening.

And yet the very emptiness of the land was a kind of openness. Here the restrictions of towns, of settlements, of crowded population—all the things that constrain people, ultimately—were absent. This is where my grandmother had traveled, on her own for the first time in her life, on a journey to an unknown destination. And yet she traveled on, completely undaunted, even exhilarated. Though she did not know it yet, exile was her gateway to freedom.

My grandmother did not fully realize what had happened until she got to New York. Slowly, along with her new freedom, she began to realize what she had lost—her country, her culture, her family, her plans for a revolution and a new way of life. But she always kept her language. The link of language—the sonorous, solemn flow of Russian, with its literary legacy, its emotional cast—was in itself a way of life, of thought, of experience. That could never be lost. For me, as child, the sound of Russian was like the portal to another kind of freedom, another kind of experience that I longed to share.

By the time she moved to Greenwich Village and built her cottage in Mohegan Colony, she had started to look for the world she'd left behind. These were the places in which I came to know her, the places that were constructed around memory, inhabited by the aura of her lost world. Like a gravitational field, she and the aura pulled me in. Though only a child, I somehow understood that there was a world left behind that was deeply important, that made her who she was and somehow also made me who I was. I wanted to follow her, to look for her lost world.

And now, as I stood in the corridor of the old Soviet railcar, watching the images of forests and rivers and villages rush up to the train window and quickly recede into the distance,

I remembered the feeling I acquired as a child, of being compelled to go searching for something essential, something missing from my own immediate world; it struck me that it was the same feeling that had compelled my grandmother to leave Pskov when she was eighteen years old—first, to go to the neighboring city of Ostrov to try to live on her own, as she informed her father she was planning to do; and though she failed and had to return home in a few months, a bit humbled, her father understood and forgave her; and then, when her naïve, fragile fifteen-year-old sister Rulia suddenly got caught up in a minor political drama of tsarist Russia (minor, but symbolic of much larger dramas to come), she immediately declared: "I'm off! To the White Sea!"

When she was young, my grandmother heard a siren song that she needed to listen to and follow, to figure out where it was calling her, the song that ultimately drew her on the journey to the north. When I was young, I heard a song, too, because of her. Now I was taking the journey she had taken, trying to figure out what she had heard; and at the same time to understand what had made me want to listen for a song when I was a child. As I watched the landscape, I listened for the faint echoes, like an astronomer searching the sky for the last light of an extinct star.

Great walls of birch trees rose up along the side of track. This was the land that my grandmother was looking for as she settled onto her acre in Mohegan, I realized. And as I looked out at this rather beautiful but forlorn land, I felt in some mysterious way that it was part of my own past. That was part of why I had to take the trip. I could not let this place simply remain part of some far-away story. I had to come myself to recapture it, to make it vivid. You have to work a little to preserve the past, to unlock its meaning. It's worth it, in the end.

As the landscape flattened, the dome of the sky seemed to flatten as well, descending lower toward the ground. The light grew duller.

We passed the town of Cheropovets across another wide river. Images of the green stucco railroad station and golden-domed church flashed across the windows. The land along the riverbank turned to a spongy, feathery light green. As we rode through the larger city of Vologda, with its red brick Victorian buildings, I realized that we were now in a part of Russia that had never been touched by war; it had reached its peak of development just around the time my grandmother and Rulia rode by on their way to Arkhangelsk and had changed very little since.

Suddenly the train slowed to a halt with only the birch and pine woods on either side. From a small break in the trees a group of locals in quilted coats and rubber boots approached the train carrying baskets—well, metal pails really, but they looked very clean—with the brightest red berries I had ever seen, pickled cabbage, pierogi, warm potatoes, sliced fish, cucumbers. The food was delicious and the scene irresistibly cheerful, an almost staged version—yet it was real—of the deep Russia of folklore, the countryside, simple virtues, the bounty of the land. This was a moment to savor. All the passengers crowded toward the platforms at the end of the cars or reached out of the train windows, smiling, utterly contented, ready to pass on a few rubles for the only good food—wonderful food—anyone had had since we left St.

Petersburg fourteen hours earlier. For a moment, the sinister mist that always seemed to envelop Russia lifted.

We started off again, passing freight cars laden with huge stacks of pine and birch logs. Toward dusk, we rode through a tiny, forlorn town. A single road from the fields beyond led into the station, then moved off into the distance on the other side. The station, with purple wildflowers growing up against the wall, was the settlement's only building. Packs of dogs roamed along the road. A group of towheaded boys watched as our train passed by.

Now, I could see only an occasional break in the woods. We rode by a small meadow with a haystack, then a small country cemetery. We continued on into the night, passing more freight cars filled with logs, like inkblots now, black on black against the backdrop of the night, and crossed the broad, dark Northern Dvina River—the last marker before entering the low-lying country bordering the White Sea, now only a few miles to the north.

We arrived at three in the morning. Katya and I climbed down from the carriage with another woman. Katya inquired whether she knew the way to the White Sea Hotel. "Oh, yes, follow me," she said. She gestured to Katya to give her one handle of her suitcase, to help her carry it. The three of us walked off into the warm night.

CHAPTER 18. ARKHANGELSK AND

THE WOODEN MUSEUM

My room at the White Sea Hotel was no more than fifty feet square, with a low ceiling and cinder block walls. The furnishings consisted of a wooden platform with a thin mattress and drawers underneath, and a simple desk with a metal stool. It smelled of dampness and neglect. And this was one of the nicer establishments in Arkhangelsk. I fell asleep to the rhythmic sound of raindrops falling on the pine trees outside my window.

I awoke at ten, went downstairs, and found Katya eating breakfast in the restaurant-bar—completely deserted except for her—a dimly lit, windowless room a few steps down from the hotel lobby.

The hotel was an amalgam of rough concrete, polished steel, and bronze-tinted glass—a classic example of Soviet style, stolid and garish at the same time. I loved its atmospheric authenticity. This was the bunker-like Soviet hotel style of the sixties and seventies, a strange combination of the desire to project a touch of class—this was a hotel, after all, and the Soviet Union was not about to let itself be seen as a second-rate country!—while at the same time keeping to the basic model of proletarian simplicity and functionality. Just as I was looking for evocations of pre-revolutionary Victorian-Edwardian Russia, the time of my grandmother's childhood and youthful escapades, I was looking for authentic relics of Soviet time, the other Russian world that had compelled her and drawn her back to Russia in the thirties.

Such an odd mixture—her early life at the end of tsarist times, amidst bourgeois prosperity and privilege, cultured and refined, which gave her the Old World manners and airs that she kept her entire life (Don't block *my* way! she thundered to the policeman on Nevsky Prospekt a half-century later) and the grim, unadorned, striving Soviet world, struggling in its own way to leave behind all those frills and that privilege, a striving that might once have corresponded to some reasonable or even noble instinct, only to end in the grotesque, sad parody that I saw before me that morning.

Katya and I pushed aside our cups of undrinkable coffee and discussed our plans.

It was Sunday. Our intention was to visit the Arkhangelsk Archive on Monday, present our letters of introduction, and begin our search of the files; a visit sometime during the week to Professor Suprun, the expert on political exiles in the north of Russia during the late tsarist period whom Ganelin had arranged for us to meet; and a trip to Kholmogory with a colleague of my cousin Sasha who had grown up there and offered to show us around.

Which left us wondering, what to do on Sunday afternoon? Katya suggested we take a trip to the famous outdoor museum of wooden churches. The far north of Russia was a kind of crucible of Russian civilization where monasteries and isolated villages had been established in the remote fastness and had remained almost untouched for centuries. The remoteness and deep history of the north seemed somehow connected with the fact that this was where my grandmother had experienced the dramatic, fateful days that determined the trajectory of her whole life.

So of course I wanted to go and see the open-air museum of old wooden architecture. Ancient churches were so much a part of the essence of Russia. It was like visiting the great medieval cathedrals when traveling in France.

The museum was set on a promontory of rolling land above the bank of the Northern Dvina River. I could never think about the Northern Dvina—which in Russian is the Severnaya Dvina—without hearing my grandmother's lilting voice: "Yes, we had to cross over the *Syeh vyeer nay yah Dvyee nah*"—six rhythmic syllables containing every characteristic trope of Russian phonics—the rolled ee vowel with the y sound in front, intensely rich and dark, contrasting with the light, airy ah sound coming after; the crushed consonants of d and v sounding together, still leaving room for the y and the ee—four separate sounds merging—when it all flowed together it was like an incantation, a summoning of the river, the green hills that rolled along the delta and opened onto the wetlands in front of the sea, like an onomatopoeia, though of course it wasn't really. When I learned to say it well in Russian, to summon it from the middle of my mouth and have it slide out easily, unlike any sound ever made in English, it was like channeling my grandmother, like communing with her. I wished she could hear me say it.

We boarded a local commuter bus for the ten-mile ride out to the village. A narrow road snaked along the contour of the hills above the riverbank. The brick buildings of the city gradually gave way to wooden dachas surrounded by carefully tended garden plots and sandy pinewoods. From the crest of the hills, long vistas opened onto the river delta, with lush marshland slowly giving way to the sea. It reminded me of the coast of Finland as I rode into Russia with my grandmother in 1963—the forest, the breaks in the trees revealing glimpses of the dun-colored, wet sand and gray water beyond, shallow for a long way, before opening out to the sea. Mysteries seemed to be hidden there; this is what my grandmother had looked at, loved, and could never forget; drawing her back and back to Russia in the 1930s, '50s, and '60s. This is what she was looking for upstate along the shores of the Hudson River and in the woods of Westchester, never quite finding it.

We arrived at the museum and began our tour. There was an array of ornately carved churches and domestic buildings from various sites across the vast expanse of Arkhangelsk Province, all of which had been made by hand with tongue-and-groove construction, without nails or screws of any kind. Before me stood the craftsmanship and deep cultural roots of Russia, at the same time both modest and magnificent.

We came upon a group of buildings arranged as if in a village square, a kind of model old town. The buildings had been transported there from crumbling villages and abandoned monasteries, piece by piece, and reassembled. As we left this evocative re-creation, we saw a sign pointing toward a section devoted to Mezen, which had its own characteristic architecture, thus meriting a separate, unique display.

I pressed Katya to hurry on to the Mezen exhibit. We both knew that Mezen was the one place we could never reach; it was a so-called closed military area, a characteristic feature of Soviet Russia—and of contemporary Russia again today. We were about to tour the actual city of Arkhangelsk, my grandmother's first stop on her journey away from Pskov. And we planned on visiting Kholmogory—whose name means "hills and mountains" in Russian—where she experienced, as she loved to say, "the most wonderful exile." But never Mezen, where she had organized her most remarkable feat, the flight to freedom that set the course of the rest of her life.

In the Mezen section there was an icehouse with a plaque explaining how it was built each spring; a lean-to shed raised over a deep pit dug in the just-thawing ground, filled with chunks of ice during the summer. It was the kind of icehouse that would have been built just as my grandmother and Rulia arrived in Mezen, alongside the house they moved into, where the salmon they ate all summer would have been stored. "Ah, the *syomga*," my grandmother marveled—using the Russian word for salmon—as she related, on the tape, what they ate. Everywhere else in Russia, smoked salmon was a rare delicacy; but in Mezen, at the source, they ate it almost every day for the entire month of August.

It was only a museum, but for a moment I indulged myself and imagined I was walking around old Mezen, looking at the kinds of houses that my grandmother could have lived in and visited. It was the closest I would ever come to time-traveling that part of my grandmother's adventure, the place where its climax took place. We strolled through the farther reaches of the sprawling exhibit grounds, past a small barn for storing fish. Against one of its gray walls a thicket of wild berries, intensely red and fragrant, swarmed up the side, as if striving to break free.

On our way back along a different route than the one we had taken coming in, we happened upon a church from the seventeenth century. The daily ringing of the bells had just begun. We paused to listen to the jangling, like chirping birds. The ringing followed no rhythm really, just a continuous sparkling trill. The middle and lower bells droned underneath, steady, determined, mournful, pulling everything downwards, back to earth. While the upper bells squawked and trilled, fighting to pull free and soar, to fly off, to evade restraint and escape.

And everywhere the gray wood was carved with elaborate decoration, tracery, scalloping, grillwork, arabesques, little eyelet holes. The projecting center beam of a storage building, a barn, ended in a carved bird's head, Viking-like. Ah yes, I recalled, the Vikings had come here in the ninth century, founded ancient Russia, and merged with the local culture. Here was the echo, hundreds of years later. And everywhere the humid, velvety green of the northern woods and meadows unfolded around us.

We arrived back at the entrance to the museum grounds around six o'clock. The afternoon light had begun to fade, and a chilly wind blew up from the river. It suddenly struck me that here in Arkhangelsk, seven hundred miles to the north, the days were ending earlier than in St. Petersburg. This was exactly the time of year that my grandmother would have realized that there were only a few weeks left to find a way to get Rulia out of Mezen before the sea route back to Arkhangelsk froze over.

Later in the week, as I read through the documents in the Arkhangelsk Archive and slowly grasped the reality of what my grandmother had done and the danger she faced, I thought back to how she always told the story and realized, with a sudden jolt of amazement, that she had never expressed any worry. To her, it was all just part of the continuing adventure. She always seemed to know what she would do next, or if she didn't exactly know, she knew something would turn up. When she left Pskov with her young sister, eager to reach a place where she could mingle with real revolutionaries, she had already made up her mind to change her life. The one thing I never heard in my grandmother's voice as she recounted the adventure was fear. She still laughed and rolled her eyes with merriment when she retold the story, sixty and seventy years later. It was the greatest adventure of her life, her intersection with history, her foray into amorous escapades which she looked back on with a wistful sense of pleasure for the rest of her life. "You should be having more love affairs," she would tell me as I wandered through my early twenties without any serious romantic attachments. "The time for these things is when you are young."

We reached the top of the last hill inside the museum grounds. I looked across the simple landscape whose very ordinariness, quiet and unassuming, was somehow what made it beautiful. The silver-red ribbon of the Dvina snaked along into the distance; across the river, on the far bank, rolling farmland rose slowly up to a low ridge with a small hamlet and a domed church.

CHAPTER 19. THE ARKHANGELSK ARCHIVE: MY GRANDMOTHER APPEARS

The next morning, armed with the instructions from Ganelin and his minions about which file numbers to request and the letter of introduction they'd provided, we set out for the Arkhangelsk Archive. The day was sunny and warm. We walked the short distance to a nondescript, three-story building of white concrete. The Arkhangelsk Archive was set in a park of fir trees with a small courtyard in front. Grass and weeds sprouted through cracks in the short path leading from the gate to the front door. The building was another utilitarian product of the Soviet sixties, like the White Sea Hotel, and had similarly been left to fend for itself in the harsh northern climate. Despite decades with no apparent upkeep, there it still sat, solidly, on its gray stone foundation.

We asked for the director at the front desk and were shown into a small office in an adjoining corridor. The inside of the building was finished in linoleum tile and cinderblock, strangely reminiscent of similar buildings built at the same time in the U.S.—my childhood grade school, for example. The director, a young man who looked more like a Soviet apparatchik-bureaucrat than a scholar, eyed us with distrust. Once again we found ourselves in the far from extinct Soviet-style world of closed networks in which everyone was considered suspect until proven otherwise.

We explained our purpose and presented our letters from Ganelin and Varustina, which he looked over indifferently. He doubted we would find any material of interest; rather, he appeared to be more concerned that he would get in trouble if he gave anything away or missed the covert action that he suspected was unfolding under his very nose, though he couldn't quite put his finger on what it was.

We explained that we had done preliminary research, that we were sure that my great-aunt Rulia had come to Arkhangelsk in 1909, and that Ganelin had given us the numbers of the files we needed to search. Grudgingly, he gave us the phone number of the head of the card catalogue division and sent us back to the reception desk. We phoned her office, and she agreed to meet us in the catalogue room upstairs.

We went upstairs to the third floor and found her waiting for us. Once again, we quickly sketched in the details of our story. Katya had by now become an almost full coequal in our quest, displaying at times a delightful (to me, secretly) sense of proprietary ownership of the project. She occasionally slipped into the first-person plural when referring to Rulia or my grandmother—"our great-aunt," or "our grandmother." The director of the catalogue division looked into the general file and reported that there was no card for Bamuner. She did, however, proudly present us with the card listing the file and sub-file numbers for Voroshilov. The scratchy writing covered both sides of the card. Ah well, we thought, at least we can find out more about Voroshilov, what he was doing here and where he was living. Perhaps—here we were dreaming—there would be a document under his name mentioning something about my grandmother as well.

We pressed her to check the particular file number that Ganelin had given us. The pre-revolutionary files had survived the fighting around Arkhangelsk during the Russian Civil War when British, French, and American forces intervened on the side of the armies of the deposed tsar in a futile attempt to turn back the Bolshevik tide. But the Soviets had reorganized them all under a new numbering system, making it very difficult to find anything. As we learned a few nights later when we met him, Mikhail Suprun had painstakingly cross-referenced all the numbers and was able to tell us which ones to look for based on his system. Lacking that information, our librarian listened to our request with a dismissive frown (we have already seen this movie, with Svetlana in the State Historical Archive, we said to each other with a silent look); but at our insistence irritably continued thumbing through a different section of the catalogue. Moments later she withdrew a card— the original card, filled out in swirling pre-revolutionary script nearly a hundred years old—with the heading, "Bamuner." The card contained a list of file and sub-file numbers.

Katya and I looked at each other with a mixture of triumph and amazement. We had arrived in Arkhangelsk with low expectations; who really thought there would be files about an unimportant girl from Pskov who got arrested in 1908? Merely reaching the city, experiencing the train trip there, going to the wooden museum village, had made the journey seem worthwhile. Now we felt vindicated. We had planned well and it appeared that the tale of the Bamuner sisters merited a place in the historical record after all!

Katya read over the card and handed it to me. I looked at the ornate script, deciphering small bits. Just as when I had first seen the name of my great-grandfather in the Address-Calendar in the library in St. Petersburg, for a moment I seemed to simultaneously inhabit two separate points in time. Standing there, on the top floor of a run-down Soviet office building in August 1998, looking out over present-day Arkhangelsk, I suddenly experienced a very specific moment in 1909 as well. I held the card that had been filled out in the same city at the time that my grandmother arrived there, looking at the same ink that had dried on the piece of paper ninety years before. I looked out the window and saw the contemporary city of blocky postwar buildings and factory smokestacks. I could also see the city of wood, the old city, with the domes of churches just like the ones I had seen the day before from the hillside in the museum of old wooden buildings.

We wrote down the file numbers and went to the main reading room where we filled out the request forms and handed them to the clerk. The reading room was a modest version of the grand ceremonial halls in St. Petersburg where Katya and I had made our first discoveries. The same rows of tables with leather insets, the same old-fashioned, velvet-seat chairs, the same ornate lamps hanging low over the individual workspaces. Almost every seat was occupied. Even here in the remote north, the Russians continued to toil away, cataloguing the past, recording and interpreting it, trying to make it comprehensible.

The reading room overlooked the courtyard of an old factory with a tall smokestack, surrounded by a high wall. The factory buildings, smokestack, and wall were made of Victorian-era red and white brickwork with decorative flourishes, all of it strangely well preserved. A slagheap leaned against the wide base of the smokestack. A group of workers sat on benches, chatting and smoking under the "No Smoking" sign hanging on the wall above them.

It was a scene, it struck me, as quintessentially Russian as the view from the Wooden Museum across the Severnaya Dvina to the farmland and hamlet. The beautiful Victorian-Edwardian brickwork evoked—was the perfect stage set for—the first decade of the twentieth century, the time of my grandmother's stay in the city. She and Rulia could have walked down the narrow street, or one just like it, below the reading room. They might have lived in one of the old brick or wooden houses nearby and walked along the same raised wooden sidewalks. In the distance I could see scrabbly earthen hills leading onto the riverbank. It all looked exactly like the old photos of Arkhangelsk I had seen in one of the books Katya and I read together in the Publichka in St. Petersburg—the bare hills dotted with small wooden houses. According to the book, Arkhangelsk at the turn of the century was bustling, filled with theatre and library societies, evening performances, and even societies of exiles.

We received the first file and found a place at one of the tables. On the first page, we gazed in mild wonderment at the notice from the Interior Ministry, no. 75387, dated 1 February 1909, to the Governor of Arkhangelsk Province: "Bamuner, Rakhil Samuilovna, merchant's daughter. Sent under supervision for three years from 11 February 1909 to the Mezen district, for membership in the Pskov section of the Socialist Revolutionary Party and active participation in terrorist activities of the aforementioned." And on one of the sheets a few pages later: "I report to your Excellency the arrival of the sister of Rakhil Bamuner, exiled for membership in the Socialist Revolutionary Party, Eda Samuilovna Bamuner. She is known to associate with several of the political exiles in the city."

My grandmother had finally made her appearance in the official record, drawing the attention of the police for suspected revolutionary activities.

We spent the rest of the afternoon reading through the file, cross-referencing, uncovering additional file numbers. We filled in the request forms and left them at the reception desk. The clerk promised that everything would be ready for us Tuesday afternoon.

When we got back to the White Sea Hotel, we called my cousin Sasha's colleague Lyena, who worked in Arkhangelsk but had grown up in Kholmogory and had offered to take me there. She was delighted to hear from me—Russian networks of friendship and hospitality humming into gear, once again—and we agreed to drive to Kholmogory on Saturday. I kept saying, "*Spasibo*"—thank you in Russian—since it was the word I knew best. "You don't have to keep thanking me," she interjected kindly, after my fifth or sixth time.

After which, we tried calling Suprun. After eight or ten rings, someone answered. I listened as Katya began explaining who we were and why we were calling. It turned out to be the wrong number, a somehow unsurprising turn of events (in Russia one becomes gradually accustomed to the often circuitous way things unfold).

"And of course, there are no phone books in Russia," I said, repeating something Sasha had told me, which in his mind was an allegory—that in Soviet times nobody wanted their names listed on anything; and even though the end of the Soviet period had eased this concern, well, still things were the same: inertia, people remain suspicious, nothing ever gets done in this country anyway.

Katya replied, "No, I saw one yesterday at the post office when I went there to call my parents." We agreed to go there the next day and check the number.

The next morning, after breakfast in the dark cave of the hotel restaurant, we emerged into the warm morning and walked out through the city toward the waterfront. We came to the center of town, crossed a tranquil square, and walked out onto the embankment boulevard above the Severnaya Dvina, at this point quite broad as it opened out toward its delta, with a broad beach below us. In the distance stood the delta islands with radiant white stripes of sand lining their shores alongside shimmering green patches of pine trees. Across the boulevard the side streets leading back into the populated part of the city were lined with turn of the century brick-stucco mansions, monastery buildings, and wooden houses. This was the historic waterfront district from the time of Arkhangelsk's apogee, at the turn of the twentieth century; once again I found myself amidst a long-surviving relic of pre-revolutionary Russia: an essentially poor country that could not afford to rip out everything old and replace it with something new; so here it all still sat, a century later.

Two young boys with their father were fishing on the beach below the embankment, the water lapping gently onto the shore. The scene radiated a quiet, concentrated quality out of time, looking just as it might have, I thought to myself, a hundred years earlier.

CHAPTER 20. GOOD RUSSIANS: WE VISIT PROFESSOR MIKHAIL SUPRUN

On our way back, we stopped at the post office to look for Suprun's number. There was, indeed, a worn phone book bound in black plastic covers hanging in the lobby. We looked under S—which looks like C in Russian—and found a number for Suprun, M. We went up to my room to place the call.

With its damp, bare concrete walls and cellblock-like furniture, the room was like a stage set for a scene from a Cold War potboiler. Katya watched with anticipation as I dialed— she had begun chiding me that my Russian was adequate and that I should do more of the talking myself, I didn't always have to depend on her—and the phone began to ring. We had already gone through enough cycles of anticipation that ended in failure to be prepared for disappointment; but by now we also knew that some forays could end in unexpected, intoxicating success.

Suprun picked up. I started to explain who we were, then lost my nerve and handed the phone to Katya. Yes, he had heard about us from Ganelin in St. Petersburg. "I have a file card on every political exile sent to Arkhangelsk in the decades before the Russian Revolution, let me check the name," he said. "Call me back in an hour."

We called back. "Ah yes, Rakhil Bamuner and her sister Eda, oh yes, I have a card on them." We wrote down a bit of the information he gave us, which promised to be of great help in our next day's work. The rest we would collect when we went to see him. He invited us to his house on Friday evening, but Katya replied that we might be leaving by then. "All right, then come Wednesday evening," he replied, warning, "it will be modest," since he wouldn't be getting his salary until Friday.

Katya smiled at me in the knowing way I had come to recognize. Her look communicated the following: Remember, everything in Russia is done by "connections," the context of which was typically sinister or corrupt, but in our case the cause was noble, and Katya was taking satisfaction in the fact that that we had gotten the system to work for something good. "You see, I told you so," her look said. In Russia, it could be difficult to maintain one's perseverance, but—Katya was reminding me—it was essential to any kind of success.

Early Wednesday evening, after a long day in the archive, we left the hotel and walked out into the balmy evening. Suprun's apartment was a twenty-minute walk along quiet, tree-lined streets. Arkhangelsk, the far northern city normally evoking images of icy winds and snowdrifts, seemed on this evening to be suspended in a soft, forgiving glow. Summer in Arkhangelsk was a kind of paradox; by now, in late August, even we—though neither of us had ever been there before— sensed that the weather could turn severe at any moment; that the calm evening was a kind of gift. In Russia, moments of softness and ease were like little treasures, since everyone knew by long experience how easily things can turn dark.

We continued along the quiet streets, in a forgotten quarter of this northern city on the very edge of the vast Russian continent. A few blocks away, the Severnaya Dvina River—which had conveyed my grandmother and her sister to internment in Mezen, then back to Arkhangelsk where they stepped off their boat into a secluded district like the one we were now walking through to take shelter among their fellow exiles overnight before crossing northern Russia into Finland and continuing on to Germany and America—flowed silently to the White Sea.

We stopped on the way to buy a cake and some wine. "What kind of cake would be appropriate?" I asked Katya. I had been thinking of something elegant, perhaps a chocolate mousse cake or pastry tarte. But as usual, all the cakes in the little shop we visited were rich and syrupy; the Russians had their own concept of cake. We chose a cream-filled cherry torte. I realized I had mistakenly been planning my visit as if I were in New York City or Paris; a bit of misplaced culture-centrism. "They have a young son," Katya said. "Don't worry, the cherry cake will be a hit." I suggested that we bring some bread and cheese as well, to strike an informal note and show that we were sympathetic to the economic pressures that all Russians continued to face; a dominant theme with my Russian relatives all through my childhood, and one which persisted through the post-Soviet 1990s. As an academic, Suprun was by definition under economic stress.

"And the wine?" I asked Katya. Moldavian, of course, slightly sweet. Avoiding another round of cultural miscues, I had correctly concluded that the occasion did not require

French wine, especially since nobody drank it on a routine basis, if ever, anyway. Semi-sweet Moldavian wine was the national staple. I thought back to the visit, a few weeks earlier, of a long-lost cousin from my grandfather's side of the family who had come to see me on Vladimirsky Prospekt at Sasha's apartment. Sasha, displaying as ever his eccentric and perhaps capricious manners, conducted Saul rather formally to the living room at the back, instead of to the kitchen, where more homey social encounters would normally take place. He then proudly produced a bottle of dry French white wine to further display his cosmopolitan sophistication. "Some dry white wine?" he kept asking my baffled cousin Saul—a simpler, more typical Russian citizen—emphasizing the word "dry." Saul looked at him in bewilderment, repeatedly answering, "No, thank you."

We gathered up our packages and continued on to the bookstore to buy a copy of Suprun's volume, for him to sign, on the (little-known) impact of the American Lend Lease program on northern Russia during the first part of World War II, as the Soviet Union struggled for its very survival following the surprise Nazi invasion launched in the early hours of the summer White Night of June 22, 1942.

We continued along a street lined with low buildings with cracked concrete facades, built sometime after the war. Every few blocks the succession of apartment buildings was interrupted by a stately house from the turn of the century, painted in a bright hue—a souvenir of Arkhangelsk from the time of my grandmother's brief sojourn. The look of the street, the entire atmosphere, was unmistakably Russian. Partly it was the general state of ill repair, but ultimately it was something more abstract—a forlorn, slightly threatening, slightly sinister look. An atmosphere that proclaimed Russia's vastness, a place almost too far away, beyond Western Europe, at once exotic and uncomfortably unfamiliar. Yet together with that, I was always looking for another atmosphere that also existed, more subtly. The atmosphere that corresponded to my grandmother's Russia.

This was the balance that was Russia—the beautiful and fine amidst the sinister, vulgar, and decayed. The good Russia and the bad Russia. The bad Russia was the well-known oppression of Soviet times—the crassness, the poverty, the vicious tyrannical politics with its stupefying Orwellian babble, suffocating the exquisite Russian language. The good Russia was the culture that endured, fought back and transcended oppression with a language that could never be suffocated and a bedrock of human warmth—the Russia that my grandmother had revealed to me, and which I had seen with my own eyes as a child.

As Katya and I walked along on that warm evening we seemed to share a tacit sense of satisfaction that we were heading for an encounter—in our visit to the Supruns—with the good Russia. It was a kind of lovely mutual understanding we had developed over the weeks of our work together; we were on the same side, striving toward the same goals.

The apartment was on the second floor of a Soviet-style two-story concrete apartment block built at some forgotten time during the postwar years. Shoddy and inelegant in every way, it nonetheless felt somehow solid and cozy, a shelter in this remote northern place. Suprun opened the door and greeted us warmly. We took our shoes off and waited for him to point out which pair of house slippers lined up by the door we should put on. "No, no," Suprun protested, implying that such humble customs were not necessary for honored foreign visitors. But I insisted, casting an eye to the shiny wooden floor and wanting to show deference and my knowledge of Russian manners.

Inside the apartment was neat and clean, with hardwood floors, bookshelves, and modest Scandinavian-style furniture. Suprun lived there with his wife and young son. He was the model of the aspiring academic, Russian style—ambitious, energetic, attentive if slightly watchful, and modestly dressed. The apartment consisted of one long, narrow main room, with a couch and coffee table toward the far end. The kitchen was off to the left, near the entryway. Directly in front of us sat a long table, half piled with papers, with the other half set for the evening supper. We sat down and began to discuss our project.

His wife, a journalist, asked if she could interview me for a segment on the local radio station—of course she wanted to interview this curiosity, the American returning to Arkhangelsk to research the story of the pre-revolutionary exploits of his Russian grandmother. When did an American ever come to visit, no less one so interested in Russian history and culture? I protested my bad Russian. "Oh, go ahead," Katya said. "You speak Russian perfectly well."

She asked how I had gotten started on the whole thing. "Well, Russian culture was always part of my life. I was fascinated by the sound of my grandmother's voice as she spoke the language, and I always wanted to learn it myself." I then began to recite the verses of Pushkin that every Russian knows, from Eugene Onegin, which I had learned from my grandmother—the first few lines of the famous soliloquy in which Lensky, before his duel with Onegin, wonders:

Whither, whither have you gone,
Oh, golden days of my youth?
What awaits me in the coming day?
My gaze searches vainly, I cannot know.

Katya and Suprun interrupted their parallel conversation and, together with Suprun's wife, smiled at me quizzically, with slight embarrassment. Here was an American visitor reciting the poetry they all learned in school but which sounded terribly old-fashioned to them now, really just an oddity; yet there he was —dressed in his gray wool, formal summer slacks and pin-striped Oxford shirt, creating a somewhat jarring contrast to the lumpy chinos and polo shirt of Suprun and the modest dress of his wife; though at least we were all wearing tapochki house slippers, which I always felt functioned as a welcome social leveler during the calls I paid that summer—nonetheless holding forth, a bit of out of his depth, no doubt, but seemingly determined to press forward.

And then I launched into my grandmother's adventure— revolutionary activities during her student days, arrest, exile, escape, Voroshilov, coming back to the Soviet Union in the thirties. It was much easier for Suprun and his wife to understand that interest—it was connected to the same extremes of history that had shaped their own lives and brought them to where they now were, extremes that had been inconceivably destructive but were also connected to times that had been more compelling, times when it was perhaps easier to understand the imperatives of life; and times whose events were still a confusing conundrum in so many ways. Why had everything after the Revolution unfolded with such brutality?

Had any of it been even slightly well-intentioned or valuable? Who were the guilty and who were the innocent? Was the line of demarcation absolutely sharp? And, most important of all, why did everything turn out the way it had after the promising decades before the Revolution?

Most Russians wanted to know the answers, now more than ever, with their new-found freedom of thought and expression; Suprun was no different, except that he toiled away in pursuit of the answers professionally. The time that I had come to investigate, when my grandmother came to Arkhangelsk in 1909, was the acme of Russia's pre-revolutionary Silver Age. As Suprun compiled his lists of exiles and catalogued their experiences, he was working to understand that time, to understand what had come afterwards, and whether it could have been different.

The Russians still maintained the old-fashioned custom and had their main meal at midday. In the evening people gathered for tea around nine o'clock and ate some bread and preserves with a few small dishes of cheese, salad, or fish. The Supruns had laid part of the long table, halfway between the kitchen and the far end of the room containing the couch, for the evening meal. They thanked us for the wine and cake and found a place for them amidst the jumble of papers and dishes. The table, floating in a slightly ill-defined space near the front door, nonetheless belonged clearly to the kitchen. In Russia, any serious business, not to mention deep interpersonal revelations, took place at the kitchen table.

Suprun was a classic Russian intellectual type (as my grandmother would have put it; she loved to describe people as "a type"). His face was soft and round with pink cheeks, intense eyes behind rimless glasses, dark silky hair, and a neatly trimmed beard. His expression radiated curiosity, amusement, and slight irony. His wife possessed an irresistible warmth that I always associated with certain Russian women, beginning with my grandmother.

Their son, Kolya, was eleven or twelve years old. With his shock of dark chestnut hair falling over his forehead, his glasses, and his serious look, he was an almost perfect miniature of his father. He tried a few words of his English on me and listened attentively as Katya and I spoke English, then switched back to Russian with his parents, interspersed with some English again. He reminded me of myself as a child, listening to my grandmother speak Russian with the other adults.

We began working through Suprun's files. Katya took down the list of file names and numbers, sorting and organizing them as best she could as we went along. There would be plenty for us to do in our remaining day and a half in Arkhangelsk, although some of the entries in the extensive list of cross-references led on to other archives, either back in St. Petersburg or, in that most formidable archive of them all, the State Archive of the Russian Federation in Moscow, known in both Russian and English by its acronym, GARF.

I produced the picture of my grandmother with her fellow exiles in Kholmogory, with all their names and the year, 1909, written on the back—the photo sent by my cousin Sven that had corrected my mistaken understanding of the year of my grandmother's trip to the north. Suprun cleared away some papers and set it down on the table. He leaned in closer, studying the photograph with rapt attention, like a classical archaeologist examining an exquisite bronze figurine just unearthed from an Attic dig site. "Remarkable," he murmured, as he turned the photo over, then back again, trying to line up the names with the faces. "There is Klim Voroshilov," he said, recognizing by sight the short, stocky figure with a military-style tunic gathered tightly in at the waist by a broad belt. Others were familiar to him by name; he would check further into them in his files. The group, almost twenty in all, posed around a kind of large rock, a boulder, with a few of the men sitting on top, set into the earth somewhere in a treeless plain with low hills rising up in the distance. Most of the group were young men—some more boys than men, by their appearance—together with four or five women, including my grandmother and Rulia. The men wore mostly worker's caps and Russian-style shirts, buttoned up the side to simple round collars, and rough jackets; the women wore long skirts and light-colored, high-buttoned blouses under tightly fitting, rough jackets as well. They looked like people—elaborating slightly with the romance of historical hindsight and my grandmother's descriptions—who were ready to sacrifice everything for their revolutionary beliefs; but also people who were young, artistic, and passionate, people eager for the White Night revels that my grandmother so longingly described decades later, as she spoke into the tape. My grandmother was smiling invitingly, excitedly, almost as if to shout, "Here I am!" from inside the sharp but aging black and white image. Next to her stood Rulia, looking timidly into the camera, shrinking back but exquisite, with her almond face and long, gently wavy hair, and smiling sadly, as she did in almost every photograph taken of her until the end of her life.

As we worked, Kolya watched over his father's shoulder. From time to time he went to the living room, making a show of paging through a book, but he kept coming back to the kitchen table. His parents gently told him to go to bed in the adjoining room. He looked at them reproachfully and kept listening. In truth, his parents didn't seem all that worried about putting him to bed. In Russia the night was the time to exchange confidences. The most important conversations took place very late at night—at the kitchen table.

Though this family was cosmopolitan, a visit from an American was still a bit exotic and had produced a feeling of excitement in the household. I was aware of the same reaction when I visited Leningrad with my grandmother as a child; apparently the allure of the American visitor still retained some of its special power. Americans were messengers from a distant and inaccessible world, like those travelers in a fairy tale who visit a remote village, telling of strange and wonderful things that happen far away.

One of my cousin Lyena's friends, Seryozha, after a few vodkas, inevitably recounted to me the following story: "Steve, listen. My mother had a cousin who went to America, to Pittsburgh. He opened a dry goods shop and then another, and by the time he died he was a millionaire. And he died without any heirs. The business is still worth millions of dollars. Do you think I could go there now and claim it for myself? I think if you have enough money, you can become a citizen. Is it true?" I felt like I was listening to a Sholom Aleichem story from 1895. The mythical land, America. Seryozha, of course, knew that it sounded that way; he was mostly being ironic and humorous. But the pull, the association to America, the chance to air out this little charade on an actual American, retained its appeal.

And when I met some elderly cousins from my grandfather's side, Boris and Asya, during my stay that summer, they told me a story about being called home urgently from work one day. Both worked as librarians in a factory collective—any self-respecting Soviet factory would of course have had a library!—on the outskirts of Leningrad. They received a message: "There are some Americans, your relatives they say, who have come to see you. They are waiting for you at home." So Boris and Asya immediately left work and rushed home, but there was no one there. The neighbors told them, "They waited and waited, then they said they couldn't wait any longer. They came in a big, black car. They said they'd come back." For the next month, Boris and Asya went home early every day, waiting for the American relatives. But no one ever came. They still smiled ruefully when they told the story—either because they understood how gullible and childish they had been; or because they still regretted missing the mysterious visitors who might have arrived bearing some kind of deliverance. Or at least a break from the monotony of their Soviet lives. They, like the relatives on my grandmother's side, were too well educated, their cultural DNA too strong, not to know that they were living a kind of marionette farce of a life, like sleepwalkers, going to their meaningless jobs, watching the meaningless news reports on television when they got home. A visitor from America could have changed all that, at least a little.

Yes, having an American show up for a visit was still a bit exciting, a little badge of honor. The whole family, not just Kolya, was caught up in it.

In their own way, they were like my cousins in St. Petersburg, if much younger. Intelligent, sensitive people who valued knowledge and decency. Like the Russians of my grandmother's day I imagined, with the after-effects of Soviet life of course stamped on them indelibly. A beautiful family, except that now all families were tiny. Before, they were all enormous, with a dozen children, like my grandmother's. In Soviet Russia, people only had one or two children. It was a kind of a pervasive symbol of the impoverishment of life.

We worked for two hours, then took a break for some food and wine. The Supruns cut the cherry cake and passed it around; the first piece went to Kolya, who had been waiting patiently. Afterwards they served tea and blini with preserves and sour cream. We resumed working through Suprun's files and finished around midnight. Katya and I thanked Suprun, said our goodbyes, and stepped out into the cool night air.

As we were walking back through the deserted street, it struck me: that just as the Supruns were experiencing the excitement, the satisfaction of the visit from their American guest, I was having the mirror-image experience. Growing up, trying to understand who I was—the child of American parents or the grandchild of my imposing Russian grandmother—was like a fugue, a two-part invention in music. I heard two melodies; they overlapped, they related to one another, they wove in and out; the listener always trying to decide which was more important, which one to pay attention to. I tried to follow the different lines. The American theme came first, but the theme introduced by my grandmother kept re-entering, always a part of the counterpoint.

In the end, after all the complex admixture, the variations, the inversions and repetitions, the two themes had come back in their simple, original forms. It had been happening since I arrived in Russia this time, as it had when I went there as a child. I heard the two themes, simple and separate, yet conjoined. The visit to the Supruns was a passage in the two-part invention. Kolya was the Russian version of my young American self.

The next day we flew back to St. Petersburg. Katya's parents came to meet her at the airport and kindly offered to drop me on Vladimirsky Prospekt. I went upstairs, eager to tell Sasha and Marina about my adventures in Arkhangelsk and Kholmogory. But before I could get started, Sasha handed me an envelope with the return address of the Pskov Archive. "This came while you were away," he said.

Inside, there was a single sheet filled with typescript on both sides:

"From the Local Historian Natan Feliksovich Levin, in response to the request from the American, Stephen Saletan, to the Pskov Archive.

"Information in Print on the Bamuner Family."

A page and a half of citations followed, numbered one through five. The first three contained entries in address calendars and newspaper advertisements for my great-grandfather's business over the years. One was annotated by Levin with the comment, "The building has been remodeled, but in my collection I have a postcard with a view of the original building; on the corner there is a sign visible that says, 'Sh. G. Bamuner, Civilian and Military Tailoring.'

Number four was headed, "Information about the Bamuner family in newspapers."

The list began with an article about the drowning in the Pskov River of my grandmother's brother, Nakhim, in 1893, at the age of six. Following which, eight articles about Rulia's arrest, the events leading up to it, and its aftermath. I suppose I might have found the articles by paging through the four or five different Pskov newspapers for the years 1905-1909, if I had had enough time. But now I had the roadmap.

In entry number five, Levin added the following:

"I am in possession of a copy of a group photograph of seven Pskov girlfriends from the year 1906. The first on the left is Eda Bamuner, the fourth is Estia Borkhova. The original is with the descendants of Professor Nikolai Ivanovich Sokolov, the future husband of Borkhova. I am in correspondence with his grandson Valentin Pavlovich Sokolov, who resides in St. Petersburg and can be reached at the following address and telephone number."

Sasha and I called Valentin the next day. I asked Sasha to begin the conversation. He started in his typically formal, somewhat circuitous fashion. I followed along as he explained who we were and why we were calling. As he struggled to weave in all the threads—my grandmother, Sokolov's grandmother, Pskov before the Revolution, Ganelin, Levin, the photo—I started to worry that Valentin would lose interest before Sasha got to the point.

Suddenly Sasha began to smile, and I tried to decipher what had changed in the conversation. I started to catch fragments—Sokolov's grandmother and mine were girlfriends, a box of medals, the Riga seaside. Suddenly, I understood. Valentin was the boy who had come with his grandmother to Vladimirsky Prospekt to visit my grandmother and me in the summer of 1963 and had given me a box of medals as a gift. The visitors that day, it turns out, had been Estia Borkhova, my grandmother's closest childhood friend, and her grandson!

At the end of the summer, Sasha had gone back to Moscow for several years. He and Valya, as Sasha began calling him, had not seen or spoken to each other since.

We promised to pay him a visit later that week.

Portrait photograph of my grandmother Eda (Riga, 1908).

Portrait photograph of my great-grandfather Sh. G. Bamuner (Pskov, 1890s).

1906 newspaper advertisement for my great-grandfather's shop in Pskov. "English Emporium—Military and Civilian Tailoring. Wide selection of domestic and imported fabrics. Winner of the Gold Medal for Men's Clothing, 1905 Brussels Exposition."

My grandmother (last row, third from left), Kliment Voroshilov (to her right), and great-aunt Rulia (front row, second from left) with fellow political exiles in Mezen (1909)

Kliment Voroshilov in exile in Mezen (1908).

230

Его - Превосходительству Господину
Архангельскому Губернатору.

Политической ссыльной
Рахили Самуиловны
Балумеръ г. Холмогоръ

Прошенiе.

Въ виду того, что годъ сидѣнья въ тюрьмахъ
сильно расшаталъ мои и до этого слабые нервы
и крайне тяжело отразился на моемъ здоровьѣ,
которое требуетъ радикальнаго леченiя, то я
прошу Ваше Превосходительство, оставить
меня въ г. Холмогорахъ; по освидѣтельствованiю
мѣстнаго врача я не могу ѣхать.

Рахиль Балумеръ

16го мая 1909г.

г. Холмогоры.

Letter from my great-aunt Rulia to the Governor of Arkhangelsk
Province, requesting that because of her weakened health she not be
sent further into exile to Mezen (1909).

My great-grandfather Sh.G. Bamuner in old age near Riga (late 1920s) with his second wife, Anna Mikhailovna (seated on the ground), and son Arkady (standing behind).

КОПИЯ.

Уважаемый

Климент Ефремович !

К Вам обращается с просьбой брат Иды и Рули Бамунер, находившихся с Вами в ссылке в городе Мезени
в 1907 г. и бежавших оттуда в Америку. Сейчас они в
письмах выражают сильное желание приехать в СССР. Нам
придется хлопотать о получении для них визы.

Климент Ефремович, вы единственный живой свидетель,
знавший сестер в ссылке. Возможно, что в ходатайстве
нам придется сослаться на лицо, знавшее их в ссылке.
Не возражаете ли Вы против указания на это обстоятельство

Был бы очень обязан , если бы Вы уделили лично
2-3 минуты , о чем бы я узнал от Вашего секретаря. По
профессии я - советский журналист , до последнего времени
работал в Ленинградском отделении "Известий ЦИК", откуда
приехал специальному по этому делу.

Аркадий БАМУНЕР (газетный псевдоним АЛМАЗОВ)

2.II. 1931 г.
Ленинград, пр. Нахимсона
8 кв.5.

ВЕРНО: Вирбунь

My great-uncle Arkady's 1931 letter to Kliment Voroshilov seeking his help in obtaining visas for my grandmother and Rulia to enter the USSR.

Family portrait taken shortly after the arrival of the American relatives in Leningrad in 1932. Back row (right to left): my great-uncle Volya, my grandmother, my great-uncle Arkady. Middle row (right to left): my uncle Eugene, his cousins Lusya and Alek.

Summer theatrical at the Tarkhovka dacha (1932), organized by my great-uncle Arkady (standing).

My grandmother (left) with her brother Arkady and sister-in-law Nina in Sochi, mid-1950s.

Family photograph taken during our visit to Leningrad in 1963. Back row (right to left): my cousin Sasha, my cousin Gina, great-uncle Arkady, and me. Front row: my grandmother (right) and her sisters.

PART III

YOUNG REVOLUTIONARY

CHAPTER 21. PSKOV

My earliest memories of my grandmother's Russian stories begin in sound—with the exotic, nearly unpronounceable name of the city where she grew up: Pskov. Four sharply etched consonants barely held together by one soft vowel. A sound unlike any I ever heard at home or at school, one that evoked my grandmother's Russian world with startling clarity. A sound that only my grandmother could articulate with ease.

We must have talked about many things on those Friday evenings all through my childhood when she came to visit. But the only topic I can remember is Russia, and my grandmother's Russian stories always came back to Pskov. As much as she had become an American, the mother of American sons and grandmother of American grandchildren, it always felt as if she had just returned from Russia or was about to set off on another trip back there. That was the person I waited for eagerly on Friday evenings—the traveler from Russia. For my grandmother, stories were the way to construct the world. That alone seemed very Russian to me, part of the essence of the spell that she cast. Her stories were always about Russia, and everything having to do with Russia came in the form of a story.

The rest of her adventures, the ones that came afterwards—exile to the remote Russian north, the flight across half of Europe, escape to America, the return to Soviet Leningrad in 1932—took shape for me in stark images of black and white. But amidst this dizzying array, which tumbled backwards across time and yet still seemed to exist in the present, a single image appeared in vivid color: the ancient and serene city of Pskov, like a tiny golden thread at the center of a vast tapestry.

My grandmother was born in 1888, the third of my great-grandfather's twelve children with his first wife, Sofia Wolf, in the Finnish city of Viipuri. In Russian it was known as Vyborg, as Finland was then part of the Russian Empire. After World War I Finland became independent, but Stalin managed to take back the piece containing Vyborg just before World War II. My grandmother recounted such huge shifts of land and people—the violent vortex in which the history of central and eastern Europe played out over the twentieth century—with calm detachment. Similar stories involved her father's move to the larger city of Riga, in Latvia, after his early success in Pskov; Latvia's independence after the Russian Revolution followed by its subsequent reabsorption back into the Soviet Union after World War II; the travels of her brothers and sisters from Riga to Petrograd, soon to be known as Leningrad, and back again, across dangerous borders with threatening government authorities on either side. All made the more vivid to me as a child by the names of the places whose sounds were nearly as compelling as those of Pskov and

Russia. The idea that history kept washing over these lands, shifting borders, forcing people to rethink their lives and contend with gigantic, inexorable forces sounded frightening but irresistibly exciting. So much more compelling than the uneventful life we were living in suburbia.

It was in Vyborg that my great-grandfather started his tailoring business, making uniforms for the army regiment garrisoned there. Every regiment in the Russian army had a different uniform, each requiring a dedicated tailor; appointment to a regiment was coveted. "Papa was the regimental tailor," my grandmother would explain with a note of pride. When the regiment was posted to Pskov, my great-grandfather moved there with his family and opened an elegant new shop.

In Pskov his business prospered. He became one of the prominent businessmen of the town. By the turn of the century his shop was big enough to take out full-page advertisements in the local newspapers, as Katya and I discovered during the course of our research, bragging that he had won first prize in an international trade exposition in Brussels. Making uniforms for the military was a profitable business; eventually the shop sold clothes for civilians as well. "English Style Emporium, Sh. G. Bamuner, Civilian and Military Tailoring," his advertisements proclaimed. By the time my grandmother was old enough to go to high school (the Gymnasium, as she called it, using the Russian word for an academic secondary school), the shop employed thirty master tailors and apprentices. My great-grandfather's name started appearing in the annual lists of Merchants of the First Guild.

Under tsarist rule during the nineteenth and early twentieth centuries, Russian Jews were allowed to live only in restricted parts of the country, along the western borderlands in designated areas known as the Pale of Settlement (in Russian, literally, the more forbidding-sounding "Line of Settlement"). But exceptions could be made, as the process of Jewish assimilation that had begun in Germany, France, and England in the early nineteenth century slowly filtered into the backwaters of Russia. Some Jewish families began to live in the big cities, to attend Russian schools, and rarely, even universities. One basis for the exception was success in business. As a Merchant of the First Guild, my great-grandfather was entitled to live outside the Pale. And so my grandmother grew up in the traditional, very Russian atmosphere of Pskov.

Pskov was small, historic, and beautiful. Since medieval times it had been known as the city of merchants; situated as it was on the very western edge of Russia, it became a natural point of defense but also of trade with the neighboring lands of Germany, Poland, Lithuania, and Sweden. By the time my grandmother was growing up, it was also known as the city of schools. The city's five-hundred-year-old fortified citadel, called a "kremlin" in Pskov just as it was in Moscow or any other old Russian city, stood at the center of the town on the high bank of the Pskov River. The meadowlands on the city's outskirts were dotted with ancient churches and monasteries decorated with medieval icons and frescoes.

My grandmother's accounts of her early life in Pskov had the quality of a double exposure: on the one hand traditional and remote as a fairy tale, on the other filled with things that sounded not very different from the world I lived in. Her stories of her family of thirteen children, not all of whom survived childhood, came from a world completely unknown to me, one that had seemingly disappeared. Two of her brothers died as small children, one by drowning in the Pskov River, the other of a childhood fever. These stories she recounted with deep melancholy, a kind of still-raw emotion, but without shock or surprise, as if such things were to be expected and life simply continued. To me they were incomprehensibly alien. Yet against this background of a time and place very distant and antique, against the pictures of my grandmother and her sister Rulia in floor-length skirts, high-collared blouses, and old-fashioned, elaborate coiffures, Pskov already had streetcars and electric lights, and my grandmother's memories of going to school, traveling around the town, and visiting her friends sounded rather like the world I knew. By the time she was finishing school, people could travel easily throughout Europe by train and to America and back by steamship. Her sense of the world, of herself and relationships with other people, of culture, education, and work seemed not so terribly different from the world that surrounded me, more like modern times than storybook, bygone days.

Indeed, as she grew up in Pskov, my grandmother lived a kind of series of dualities: she was a Jewish girl living in a prosperous, assimilated family in full Russian style, speaking only Russian rather than Yiddish, yet she would never be seen as unconditionally Russian by the dominant gentile population around her; she was a bright student and well-educated, but in a world where only the tiniest fraction of women went on to a university education and the professions, which she did not; she was devoted to the idea of revolution from an idealistic point of view but had no taste for the violence inherent in revolutionary politics, though eventually she began to visit the meetings of the revolutionary societies and eventually joined the party of the Socialist Revolutionaries. These were the tumultuous times in which my grandmother was formed.

She and her gymnasium classmates were steeped in ideas about materialism, historical determinism, Marxism, class warfare, and revolution. The doctrines that were to fuel the violent political struggles of the twentieth century were assuming their recognizable form during the years she grew up. In 1880, Russia was a rural backwater. By the time my grandmother finished high school, the western part of the country was rapidly industrializing and a new class of factory workers, as opposed to simply agricultural laborers (still referred to as peasants), made up a significant part of the work force. Strikes and protests, sometimes violent, had begun.

In 1904, the year my grandmother turned sixteen, her mother died giving birth to her twelfth child. At first, my grandmother could barely comprehend what had happened. In contrast to her father, who was strict, remote, and preoccupied with his own affairs, her mother had always been warm and affectionate, the emotional center of my grandmother's young life. To the end of her own life, whenever she spoke of her mother's death, I sensed that my grandmother still felt the shock and trauma—the void that it suddenly created in her life—acutely.

Her older sister Lyuba would normally have taken on the role of surrogate mother to the remaining children, but Lyuba was even more profoundly affected by her mother's death than my grandmother. Paralyzed with grief, she cried inconsolably for weeks. At the age of sixteen, my grandmother was left to watch over Rulia and six younger siblings, all under the age of ten. She grew up quickly, responsible suddenly both for her siblings and for her own future in a rapidly changing, increasingly unstable world. The abrupt shift in circumstances, together with her father's remoteness, sharpened her natural inclination toward decisiveness and independence. She began to help her father in the shop and looked after her younger siblings until he remarried two years later. All of which prepared her to play a similar role throughout her life as unofficial matriarch to two extended families, one in America and the other in Russia.

My great-grandfather had opposed sending—or, more precisely, paying for—any of his daughters to go to university. But like my grandmother, Lyuba was a bright student, and after much resistance her father finally gave in and agreed to let her enroll on the condition that she study to become a dentist. Following my great-grandmother's death, under the burden of her intense emotional distress, Lyuba left the university whereupon my great-grandfather announced that he would revert to his original plan—none of his daughters would go on to higher education. Lyuba and my grandmother were to help in the shop and, eventually, get married. A year later, my grandmother's older brother Volya enrolled in the prestigious Riga Polytechnic Institute and went on to become a successful, well-known engineer. There was never any question that the three surviving Bamuner sons would continue on to a university education.

And so, at the age of sixteen, coping with the trauma of her own mother's death, my grandmother was thrust into the role of surrogate parent with responsibility to manage her father's large household—while at the same time receiving the message that she was to remain under his rigid authority and not harbor any expectations about deciding her own future.

Yet, powerless as she was in one way, like other young women of her social background she obtained a secondary education, and from the way she described her peer group relationships at school I got the impression that she was treated seriously and respectfully, that she did not feel constrained. The whole mixture was a kind of perfect brew for generational rebellion. A young woman who was part of an educated, forward-looking generation, with a father who was old-fashioned and backward-looking. (Though, in the end, apparently loving and caring, since my grandmother complained about him with the kind of affectionate tone one uses for a beloved relative whose endearing human and emotional qualities overcome one's irritation at their wrong-headed political or social views. My great-grandfather, I got the sense, was tender-hearted and devoted to his children; stern nineteenth-century-style patriarch though he may have been.)

The fuel waiting to feed the fire was the revolutionary passion that had begun to stir in a country whose government was in the hands—literally—of a single individual, the tsar. No representative democracy of any kind existed in Russia in 1904, in baffling contrast to the rest of Europe, as my grandmother and her classmates well knew. Revolutionary ideas had been seeping into—and undermining—Russia's rigid social and political structure for over half a century by the time my grandmother was in school but had only recently begun to infiltrate more widely into the new middle class to which my grandmother belonged, just as she began to chafe under her father's authority. And at the end of the year, a political earthquake that was to violently shake Russian society to its foundation arrived, providing the powerful catalyst that accelerated the reaction.

When I asked my grandmother during our taping session to tell me about her father, she reflected for a moment then declared emphatically, "We called my father a despot," with a mixture of indignation and affection. She used the Russian version of the word, more or less the same as in English, but sounding sharper and more despotic in Russian, as her voice lingered on the drawn-out first syllable "dyes" before landing decisively on the short, accusatory second syllable, "putt."

"He demanded that everything be done just as he insisted, and I, well, I was a revolutionary from the age of sixteen, so I didn't agree with him about anything. His son Volya, my older brother, was just like him. Everyone in the shop called Volya 'the boss's boss.'

"I disagreed with my father about so many things, for instance, about his attitude toward my sister Lyuba. The sudden death of my mother had a terrible effect on her, and she remained sick for years. She was engaged to be married, but she broke it off. She didn't finish her course in the university to become a dentist. She was a highly neurotic person, but my father only cared about her getting married. And I considered him a terrible despot to his new wife, Anna Mikhailovna, though she loved him and always took care of him. And I didn't like his attitude to the workers."

As her father grew wealthier and the number of children increased, the house filled up with nannies, cooks, and maids.

"Papa told us never to speak to them while they were working," my grandmother remembered. "I thought it was terrible, because of course all of us kids knew them well and were friendly with them. It was the maids who used to take notes for me across the city to my girlfriends."

Indeed, like the other students from well-to-do families who discussed revolutionary ideas among themselves at school, my grandmother was incited to her beliefs partly by what she saw right in front of her. As her father's business prospered and his shop and workrooms grew larger, she saw for herself the long work hours, the rules that forbade employees to speak or make any complaint, and the low wages they received.

"Papa never spoke to me inside the shop in front of the workers, when I would help there," my grandmother continued. "And he told me never to speak to him when he came downstairs to look things over, either, because anything I had to tell him should be discussed only in private."

If she had a question or a problem, she explained, she had to go upstairs to the house and see him in his study. She would knock, enter the study, and wait silently until he looked up from his papers. And as she waited, she remembered, she would twirl the globe that always stood on his desk, looking at the shapes and names that stretched along the curve of its shiny surface. I will go to those places, she told herself, as she waited for him to look up.

CHAPTER 22. SCHOOL,

REVOLUTIONARY AWAKENINGS

As much as my grandmother told me about the extraordinary things she had done growing up in Russia, she never really explained why she had done them. It seemed to have happened almost spontaneously, as if the times themselves, the roiling ferment of prerevolutionary Russia, had determined who she was to become. She never claimed any special credit for herself, though grace notes of pride and self-dramatization crept into her narrative from time to time.

She seemed to take everything she had done—and the enormous consequences that resulted—for granted. And the consequences were profound: involving herself in revolutionary politics, she managed to get her young sister tangled up in them as well; she was forced to leave her home, after nearly getting arrested herself, together with the sixteen-year-old Rulia, who had spent a year in jail before being sent to a part of Russia where she was unlikely to survive her three-year term of exile; a place where the nearest city was three hundred miles away and winter temperatures dropped to twenty degrees below zero, as the wind blew continuously for five months and the daylight dwindled to four or five hours a day; where only at the last minute did my grandmother manage to get them out, but at the cost of leaving behind everything they had known growing up and everyone they loved.

She somehow communicated that it had all simply been her destiny, as if she had been the vessel for a higher calling—the moral obligation to fight for justice, yes, but in some even more fundamental sense the urgent drive to take up a more exciting life than the comfortable one she had been handed. She was not going to be the dutiful child of the stolid bourgeois world that her father had so skillfully crafted for the family.

At the end of our taping sessions on 66th Street, when she was almost ninety years old, I asked her, "But why did you do it all?"

She looked out over the gray expanse of the Hudson River. "I don't know, that's just the way I was," she answered. "I always wanted something new, some kind of adventure," she continued, with a heavy Russian-accented emphasis on the second syllable of the key word, adventure. "Yes, that's just the way we were," she concluded. "We had such audacity."

As much as my grandmother conflicted with her father, the family was the secure center of her life. She knew that no matter how much she defied him, he would forgive and protect her in the end. Though they disagreed, their relationship was loving. She remained attached to him until the end of his life, returning twice to Latvia between the wars to see him. My uncle remembered how she sobbed when she received the telegram with the news of his death on the eve of World War II. And she maintained her relationship with each of her siblings as well, exchanging letters, sending packages, and visiting them over the course of four decades in the family apartment on Vladimirsky Prospekt. As much as she rebelled against it all, the afterglow of her early life in Pskov—the comfortable bourgeois world of school friends, books, and poetry, well-appointed houses, school pranks, and intrigues—never left her.

Rulia was four years younger than my grandmother; the brother between them in age (as a new child was born to the family every two years from 1884 until 1906) had died in childhood. Both sisters were attractive, but in entirely different ways. My grandmother's hair was dark and wavy; she was short but sturdily and attractively built; her intense gaze radiated vigor and certainty. Rulia was slim and delicate; her hair, chestnut and silken, gently framed her exquisitely fragile, oval face. My grandmother was confident and forceful. Rulia was shy, with a dreamy, ethereal air—a hint of hesitancy before she spoke or moved—that she retained to the end of her life. By the time I knew her, half a century later, she was an old lady living in a small Manhattan apartment at the top of a dark staircase, so badly afflicted with arthritis that she could barely leave her chair, but she remained delicate, elegant, and other-worldly, speaking in barely a whisper in her lightly accented English. My great-grandfather, though severe with my grandmother and the rest of his older children, doted on Rulia, calling her his little dove, my grandmother remembered, and delighted in making her laugh by teasing her or surprising her with gifts.

As different as their characters were, and despite their difference in age, following the death of their mother my grandmother and Rulia grew close. Gradually their lives began to unfold in parallel. They went to the same schools, followed the same interests, and cultivated the same tastes in clothes and boys. Starting from the age of twelve, both attended the academic Girls' Gymnasium of Pskov.

My great-grandfather emerged from a world in which the Jews of Russia had lived entirely separately. Over time a small group entered the mainstream of society. All of this had come about over the course of one generation. He, presumably, had been part of the first wave of Russian Jews who heeded the call for "Enlightenment" that had been sweeping through the Jewish communities of Europe for the previous century and had finally reached Russia. Speak the language and adopt the outward customs of your country, the new thinkers advised. Be Jewish Germans, Jewish Frenchmen, Jewish Russians. Jewish, but part of the common society. My great-grandfather was born around 1860 and must, given the timeframe, have grown up in a reasonably traditional Jewish milieu. Yet he apparently had attended Russian schools, since he was highly literate in the Russian language and comfortable in Russian culture. He was part of the first transitional generation.

And since Jews in Russia could not own land, many entered the professions and business. The ones who succeeded on a grander scale, like my great-grandfather, eventually became well educated and deeply cosmopolitan (to use the word appropriated later by the Communists, and so many others, to viciously assault the very same people).

This relatively small, specific world of the assimilated Jews of Russia, the educated, cosmopolitan sphere of the prosperous

Jewish families of Pskov, was the milieu in which my grand-mother grew up. But such was the complicated status of Jews in Russia, that while some, like my great-grandfather, could live as prominent businessmen and honored citizens in one of the country's oldest cities, renowned for its Russian Orthodox churches and monasteries, only a few hundred miles away in the backwaters of the Pale of Settlement, Jews could suddenly and without warning become the victims of savage pogroms.

Following the example of her father and her older siblings, my grandmother enrolled in the academic gymnasium when she was twelve years old. Her closest friend at school was Estia Borkhova. Estia's father, Isaak Borkhov, was Pskov's most successful Jewish businessman. He owned the city's largest factory, employed hundreds of workers, and was far wealthier than my modestly prosperous great-grandfather. The Borkhov family lived in Pskov's grandest, most historic mansion, renowned for having hosted Peter the Great when the fearsome tsar visited Pskov in the early eighteenth century.

Estia and my grandmother went to school together every day. They met in front of the turreted, red brick building on the city's main square that housed my great-grandfather's shop on the ground floor and the family's sprawling apartment on the second, and walked together down the narrow street that ran below the walls of the Pskov kremlin toward the gymnasium. "The reflection of the sun from the five golden domes of Trinity Cathedral used to light up the street as we walked," my grandmother remembered. Each day they looked forward with pleasure to the academic routine of reading the classics of Russian literature—Pushkin, Lermontov, Gogol, and Tolstoy—and studying history, French and German, mathematics, and science. But they bridled at the school's system of arbitrary rules and strict discipline.

Like everything else in Russian society at the turn of the twentieth century—and afterwards—the educational system was complex and bureaucratic. Different students took different examinations and attended different types of schools, some geared toward professions like science and engineering, others toward specific trades, resembling vocational schools. At the highest level, students attended the academic gymnasium, a word borrowed, like so many Russian technical terms, from the German. There the students studied languages—Russian, Greek, Latin, French, German— history, literature, philosophy, and other academic subjects. The best students could continue on to the university in St. Petersburg or Moscow, though places for Jewish students were severely limited by the quota system. This traditional academic education of the gymnasium was the education that my grandmother received in Pskov. But at the same time, it was in the schools that young people passed around the forbidden works of literature and philosophy that served to build the ideas of political and social freedom, of workers' rights, of the Revolution. The Russian Revolution was born, to some very great extent, on the page. Every Russian revolutionary, my grandmother included, knew the great works of philosophy prefiguring Marx and socialism; knew the Populist writings of the socially conscious Russian authors of the nineteenth century; and passionately discussed and debated the ideas they had read about.

"Of course I belonged to a student circle in the gymnasium," my grandmother told me. Student circles had been a time-honored activity of intellectuals in Russia for almost a century. In the beginning the activity belonged to aristocrats, but as the middle class grew, students like my grandmother had the time and education to join the tradition. As it had been for their forebears, the allure, the idealism, the sense that they could change and improve the world, was irresistible. The very existence of the new middle class to which she belonged was emblematic of the fact that life in Russia had already changed remarkably. The emergence of an educated, politically aware middle class was part of what made the bursting of the dam of the old order in Russia inevitable. By the time she entered the gymnasium, my grandmother, together with her young friends among the sophisticated Jewish families of Pskov, sensed that Russia was on the brink of a volcanic eruption.

The situation in Russian schools at the beginning of the twentieth century was indeed paradoxical. The bureaucrats in St. Petersburg worried and wavered; on the one hand they knew that Russia had fallen behind western Europe and needed educated citizens to serve in the government and enter business and the professions so that Russia could catch up and compete economically and militarily. Yet they were afraid of the subversive political influences that education could bring. Waves of educational reform that opened the schools to more students and expanded the old-fashioned, restricted reading lists alternated with periods in which the government issued decrees intended to suppress the development of dangerous political thinking. But the strict codes of conduct and bans on books served only to inflame the students to circulate the forbidden reading material among themselves in secret, gather in small groups to read and discuss them, and organize protests. In spite of the best efforts of the government and school authorities, despite the controlled reading lists and curriculum, my grandmother and her friends were learning about what was happening in the world beyond the placid waters of the Pskov River, flowing slowly by the rough-hewn walls of the ancient town fortress, and where boys fished for crabs on the sandbars along its banks. Russia could no longer remain completely walled off from the spread of newspapers, electricity, railroads, and the newfound ease of crossing the ocean by steamship. The vast nation was no longer the world of the closed village, cut off from the world by snow through the winter and mud throughout the spring and fall.

Russia in the first decade of the twentieth century was officially conservative but porous—despite the work of the censors, the newspapers continually brought news of the outside world, of the early failures of the war with Japan that began in 1904, of the ensuing strikes and riots across the country, of the activities and arrests of suspected revolution-aries. Paradoxically the outside world was more accessible to my grandmother growing up in Pskov than it would be to any of her siblings after the Revolution. And after the Revolution, news from inside the country stopped flowing outward as well. By the time my grandmother returned to the Soviet Union in 1932, she had little idea of what was actually happening there. This was one of the reasons that she went, besides wanting to rejoin her beloved brothers and sisters.

By the time my grandmother enrolled at the gymnasium, the cycles of greater openness followed by harsh tightening had been going on for two generations. Coinciding with the sudden arrival of a war—ultimately disastrous—with Japan, the cycle that began in 1904, when my grandmother finished her fourth year of school and celebrated her sixteenth birthday, would prove to be the most explosive. And so as much as my grandmother and Estia looked forward to their academic pursuits and the meetings of their student circles, they rebelled against the discipline that awaited them each day, even as they arrived at school.

"The headmistress waited for us at the top of the stairs and examined our clothing and school bags as we went inside," my grandmother remembered with undimmed indignation. Girls could be sent home if the headmistress judged them to be immodestly dressed. If a book that was not included on the school's curriculum was found among someone's possessions—like the poems of Russia's great civic poet, Nekrasov, who wrote in praise of the common people and was forbidden to the students—they would be sent home with a failing grade in their journal for the week. (Nekrasov, unsurprisingly, was one of my grandmother's favorite poets. When I was a child, she recited and taught his verses to me, helping me to mimic the Russian sounds and translating as we went along.) After all the girls had entered, they were obliged to wait in the entry hall in silence until the headmistress accompanied them to the cloakroom where they put away their heavy winter clothes and boots. The length of their skirts and the cut of their blouses were precisely prescribed and closely examined. Infractions led to more failing grades. With a second infraction, a student could be expelled for a semester, unless her parents came to the school and used their influence to reverse the decision. The wealthy parents usually succeeded. Scholarship students from modest homes were often not as lucky.

At the same time, my grandmother's bitter memories of the headmistress were leavened with the mirth of her adolescent rebelliousness:

"We had to curtsy whenever we passed her—as we came into school, in the hallway, even when we met her in the street. She was a sour-faced older woman, but with a beautiful figure, it's true. She always wore a long dress with a tiny, pinched waist and a train that trailed after her like the tail of a fish. But when she turned to look at you, her face was like a wrinkled cucumber," my grandmother remembered, laughing good-humoredly.

The Russo-Japanese war began in February. By the autumn of 1904, the somewhat abstract and aspirational political yearnings of students like my grandmother were suddenly thrown into sharp relief by actual events—transformed into something approaching reality, an actual time of reckoning, by a series of completely unanticipated developments. A war with Japan, early defeats, protests and demands for greater accountability from the government, crackdowns from the autocratic center—all brought the country, by year's end, to the verge of open, full-scale Revolution.

The moment created a kind of perfect storm: a headstrong, fearless young woman denied access to higher education and a professional life; a tyrannical father who not only inhibited her own ambitions but mistreated his workers; a school system designed to pacify and co-opt a small group of elite secondary and university level students but which more often merely provoked their defiance; and now, a political earthquake that threatened to destroy the autocratic regime of the vast Russian Empire and utterly change the political and social life of the country. It was a set of circumstances ideally arranged to encourage the revolutionary outlook of someone like my grandmother—idealistic, intellectually curious, emotionally intense, naturally headstrong, and thoroughly rebellious.

Even as a child I was struck by how modern my grandmother's childhood sounded, how similar in many ways to my own world, as far away in time, space, and language as it was. She seemed to be independent and free, she pursued her own friendships, love interests, political passions, and adventures with an esprit and sense of self that seemed completely contemporary. She refused to be bound by tradition, as much as it surrounded her, or by traditional authority or any sense of limitation about who she was or what she might do. She was self-aware and autonomous. Nothing terribly Old World about any of it. Quite the opposite—familiar, rather like the people I knew, the kind of person I wanted to become. Except that the frame was turn-of-the-century, tsarist Russia, Pskov, onion-dome churches, old fortress walls, high collars and long skirts, long hair pinned up in a bun. The frame was antique; the people modern and free. This fascinated me. It seemed very far away, and very close at the same time.

CHAPTER 23. REVOLUTION

In 1904, Russia plunged into political chaos. The First Russian Revolution, well-remembered to this day in Russia if little known in the West—overshadowed as it was by the Bolshevik Revolution of 1917—is also known as the Revolution of 1905, though it actually began in 1904 and ended in 1907.

The wave of violent political unrest was triggered by a war with Japan that began in February of 1904. Russia had been on a centuries-long mission of conquest eastward, ever deeper into Asia, finally reaching the coast of the Pacific Ocean. A new city, Vladivostok, was founded in 1860 to provide a port on the Pacific, but it froze over in the winter. Toward the end of the century, Russia established a new, year-round naval base at Port Arthur, farther south in Manchuria, on what was officially Chinese territory.

Russia's expansion into the vast Far East, purportedly a backward and thinly settled wasteland but actually inhabited for millennia by indigenous people, bore an eerie similarity to the one undertaken later by the United States to conquer its West—although America managed to accomplish in seventy-five years what took the Russians more than three hundred. The two mirror-image campaigns of conquest ended on opposite shores of the Pacific, after brushing up briefly against one another in Alaska and northern California.

At about the same time, the Japanese, following their Meiji Restoration, rapidly industrialized, militarized, and set out on a program of conquest of their own. When they decided that Korea was to be their vassal state, Russia's presence in nearby Manchuria presented an unacceptable obstacle. Through a combination of poor judgment (a theme that persisted throughout his reign until his downfall) and racist views ("You are the last bastion of Europe against the rising Yellow Peril, the new Mongol Horde," his incendiary and bellicose cousin, Kaiser Wilhelm of Germany, wrote to him), Tsar Nicholas II rejected Japan's demands to withdraw to the north. The Japanese will never dare attack us, his advisors assured him.

The war began with a surprise assault on the Russian fleet in Port Arthur. Russia suffered serious losses but continued to believe the Japanese could easily be overcome. At first, Russians at home paid little attention to the smoldering conflict thousands of miles away. The government continued to whip up racial sentiment and promised easy victory. My great-grandfather was initially pleased as orders for winter uniforms flooded into his shop.

But within months, what remained of the Russian Pacific fleet at Port Arthur was destroyed and the Russian land army suffered a shocking defeat. The first bell of a century-long series of ill-fated western military adventures in Asia had sounded. And public opinion in Russia began to shift dramatically. Criticism of the tsar and his autocratic administration as backward, deaf to the democratic developments that had taken root across the rest of Europe, and—as a result—grievously incompetent suddenly moved from the relatively small reformist and revolutionary groups at the margins of society into the mainstream.

In the summer of 1904, the terrorist wing of one of the two main radical parties, the Socialist Revolutionaries (the other was the Social Democratic Party, better known by the name of its dominant faction, the Bolsheviks), assassinated the reactionary Minister of the Interior, Plehve, who had long exercised almost unlimited authority in implementing the autocratic, ineffectual policies of the tsar. Even moderates were pleased to be rid of him. The pressure for some kind of political reform now appeared to be irresistible.

Sviatopolsk-Mirsky, the tsar's new chief minister, advised him to address the burgeoning calls for reform and allow greater freedom of public discussion and assembly. A country-wide convocation of local district councils, the National Zemstvo Congress, convened in St. Petersburg and issued a ten-point manifesto calling for the rule of law, civil liberties, and an elected national assembly with the right to pass independent laws—a virtual demand, up to then anathema, that Russia adopt a constitutional form of government. At the same time, the country's scholarly and professional societies announced a country-wide program of political assemblies, the so-called "liberation banquets" patterned after the ones held in Paris before the Revolution of 1848 in France. (Russia's love affair with all things French permeated politics as well; the Bolsheviks conceived of themselves as the second coming of the French Revolution, referring to one another as "Marat" and "Robespierre.") Thousands of citizens were suddenly meeting and debating the country's political future. Nothing like it had ever been seen in Russia.

Despite official censorship, it was all reported in detail in the newspapers. The new openness of public dialogue brought about an irreversible change in the political landscape. Though not so named, it was essentially the same phenomenon as the famous "Glasnost" unleashed by Gorbachev—and as much a harbinger of the collapse of the old regime as it turned out to be for the Soviet Union. The days when revolution was mostly discussed in the salons of aristocrats, debated and written about by exiles in London, Paris, and Zurich, were coming to an end. Now masses of people within Russia itself were ready to join the uprising and lead the cause.

As the events of the spring and summer of 1904 unfolded, my grandmother, still recovering from the recent shock of her mother's death, watched with a sense of amazement. "We started reading all sorts of things in the newspaper about the tsar, how he wasn't making the right decisions," she remembered. "People had only whispered about such things before that. Suddenly everyone was talking openly."

The revolutionary ideas that she and her classmates had read about and discussed, which had always seemed mostly theoretical and aspirational, were suddenly coming to life around her. My grandmother was enthralled. This was everything she and her friends had been discussing and dreaming of, what they had longingly read about in the poems of Nekrasov and the deeds of the Decembrists.

As the war continued and the calls for reform mounted, unrest among workers began to sweep through the country's factories and workshops. The labor movement in Russia at the beginning of the twentieth century was less developed than in the rest of western Europe, but harsh working conditions had created a reservoir of discontent that was ripe for agitation. Study circles where workers could receive a basic education in Socialist ideas had been meeting since the 1880s. These, like trips to the countryside to work among and commune with the peasants, were in the beginning the province of progressive-minded aristocrats and intellectuals but now were practiced eagerly by students and members of the burgeoning middle class. My grandmother never mentioned any politically-inspired expeditions to rural villages, but I saw the echo of the sensibility behind them, which I knew she harbored, half a century later, when on summer afternoons in Mohegan she would seat herself in a folding chair on her modest back terrace, amidst the white birch trees, and paint evocations of the landscape into which she fancifully inserted rustic figures she referred to as *muzhiks*, using the old-fashioned Russian word for peasant. She did remember attending the worker study circles in Pskov. "Nikolai, who was kind of sweet on me, was one of the boys in the gymnasium. He used to teach in the circles, and he invited me to come along. That's where we discussed the doctrines of Plekhanov, Marx, and all the other famous Socialists."

The study circles in Pskov were sponsored by the Socialist Revolutionary Party. The so-called SRs were the successors of the Populist movements of the nineteenth century. With their emphasis on "going to the people," the SRs had great success in enrolling the students from the secondary schools, especially the elite humanitarian gymnasiums like the one my grandmother attended. The doctrines of organizing workers, distributing land to the peasants and ending the tsarist autocracy all appealed to the rebellious, idealistic students—such were the beliefs that formed my grandmother's revolutionary catechism. In particular, the Socialist Revolutionary leaders knew they would find fertile ground among the wealthy children of the merchant class, especially the Jews, who, though moving more and more into Russian society, were still outsiders, dreaming of a different society and a different world.

"Once the war with Japan started to go very badly and they called for the Zemstvo Congress in Petersburg, Nikolai stopped holding meetings in the shops and factories," my grandmother recalled. "He said there wasn't time to study anymore because the workers were already calling for strikes. And it was too bad, because I had always wanted to start a study circle in Papa's shop."

In St. Petersburg, a religious leader named Father Gyorgy Gapon established one of the country's largest labor associations. Father Gapon was a charismatic priest who had devoted himself to working among the impoverished and disenfranchised workers, encouraging them to organize and improve their lot, on the one hand, while maintaining faith in the mystical union between the tsar and his people on the other. In 1903 he founded the Assembly of the Russian Factory and Mill Workers of St. Petersburg.

The Assembly was a successor to the government-controlled labor unions, so-called 'police socialism' that the secret police had experimented with at the start of the decade to defuse worker unrest—a singularly Russian phenomenon that combined elements of orthodox religiosity, support for the autocracy, and belief that the merciful father tsar was best positioned to solve the problems of the peasants, while at the same time providing nominal support for the workers' demands for improved conditions, higher pay, and the right to form unions. This curious attempt to co-opt the burgeoning labor movement was abandoned when the SRs managed to take control of one of the largest unions, in Odesa, and called a general strike. But the government's security agencies did not completely relinquish their efforts to infiltrate and control the labor movement. Father Gapon's Assembly was founded with the secret approval and covert financial support of the same officials who had sponsored police socialism.

History has still not figured out whether Gapon was a passionate advocate for workers and the poor, a government agent, or both. In all likelihood he was an example of the peculiarly Russian form of double-agenting that had been going on throughout late tsarist times—infiltrating the opposition to surreptitiously foment illegal activity, thereby justifying a crackdown. Activity which might, however, spontaneously catch fire and blaze out of control—the peculiarly Russian form of double-agenting that, from all appearances, goes on in contemporary Russia now again. As in the case, for example, of Vladimir Putin and Yevgeny Prigozhin.

As the reversals in the war and waves of political unrest mounted through the fall of 1904, Father Gapon decided that the Assembly of Workers should act. A petition, to be presented to the tsar at the conclusion of a solemn processional march through the capital city, would be delivered on February 19 to mark the anniversary of the emancipation of the serfs in 1861. But in December, several workers who belonged to the Assembly were dismissed from the city's largest armaments and shipbuilding factory. Following the failure of negotiations to reinstate them, a strike was called in early January, which quickly spread to other factories across the city. The petition to the tsar, Father Gapon and his advisors concluded, had to be drafted and presented immediately. On the morning of January 9, nearly one hundred thousand marchers, including families with children, gathered at selected meeting points on the outskirts of the city. Each group was to form a procession and march to the city center, to gather on Palace Square in the early afternoon and present the petition to the tsar.

As the columns of marchers moved forward, the troops deployed to block their route formed up along the roads and bridges and opened fire. More than two hundred people were killed and hundreds more injured. Several hours later, the troops stationed in front of the Winter Palace followed suit, firing into the crowd that had gathered on Palace Square to await the processions of petitioners, which never arrived.

"We couldn't believe it, when we read about the shootings in St. Petersburg," my grandmother remembered. "We all wanted to get on the train and go there, to join a demonstration, but Papa and my brother Volya absolutely forbade it. To make sure, they took away all the money I had and hid the rest."

Bloody Sunday, as the day immediately became known, marked the definitive beginning of the Revolution of 1905. A wave of indignation against the actions taken by the authorities, and against the tsar himself, swept the country. Strikes erupted throughout St. Petersburg, and by the end of the month nearly half a million workers were on strike across the vast territory of the empire, from the Baltic provinces and Moscow to the cities of the Caucasus thousands of miles away.

And Bloody Sunday proved to be a crucial turning point in one additional respect: it provided the catalyst that finally galvanized the alliance of workers and radical activists that the revolutionaries had been working toward for decades.

CHAPTER 24. THE PETITION

"Oh yes, I was already a big girl when all the trouble started," my grandmother said, when I asked her to tell me about the beginnings of her revolutionary involvement. "When I was sixteen, I made a strike in Papa's shop," she added, still beaming with pride.

I suspected a touch of hyperbole; but twenty-five years later, as I sat in the library on the Fontanka River in St. Petersburg reading through the newspapers from those years, I came across an article about the demonstrations on May Day—since the late 1880s, May 1 had been celebrated around the world as International Labor Day by workers and their left-wing allies—in Pskov in 1906: "Workers declared a strike and production came to a halt in the tailor shops of Bamuner, Borobyev, Krupp, and others."

After Bloody Sunday, in response to the waves of unrest, regiments of Cossacks and an organized group of vigilantes known as the Black Hundreds, a kind of tsarist Ku Klux Klan, carried out violent counterattacks against workers and protesters and a series of vicious pogroms in the Pale of Settlement. Disorder erupted in Poland and the Baltic provinces, where the general political upheaval was exacerbated by long-standing anticolonial resentment of Russia. On one of the fleet's most powerful battleships out on maneuvers in the Black Sea, sailors mutinied and threw the commander overboard, then set sail for Odesa, where mass strikes and demonstrations had been going on for weeks. After docking in the harbor, the Potemkin became the rallying point for the revolutionary crowds, waving red banners, who gathered on the embankment. The government called in squadrons of Cossacks who fired on the protestors, indiscriminately killing thousands, in the sequence of events immortalized by Sergei Eisenstein in the film, *Battleship Potemkin*.

Predictably, the country's schools became a key breeding ground for protest and agitation, as they had been for decades. Students at the universities in St. Petersburg and Moscow staged strikes and held mass meetings demanding political and educational reform. Students in the secondary schools also boycotted classes and joined demonstrations. "In February, there was a demonstration in Pskov led by students from the boys' gymnasium and the agricultural academy in the next town," my grandmother recalled. "Estia and I wanted to go, but we knew we'd be expelled from school and that our fathers would never forgive us. And don't you know, at the end of the march a bunch of hooligans attacked the kids and beat them all up.

"Well, a lot of schools around the country started to close—Volya had to leave the Polytechnical Institute in Riga and Papa even sent him to Germany for a year to study—but they kept the girls' gymnasium open. Estia and I met with some of the other girls to talk about calling a strike, but a lot of the girls were afraid and we couldn't agree on things in the end."

By 1905, students in Russia had come to be seen (and saw themselves) as a separate social group within the rigid system that placed every citizen into one of a set of prespecified categories corresponding to social status and privilege, or lack thereof—the *studenchestvo*, as they were known in Russian. The studenchestvo was anti-authoritarian, anti-sectarian, and egalitarian in terms of ethnicity and religion. This was my grandmother's mindset growing up—rather like the mindset of my fellow students during the political upheavals of the 1960s. As I listened to my grandmother recount her adolescent adventures, I identified with her. She grew up amidst one kind of epochal change; I grew up in another. But they were strangely similar in certain ways. An enormous change in perspective, a time of transformation, after which things could never again be the same.

The disaffection of the students, often joined by their professors, was seen by the government as an ominous bellwether of social attitudes on a larger scale. In March 1905, the authorities announced the closing of universities across the country; but at the end of August, in a gesture designed to restore calm, they were reopened, and the government issued a decree restoring the schools' autonomy to manage their own affairs—including, most fatefully, the right for faculty councils to decide whether students could convene meetings. This decision, in totally unanticipated fashion, triggered the climactic phase of the Revolution of 1905.

The revolutionary leaders immediately persuaded the students to abandon their strikes and open the universities "to the people" for meetings. On October 4, the nationwide Railway Union, with a constituency of nearly a million workers, called for a general strike. A week later, a mass meeting at St. Petersburg University called on workers in all occupations to join the work stoppage. Within days supplies of food, water, and electricity in Petersburg and Moscow disappeared and life throughout the empire became paralyzed.

"Papa couldn't get anything from St. Petersburg at that time," my grandmother recalled. "He was afraid he would have to shut down his business, or maybe move it to Riga where he could get things by ship from overseas."

Bowing finally to circumstance and the advice of his councilors, the tsar agreed to issue a decree promising reform. The Manifesto of October 17, famous forever after in Russian history, pledged to introduce a series of measures guaranteeing personal freedom, freedom of the press and assembly, and elections to a national representative body—the State Duma—whose approval would be required before any new law could be enacted.

The Manifesto was meant to assuage the progressives and restore calm to the country, but in response both the left and right-wing forces merely escalated their efforts. The St. Petersburg Workers' Council (better known from the Russian word for "council" as the St. Petersburg Soviet) declared victory and called for more strikes. The right wing reacted again with violent attacks on progressives and, as always, the Jews, in a fresh series of lethal pogroms. In December the Moscow Soviet called for a general strike to shut down the city. With armed revolutionary patrols roaming the streets to maintain order, the movement's leaders believed that workers throughout the country would stage similar uprisings and that the army would refuse orders to attack Russian civilians. Both were to prove true in 1917, but in Moscow in 1905 neither came to pass. As government troops, including a crack regiment from St. Petersburg, began to arrive in the city, the insur-rectionists barricaded themselves in the Presnia District, the center of the city's textile industry and of working-class militancy. The government surrounded the area with cannons and issued an ultimatum for the workers to surrender. When they refused, the regiment's commander unleashed a barrage of artillery fire that lasted for two days. Over a thousand Muscovites died and the district was reduced to rubble.

One of things that fascinated me, as I listened to my grand-mother, was the realization—the reality—that this was the kind of Europe she grew up in, a place where pitched battles with thousands of casualties were a regular occurrence in the great cities—St. Petersburg, Moscow, Paris, Berlin. It was hard to connect this background, the fact that she came out of this crucible, with the old lady living quietly at the end of her life in the little apartment on West End Avenue, remembering those times that she herself had lived through.

"Estia and I were in shock after we heard the news from Moscow," she told me. "It was already the winter school break, but we talked it over and decided that when school started up again we would present a petition demanding freedom. We didn't care what our papas or the schoolmistress would do." They agreed to meet the next day at Estia's house.

The imposing Borkhov mansion stood at the end of a leafy street, surrounded by a garden with a high wall. It was still intact, if somewhat neglected, when I saw it almost a century later. Like many of the far-flung corners of St. Petersburg, this little spot in Pskov, with its broken sidewalk, towering old trees, and weathered house, felt more like a lane in a country village than the center of a large city. Russia was still like that in the late 1990s. The cities had the antique quality of an era when little gardens existed between apartment houses and chicken coops and birds' nests nestled in the courtyards behind imposing Art Nouveau facades. Essentially unchanged from the morning in December 1905 when my grandmother went to see Estia, I imagined.

"A man opened the door—we used to call him a footman, strange as that was to us, because we never saw one anywhere except in Estia's house—and sent me upstairs to Estia's room," my grandmother continued. "That's how everything was in her house, very formal, since her father was so rich."

When I visited Leningrad with my grandmother in 1963, the apartment on Vladimirsky Prospekt was like a social club, filled with a stream of visitors. Not only family—the uncles and aunts, nieces, nephews, and cousins who came from Riga and Moscow to see their American relatives—but also my grandmother's circle of old Russian friends and acquaintances. They came with sad faces, smiling wanly; spoke in near whispers, exchanged a few trinkets or letters, and left. The grave sarabande of Russian social life fascinated me; it seemed to be about something terribly important, though I couldn't tell exactly what. The whispered exchanges concluded with weary nods, looks of sympathy, and condolence. The visitors, who like my grandmother were born and grew up before the Revolution, were all quite old. They seemed to accept the fate that had befallen them, not really pining for their lost world, but still inhabiting it in some abstract way.

One afternoon, a tall and stately woman arrived. At first she seemed to be dressed just like all the other visitors but she radiated an air of dignity and eventually I realized that her clothes, though worn like everyone else's, had once been elegant and were arranged with great care. Her grandson, who was a few years older than me, came with her.

It was not until thirty-five years later, during my visit in 1998, that I was to meet the grandson, Valentin Sokolov, again—through the series of fortuitous encounters that led me to Natan Levin, who, in turn, put me in touch with Valentin—and realize that the imposing visitor had been Estia Borkhova. That the spectral presence, the burdened Soviet lady who came that day to see my grandmother had been her closest childhood friend and revolutionary co-conspirator, the feisty and confident eldest daughter of one of Pskov's wealthiest men, the friend my grandmother had gone to see in her house at the end of the tree-lined street that morning in December 1905 to plan their petition to the school. Who would have imagined that she had grown up in a fine mansion? When I met her, she was threadbare like everyone else. She had married a well-known professor who worked in the Russian Academy of Sciences; somehow both had managed to survive the Stalin period. The day I saw her with my grandmother in Leningrad—half a century, two world wars, one revolution, and one civil war after that December morning—the only trace of the old life was in her bearing.

Looking back, I realized that as she and my grandmother sat in the apartment on Vladimirsky Prospekt that day looking at each other with intense attention, their old world had flickered to life for a moment. And looking back, I wondered: Had they asked themselves what had become of their youthful hopes to change the world, the hopes that had culminated in a fashion so grotesquely contrary to their dreams?

"Go on, tell me about the petition," I said, encouraging my grandmother.

She began. For some reason, she started to speak in Russian. I couldn't understand and reminded her, gently, to speak English. But the wonder of her youth, in her musical Russian, warmed by the memory of her high spirits, remained in the tape. When I learned Russian, half a lifetime later, I listened to the recording. I heard her speaking Russian and I understood. I had closed the gap of the final thing that separated us.

"Where we lived in Pskov, and where Estia's father had his house, was on one side of the river, but if you crossed the river—za-Pskov'ye it used to be called—there was the other part of the city. In the winter, when the river froze, you could just walk across the ice, but otherwise we had a bridge, which was called a floating bridge. It used to be put up for the warm months and taken apart when the river began to freeze again. And since it was in the winter, the river was frozen, and I remember a whole group of us went to the other part of the city, to a girl's home where we had a kind of a meeting, and we composed the petition. To the principal.

"Now, it was a long petition; we asked for things like the right to speak in class, to express our opinions about politics, to have the right to petition for changes to the reading list, to ask for the books we wanted; I don't remember all the things we put in there. When we finished, I took the petition, to hide it and bring it back to town. And we had to cross the river again—most of the girls lived on my side of the river—to get ready to give it the next day to the principal. We had talked it over, and everyone decided I should be the one to do it. To make things very safe, we decided to put the petition into my shoe, under my galoshes. Why did it have to be so safe? The police were after everything—anything out of the ordinary. You don't give a petition to a principal. We were asking for freedoms, that was considered against the law in a way. It had to be very secret. There was something political, too; we had written that we supported the right to elections for an assembly that could pass laws.

"So we scattered, we decided not to walk two or three together; it gets dark very early there in the winter, and it was already dark. And I with the petition had to be especially careful. The za-Pskov'ye was not where all the businesses were, it was more rural in those days. So the streets were very quiet. All of a sudden, I saw a group of what we called 'hooligans'—you never knew when they will be after you, to stop and annoy you, even rob you. I saw three hooligans, and there I was with the petition. I didn't know what to do, I didn't want to meet them face to face. And it was a narrow street, there was no place to hide. There was an empty big barrel standing there. So I jumped into the barrel and stayed there, for a long time, until I came out and went home across the ice. I was scared stiff.

"I came home, and of course I couldn't tell either my sister Lyuba or my older brother Volya. Volya was very conservative, very reactionary, you couldn't tell him about any kind of freedom or fight for freedom; he thought I was terrible, with my revolutionary ideas; and for many years, even when I used to come to Russia, when I was married, he used to tell me: It wasn't Rulia who should have gone to prison and exile, it was you, she suffered through you.

"Well, do you think we ever turned in that petition? On the way to school the next day, Estia and I talked it over.

Suddenly everyone was scared, we met in the bathroom, two at a time, and we decided that we were crazy to do it, that we would be arrested, that we would be expelled and never get our diploma. All day long we kept meeting and talking, trying to decide what to do. And then we came to school the next day, and the school was closed. The authorities became afraid of more strikes and, well, petitions like the one we had made. All the schools around the country closed for the rest of the year."

Hiding in the barrel that wintry day, as the bitterly cold afternoon turned to night, my grandmother believed she was invincible. In the years before the Revolution of 1905, she had never known anyone who had been arrested, put in prison, or sent into exile. Of course, she had read about such things happening in the previous century—to the aristocratic Decembrists, to the poets Pushkin and Lermontov, to the Populist Alexander Herzen. Those were the exploits that she dreamed about, that she was determined to emulate; but she and Estia never imagined anything dire would actually happen to them. Their fathers were wealthy and had connections to all the important city officials and officers of the army regiment. In her youthful zeal, she somehow imagined that she could be a passionate, aspiring revolutionary, but still continue the secure life she had always known.

Least of all did my grandmother think that anything she might do in pursuit of her revolutionary ideals could bring down fateful consequences on herself or her family.

CHAPTER 25. REPRESSION

RESTORED

Following the suppression of the Moscow uprising, the government dispatched troops around the country with instructions to eradicate any remaining pockets of resistance. Despite the continuing armed conflict, promised elections for the State Duma took place the following February. In anticipation, the government issued a series of preemptive laws limiting the Duma's powers and creating a complex system of voting weighted toward the wealthier classes at the expense of peasants and workers. When the actual voting took place, the authorities did everything possible to harass the opposition parties and intervene in the voting process. Rather like the conditions for elections in Russia today.

The convocation of the Duma provided the occasion for one of the most memorable, if not infamous, scenes in Russian history. The tsar decided to welcome the new members with an address—after extensive debate within the court as to whether he should even acknowledge the Duma's existence—in his throne room at the Winter Palace, naturally, rather than in their own meeting hall.

To the left of the throne, filling half the room, stood the members of the Duma—peasants in homespun jackets and rough boots, merchants and tradespeople in frock coats, lawyers in business suits, and clergy in long black robes with untrimmed hair and beards. On the opposite side, members of the court stood in their extravagant finery—officers in braided uniforms adorned with medals, court officials in velvet suits covered with decorations, members of the Imperial Council in fur-trimmed capes with jeweled accessories and plumed hats. It was as if the past and future of Russia had gathered, there on opposite sides of the hall, to gaze at one another with nearly complete incomprehension.

After half an hour, Nicholas and his entourage entered the back of the hall. Following a brief religious ceremony, he proceeded down the aisle to the throne. The members of the Duma looked on with impassive—if not baffled—expressions, failing to return his bows. The hall remained silent as the tsar rose to speak.

The address offered no proposals for action or reform. Nicholas simply admonished the representatives to behave worthily and justify the confidence the sovereign and his people had placed in them; and thereupon concluded his speech. A thunderous burst of applause arose from the side of the hall filled with the courtiers; from the Duma members opposite, utter silence.

After the tsar's ill-received homily, the Duma felt obliged to draft an "Answer to the Throne," patterned on the speech traditionally delivered in the English House of Commons following the monarch's Opening Address to Parliament. (Political conditions in Russia, however, resembled those in Britain not at all.) The resulting document called for redistribution of private land to the peasants, amnesty for political prisoners, and a government of ministers answerable to the Duma rather than the tsar, who refused even to receive the delegation sent to present him with the defiant "Answer." The government equivocated for two months, afraid to provoke further unrest, but had already made its decision. By early July tens of thousands of troops were stationed around St. Petersburg. On Sunday morning, July 9, police and soldiers surrounded the Duma with instructions not to let anyone enter. Fliers were posted throughout the city announcing the dissolution of the legislature and the imposition of martial law. Elections for a new Duma were called for February 1907.

My grandmother's gymnasium, like most schools around Russia, remained closed throughout the winter term of 1906 and did not reopen until the fall. With its steady flow of orders from the military, my great-grandfather's business managed to prosper despite the continuing turmoil. In the spring he proceeded with plans to open a second shop in the nearby and much larger city of Riga, on the Baltic Sea. His new wife, Anna Mikhailovna, had left her home in Latvia to marry him, but after a year in Pskov persuaded her husband to move back to Riga with his younger children. My grandmother and Rulia stayed in Pskov to finish school at the girls' gymnasium and help watch over their father's old shop.

Ninety years later, I spent several weeks in the public library on the Fontanka River in St. Petersburg reading through the Pskov newspapers from 1904, 1905, and 1906 to get a sense of what my grandmother's life had been like. Almost every day there was a story about a raid on a house or apartment where a group of students, sixteen to twenty years old, was taken away, accused of membership in an outlawed revolutionary party or the attempted assassination of a police official. Possession of forbidden political literature alone was enough to get a teenager sent to exile in Siberia for five years. At the end of each article appeared a list of names of the prisoners and the terms of their transport—those who could pay for their own food, and those who were forced to subsist on prison rations.

"Parents!" the newspaper admonished, "Do you want your children to become professional revolutionaries? Don't let them take up politics! Better, academic subjects!"

And, somewhat surreally, in an adjacent column there would appear the daily enumeration of picnics, theater outings, new electric streetlight installations, horse-drawn trolley lines transforming into electric trams—the impressive harbingers of modernity regularly appearing to adorn the city, as the papers brightly effused; the sunny news of civic improvements and entertainments for the new middle class. A kind of merry façade—the Gay Nineties, a Russian-style *Meet Me in St. Louis*—on top of a dark, smoldering morass.

On occasion, even the newspapers, which typically expressed conservative social views, could not suppress a tone of hostility toward the government and a degree of support for the progressive movement.

The Bee of Pskov   May 4, 1906

May 1, the great labor holiday of the entire world, was celebrated by large numbers of Pskov workers. It is clear that this year, the stubborn struggle of Russian labor against the existing order has reached even our small city.

In the morning, the workers of the Warsaw Railway Line, numbering no less than one hundred, walked off the job and workers at Sulmanson Carpentry declared a strike. Production was halted at the Shtein Ironworks, the Levin Bindery, and the tailor shops of Bamuner, Borobyev, Krupp, and others.

Out of sympathy with the workers movement and the struggles of the proletariat, the students of the upper class of the boys' gymnasium, the Theological and Pedagogical Seminaries, and the Agricultural and Surveyors Academies did not attend classes.

I thought back to my grandmother's proud announcement, "When I was sixteen, I made a strike in Papa's shop," and smiled at what seemed to be my now disproven skepticism, at her audaciousness, at the fact that my great-grandfather had achieved enough notoriety to merit a mention in the Pskov city papers on the occasion of the May Day strikes of 1906.

In September the girls' gymnasium reopened, and my grandmother entered her final year of school. She probably would have been arrested herself at the beginning of the year if the school had not closed and she and Estia had succeeded in presenting their petition. They were lucky they hadn't, as 1906 turned out to be an even more dangerous and deadly year than 1905.

Following the dismissal of the Duma, armed clashes with the authorities and terrorist assassinations of government officials increased. After a failed attempt to assassinate him at his summer dacha on the Aptekarskii Island in the Neva River, the prime minister, Pyotr Stolypyin, introduced a new decree—the notorious law on fields court martial, which stated that any civilian who had committed an "obvious" crime was to be handed over to a field court martial composed of five military officers and tried in secret within twenty-four hours; the sentence of the court was to be delivered in no more than forty-eight hours and carried out within one day. Four days from start to finish. Over the next ten months, more than eleven hundred people were arrested and executed, with only seventy acquitted. The noose used to carry out the hangings acquired the grotesque sobriquet, "the Stolypin necktie."

Stolypin was the same prime minister who masterminded the harsh dissolution of the First Duma. With the incongruity of historical hindsight, which so often views and distorts the past through rose-colored glasses, Stolypin, because he also tried to solve the problem of peasant unrest by attempting a program of agrarian reform, has since the fall of the Soviet Union been hailed by some in Russia as a visionary whose efforts at reform were on the right road, if only they not been hindered by the radicals. By this view, Russia would never have suffered the Bolshevik Revolution with all its attendant misery if only the authoritarian but clever Stolypin had been allowed to see things through; if only World War I and the Bolsheviks had not disrupted everything. Unsurprisingly, Vladimir Putin has declared himself a great admirer of Stolypin, and in 2012 decreed that a monument to him be erected in Moscow.

Elections for the Second Duma were held in February 1907, this time with participation of the major Socialist parties. Though the government again covertly bankrolled conservative candidates and channeled substantial sums of money to right-wing newspapers, the Second Duma proved to be even more radical than the First, with twice as many seats going to left-wing deputies. At the assembly's opening session, the tsar's representative began his speech with the sentiment that "with God's help your work will be fruitful for the happiness of dear Russia," which was immediately greeted by shouts of "Long live the Sovereign Emperor!" from the conservatives. The opposition deputies remained seated and silent, calling forth accusations of disloyalty to the tsar. All that remained was for the government to find—or invent—an excuse to dissolve the Second Duma altogether. In the end, the regime resorted to the tried-and-true tactic of false conspiracy theories and manufactured evidence. Deputies from the Social Democratic and Socialist Revolutionary Parties were accused of organizing meetings with soldiers promising to support their rights and pleas for improved conditions in return for pledges of aid in case the government tried to expel the deputies or dissolve the Duma. Raids on the apartments and offices of the left-wing deputies failed to turn up any evidence, but shortly afterwards the Prime Minister announced that after further searches, evidence had appeared after all. The Duma was ordered to surrender the Social Democratic deputies for arrest and trial, which the President of the Duma refused to do until the assembly completed its own investigation.

On Saturday evening, June 2, the tsar signed a new electoral law eliminating the voting rights of the Empire's non-Russian minorities, reducing the number of deputies to be elected by peasants and workers, and increasing the number elected by the landowners; the next morning the Security Services posted a proclamation of dissolution on the Duma's front doors. The tsar promised elections to a new Duma, but this one, he declared, "must be Russian in spirit."

Because the actions of Stolypin and the government were essentially illegal—promulgating a new election law while the Duma was in recess and without its approval, both of which violated the Fundamental Law recently signed by the tsar himself—the whole affair became known to history as the coup d'état of June 1907. It marked the end of the so-called Revolution of 1905—actually, the Revolution of 1904-1907.

The reactionary established order seemed to have prevailed, but the spark that would light a conflagration, as promised by the Decembrist revolutionary Alexander Odoevsky, had been struck. A nobleman from one of Russia's most ancient aristo-cratic families, Odoevsky was among the army officers who stood on Senate Square in St. Petersburg in 1825 demanding constitutional reform from Tsar Alexander I; together with many others he was arrested and exiled to Siberia, where he wrote the famous line, "One spark will ignite a flame," which in Russia became the most enduring of all calls to revolutionary action. The Bolsheviks' first newspaper, appearing in 1900, was named *The Spark*. Indeed it now seemed apparent that the old order could not last indefinitely. It took the outbreak of war in 1904 to light the first spark. It would take another war, in 1917, to light the next. But this time the fire would burn out of control, consuming nearly everything around it.

My grandmother graduated in June of 1907, just after the Second Duma was dissolved. One might say she came of age with the Revolution of 1905—she was sixteen when it began and just shy of nineteen when it ended. And so, upon gradu-ating from the Pskov Girls' Gymnasium my grandmother, the decorously raised, well-educated daughter of the prosperous Pskov merchant Sh. G. Bamuner, was more determined than ever to be a revolutionary. The only question was how she was going to do it.

The timing was ideal. Individuals make history, and history makes individuals. For my grandmother, it was a time when history was acting on people with great force. Her life was caught up in an intense, pivotal historical moment. It was partly her own choice, partly the sheer force of the times. This atmosphere, this sense of the moment and its historical sweep, was what enthralled me listening to her as a child. I found it irresistibly exciting. Revolution! Arrest! Exile! Escape! It was our family's Homeric saga—our small family version of the Odyssey—my grandmother went forth into battle; she and her sister wandered for a year; finally they washed up on the shores of America; later they returned to revisit the scenes of their youthful combat. Their adventurous journey resonated down the generations of our family across two continents.

Though my grandmother had finished with her school years and a new, more fateful phase of her life was about to begin, there would always remain a part of her that was the young, lovely, ardent student of the Pskov Gymnasium, coming of age during that remarkable time, as the old world of the nineteenth century slipped away and the new world of the twentieth century took shape; irrepressible in spirit and ambition, planning with her friends and classmates some kind of new life, unsure though they were exactly what it would be. Within a year, she would leave Pskov forever, but Pskov remained within her, and remained a part of her life and the life of our family, always. Because of my grandmother, I felt in a tiny way as if I came from Pskov, as if I had a special connection to it, just as all my cousins in Russia felt,

I later found out. There was something magical, something enchanted about Pskov that none of us wanted to give up.

My grandmother's Pskov was a place of transition, Janus-like. One face looked back to a time that was storybook, out of a past before written history. The rough fortress walls, the earthworks, the pine trees. It was not refined, not lined with elegant granite embankments like St. Petersburg. Pskov for me had that wonderful quality of duality, of two images superimposed on one another: east-west, half in Europe, half not. Pskov, the city founded by Vikings who wandered into Russia a thousand years before. The water, the fir trees, the wooden structures, the big rough walls of the fortress, sloping, because they could not figure out any other way to make them so thick and still stand up; conjuring up a feeling of Scandinavia, a place before history; iron, woods, water—a completely different kind of history than the Mediterranean, a totally different world. And the other face, looking forward, to a place existing in the contemporary, newly modern world; when there were no longer any real limits, a place from which my grandmother knew she could get on a train and not stop until she reached St. Petersburg, Riga, Moscow, Berlin, or, as it turned out, the other side of the ocean. You could go anywhere, do anything. That was new, less than a generation old. The duality of Pskov created a nuance; if my grandmother had come from a bustling city like St. Petersburg or Moscow, or even Riga, the story would have been different. She knew about the bigger world and was determined to get there. She was the most cosmopolitan person I knew, but she retained throughout her life the modesty of her young life in Pskov, a touch of simplicity versus the hardened sophistication of the urbanite. It remained a subtle note to her character. She was cosmopolitan, but she was not an urban snob. She was an enthusiast. The jewel-like world of Pskov always remained with her.

My grandmother's stories of Pskov got me started on the road to looking for the deeper image behind what we see immediately in front of us. The deeper level, the complexity, the ring of an echo as you stand and look at a place, the echo of something older, a deeper resonance. It was from her that I learned to know one world and be able to think myself, yearn for, and feel my way into another.

CHAPTER 26. ARREST

Interestingly I never heard my grandmother express strong views about the different revolutionary parties in tsarist Russia, whose internecine fighting gradually intensified as the collapse of the old order unfolded. She never mentioned which party she belonged to; she seemed to feel that being a revolutionary was a general condition, unrelated to the technical details of dogma. It was about freedom, about ending the rule of the rich and the oppression of workers and peasants. And though my grandmother's belief in revolution was idealistic, history was not on her side. Things were not to develop so poetically. The tectonic plate of the nineteenth century was grinding up against the approaching plate of the twentieth. An enormous earthquake was about to take place. No one quite anticipated it. When it came, no one knew how to turn it back. Her ideas of the Revolution were still more tied up with poetry than with bombs, artillery shells, assassinations, secret police, and prison camps. She knew who Pushkin was, who Nekrasov was, who Odoevsky and Herzen were, even faintly Hegel, Marx, and Plekhanov; but I don't think she yet had any clear idea of who Lenin was. She never imagined the Red Terror, the Civil War, firing squads and the ruthless elimination of millions of people judged to be counter-revolutionary or undesirable, communal apartments or a new secret police far more fearsome than the one she was evading. She just wanted people to be more equal, to be free.

Only later, when I found the record of Rulia's arrest in the archive in St. Petersburg, "for membership in the active terrorist group of the Socialist Revolutionary Party" and, later in Arkhangelsk, saw the report of my grandmother's activities among the exiles, did I learn that both she and Rulia had been Socialist Revolutionaries. In Arkhangelsk, I read the police dispatch, written in the swirling calligraphy of the elegant prerevolutionary Russian alphabet: "Rakhil Samuilovna Bamuner, daughter of the Pskov Merchant, Sh. G. Bamuner, arrived under transport. Accompanied by her sister, Eda Samuilovna Bamuner. Both active participants in the Socialist Revolutionary circle of Pskov."

Reading the reports was chilling—the sinister machine of state surveillance, intimidation, and destruction of human life that marked so much of the twentieth century had already been set in motion.

By reading the documents I did in fact find out more about what my grandmother had been doing, which is why, so I thought, I had come. But I also started to understand something I had sensed as a child but could not fully conceive or comprehend. Emigration is a desert, they say. Losing a language is like losing a part of oneself. In some strange way, from an early age, I felt the desert of my grandmother's emigration. Because of my grandmother's Russian, because Russian was where it all began, I somehow sensed—at least in speaking with her—that English was a kind of newly acquired tool, very familiar to me, of course, efficient, yes;

but a rather blunt instrument when it came to carving the deepest thoughts and emotions. Some deeper truth, it seemed, lay hidden away in her Russian. I felt as if *I* had lost a native tongue. And so, as I pored over the documents in the archives, in my slowly improving Russian, and began to understand what I was reading and what had happened, it was as if a lost image were slowly coming into focus, and I felt as if I were re-entering that lost world, that it was coming alive to me, that I was returning to something essential I had lost. Even though I, personally, had not lost it.

My grandmother always kept a part of the duality of Pskov, the Janus-like quality. She made a new life in America, but she always kept a foot in two cultures, two outlooks, two time periods. As a child, through her, I became a xenophile; I needed the Old World. She carried a piece of Pskov, of the history that began with the Varangians and ended with the brief heyday of its early modern era, with her, of Europe, of the Old World, which she transmitted directly to me. She carried several epochs, several sensibilities within her. She taught me that we are not monolithic; we can be metachronous. We span.

Could there be a counterfactual account of my grand-mother's life? Could she have stayed in Russia? No, I don't think so; she never would have adjusted—as much as she loved it, she had already outgrown Pskov, and she would never have adjusted to Soviet Russia—that is the irony. She was a bit too grand. Although she gave it a try in 1932. The way she spanned two cultures was her destiny, her character, her style. I suspect that's really why she came back to the U.S. in 1933. After that, she was never again to visit Russia as an aspirant; she kept visiting, but she became a foreigner of sorts, returning to her native but now former land, which had begun to evolve in ways that were alien to her. Her willingness to become an expatriate and span two cultures filtered down to me. Living in only one culture just doesn't do it for me. I can't live without the Old World and its beauty, its history, its long echo down the ages that I still hear. I am not complete without Europe, without the longue durée, without the old languages and everything they contain in sound, in image, in poetic expression, which plain American English generally does not (despite its great virtues). And yet, being American is what frees one to inhale the Old Culture, to exult but not to suffocate in it, as one might if one were in and purely of it. Can you really be fully modern, fully free, if you are European? Could my grandmother have become modern and free if she had remained Russian? I don't think so. There is no counterfactual version of her story. Without her story, I have no story.

Rulia was fourteen when she began the fall school term in 1907, for the first time without her older sister. But she continued to follow her big sister's ways. It was natural that Rulia should have emulated my grandmother so closely. Even before the trauma of their mother's death, they were unusually close. After they left Pskov, they continued to spend a great deal of time together until the end of their lives. Their attachment to one another was more like the bond between twins than siblings four years apart. My grandmother was charismatic; people were drawn to her. She changed people's lives.

After leaving their childhood home, my grandmother and Rulia stayed by each other's side for the next sixty years until Rulia died in her small, dark apartment in New York.

Just after Rulia's death, I went to visit my grandmother in the city. I was still young—only thirteen or fourteen—yet I could sense the enormity, the incomprehensible scale of what had occurred. These were the two sisters, young and dreamy, delicate, refined, who had walked along together in Pskov, hoping to turn the world upside down. Something in them never changed. And now one was gone and the other, old and a bit unsteady, the hair above her lined face no longer fine and black but a thinning puff of silvery blue, sat looking out her kitchen window, contemplating a universe without her mirror-image sibling, her most constant companion in life.

She seemed to be in a state of shock, as if somehow things had come full circle, forcing her to contemplate the enormous sweep of her life. She began to fuss with a yellowing house plant that looked as if it, too, might not last much longer, and suddenly broke down sobbing. They had been through it all together—Pskov, arrest, exile, escape, return to Russia, raising their young children while their husbands went off with other women. "Yes, it is something to spend seventy years with a person, you can't really describe it. Yes, it is certainly a huge loss," she said, with the philosophical tone she sometimes adopted when talking about her adventures, the death of her mother, the triumphs and tragedies of her youth and later life, as if it had all simply been decreed, not because she made any of it happen. There was that note of Russian fatalism in my grandmother's outlook. It wasn't dark and brooding, just matter of fact, philosophical. She was not self-involved or self-pitying, but she was attuned to the scale of the drama she had lived through.

My grandmother and Rulia spent the month of August 1907 at the Riga seaside in the sprawling summer dacha that served as the gathering place for the extended Bamuner clan well into the thirties. Returning to Pskov in September, with no prospects for further education and no firm plans for the next phase of her life, my grandmother—in accordance with her father's wishes—began to help out in the shop and keep an eye on Rulia.

"When my father moved his main shop to Riga, he didn't give up the business in Pskov; he didn't close that branch but left a certain Yakhnin as the manager, with Rulia, a kid of fourteen, and myself over him," she told me, when I asked her what she and Rulia had been doing the year Rulia got arrested. "Just imagine!" she added, marveling at the idea of two young women supervising the irascible martinet their father had put in charge. A martinet who had modeled himself in his boss's image.

"There was an apartment next to the shop, you walked in from the street. It was nicely furnished and Rulia and I were the sole owners of the place. Well, pretty soon I noticed that Rulia was getting very friendly with a high school kid who happened to be a twin. There were two boys, both of them went to the gymnasium. They looked exactly the same; I couldn't tell them apart. And Rulia, of course, was a giggly kid, surrounded by other kids, having fun, and was very friendly with that boy Vladimir, one of the twins. They had a much older brother who was an officer in the army. And a lot of the kids, the students in those days, were revolutionaries. They belonged to the Mensheviks, the Socialist Revolutionaries, or some other party. The two twin brothers were older, probably eighteen, and they were revolutionaries, even though they were still in high school.

"Just like I was," she added, nodding in affirmation.

"But what were you planning to do after you graduated?" I asked.

"Well, after my brother Volya, the marvelous son my father had, who came next? I did. And while my father expected a lot of things from me, I was much less satisfied with him than he was with me. I already told you, I considered him a terrible despot to his new wife, Anna Mikhailovna. And I didn't like his attitude to his workers. So one day, when Papa was home from Riga, I invited him for a real serious talk. And I said, 'Listen Papa, you're not very happy with me and I'm not a bit happy with you, and therefore I want to be completely independent from you. I've gotten my high school education, so good, now I want to live on my own.' And he listened to me, very quietly, because he could get angry in a second but this time he did not. And he asked me, 'What's your plan?'

"Well, nearby was a small provincial town called Ostrov. It had schools, but it wasn't as big as Pskov, where there were many special schools. 'Listen Papa,' I said, 'I'll go to Ostrov and give lessons there to prepare kids to take the exams to go to school in Pskov. And then, we'll see. Maybe I'll go to St. Petersburg and enter the university, who knows? But I will not live at home under your surveillance anymore.' My father smiled slightly and said: 'I'm not stopping you. You got your initial education—go and try, if you make a living, I'll be very happy, but I'll help you with nothing, you'll be on your own.' Somehow, I had enough money to go—it was very cheap then, just a couple of rubles. At the station I made inquiries about a place where I could find room and board and right away they gave me an address. It was a house owned by an older couple who used to rent out rooms to boarders.

Well, Ostrov was a very nice little town, and I began to ask everybody if they needed a tutor. But I couldn't get a single lesson. I was there for two months, I paid five rubles a month for rent. After two months, when I couldn't get any kind of work, I corresponded with Lyuba and Volya, but not my father. I was too proud to let him know. Volya never believed in me becoming independent in the first place and wrote to me to come right home: 'You shouldn't be there all alone, a young girl, somebody will follow you and try to get attached to you.' He sent me the train fare, and I went back.

"Well, my father didn't laugh at me but said, 'Yes, well, you go to a little town, nobody knows you, what do you expect? You should look for lessons in Pskov where everybody knows you.' But my idea was still to get away from home and be as far away from my father as possible."

In less than a year she would leave Pskov again, never to return. This time, my grandmother would realize fully her ambition to begin a completely different life.

"When I got back, I could see that Rulia was spending more and more time with that Fallevich boy, Vladimir," she continued.

Both sisters had a tendency to attach themselves to serious-minded, impassioned men. In the graduation photograph my grandmother took with her classmates and their friends from the boys' gymnasium, the young men are a combination of Tolstoy's fictional Vronsky and the real-life Trotsky—dashing in their Russian shirts, with thick wavy hair sweeping back from their high foreheads and parted in the middle, their intense eyes peering out through wire-rimmed glasses. Rulia was carried away by the young Fallevich; something similar— in adult form—was to happen when my grandmother met Kliment Voroshilov among the exiles in Mezen, a year later.

"Papa had asked me not to leave Rulia alone that fall, even though he agreed to let me go to Ostrov. And when I got back, he told me to keep an even closer eye on her and not let her go out alone. I guess he already suspected something."

On the morning of April 30, 1908, my grandmother and Rulia walked out onto the square in front of their house on Sergeyevskaya Street, as they had done almost every morning since my grandmother's return from the neighboring town of Ostrov six months earlier. The day was warm, my grandmother remembered, with the last piles of winter snow still clinging to the sides of the building in the shade at the edge of the square. "It was the kind of warm day we would have in April, while snow was still on the ground and the river was still frozen. They hadn't yet put down the floating bridge. I remember the way the steam was rising from the snow on the rooftops of the houses and the cathedral."

Steam rising across the city in the April sunlight: exactly as it was when I returned to St. Petersburg ninety years later, in April of 1996. The city was still covered in snow, but it was already warm, and steam rose from the patches of ice in the Neva River, from the field of snow in the Summer Garden, from the snowy rooftops and church spires all across the city and the icicles hanging from the roof ledges. Russia waking up from the winter—the sense of huge size and scale, of great forces marshaling, everything moving and changing; blue sky, white snow, translucent ice, wet streams of melting snow and icicles. Metamorphosis; spirals of steam rising from the thawing ground, the still-deep snow, glistening and white, basking in the warming sun.

The sisters walked out onto the square and like the butterfly effect in chaos theory, this one small act changed their lives, the lives of all their siblings, and all their descendants irrevocably. The other aspect of the butterfly effect they put into motion as they crossed the square was to set Russia—everything that had formed them and was precious to them—adrift, to send it drifting away from themselves.

Following Levin's list, Katya and I found the article recording Rulia's arrest.

The Voice of Pskov   May 1, 1908

During the night of May 1, massive searches and arrests were carried out across the city. The detainees were, for the most part, students; teenagers. The following were included—6 boys from the St. Nicholas Gymnasium and 4 girls from the Mariinskii Girls' Gymnasium, the latter including the student R. Bamuner.

All were arrested in connection with the following event: at ten o'clock in the morning on April 30, in a suburb of the city, a former student of the Pskov Gymnasium, Anatolii Fallevich, shot a revolver and seriously wounded (with a shot into his back that went through him) the former railway employee Eremin. According to rumors, Eremin was fired from the railroad for his drinking and served thereafter as an agent of the secret police. Last year, it is said, Eremin denounced Fallevich, after which Fallevich was arrested and expelled from the gymnasium. Fallevich, apparently, had been following and trying to hunt Eremin down ever since. The same day, the brother of Fallevich, a student of the seventh class at the gymnasium, was arrested when he came home from school for the dinner break. Eremin is being treated in the military hospital of the Irkutsk Regiment.

The same Irkutsk regiment for which my great-grandfather served as regimental tailor.

"The night Rulia got arrested I wasn't even at home," my grandmother continued. "I had gone to see Estia to make plans for the next day, May 1—May Day, you know, Workers' Day. We were planning to go to the parade. Well, it got to be very late and I ended up staying the night. When I got home the next morning, Yakhnin came running into the apartment to tell me what happened. He had already sent a telegram to my father."

"But why was Rulia arrested?" I asked.

"Well, one of those twins decided to go out and commit a great revolutionary act, to kill a political spy, a man who was known to be a spy for the police. And he did. He just went out and shot him and almost killed him. And the boy was caught, and after that they put him on trial in the court, as they called it, for underage criminals. And the twin brother, the one Rulia was friendly with, was immediately arrested, too, and a bunch of other kids. Because Rulia was so close with one of the twins, she was also arrested. I think there were about sixteen kids who were arrested altogether."

"But what was she accused of?" I pressed.

"Of belonging to a revolutionary society, that's all you had to be accused of! And Rulia actually knew nothing about being a revolutionary, she wasn't interested in it. I was the one who was a revolutionary from the age of sixteen, the one who belonged to the student wing of the revolutionary group."

I marveled how I could still hear in her voice the passion of her youthful zeal; and mixed with it, I sensed, a hint of chagrin that she herself had not committed the "great revolutionary act"—and that her young and vulnerable sister, whom she had pledged to watch over and protect, had become its victim.

"Rulia only got involved because of this boy. They came at night and searched our apartment and found a photograph of her with Fallevich, and that was enough."

My grandmother seemed perplexed when I asked her again to explain exactly why Rulia had been arrested, on what specific charge. She assumed I would understand and take it for granted, just as she did, that in those days right-minded students were revolutionaries, and that a revolutionary could be arrested at any time, without any specific reason or cause.

"Poor Rulia, maybe it was all my fault," my grandmother concluded. And then, a moment later, she drifted into a reverie about going into exile, how wonderful it was to meet the revolutionaries; what a great adventure it had been and how she had finally realized her youthful dreams. Her feelings about what happened to Rulia were a mixture of regret for her young sister, who was taken from home at the age of fifteen and never even finished school, and the unbridled pleasure she took in all she had experienced because of it.

The morning of May 1, 1908 marked the great caesura that separated the idyllic first part of my grandmother's life in Russia from its later, darker Soviet phase. The Russian Revolution was the official demarcation, the actual event that swept away all of what was elegant and cosmopolitan in Russia (well, almost all) and replaced it with the threadbare, the ideological, the hectoring and harrowing; and perhaps just a little bit, the heroic. But in her version of the story, May 1, 1908 was the breakpoint.

You could always see it in the photographs. Russia, Part I, was Victorian, elegant, aspirational. Russia, Part II, was intense beyond anyone's imagining.

On May 1, 1908, the camera stops. The art director orders a new mise en scène. The photographs of old Pskov, of Edwardian clothes, of my adolescent grandmother with her well-heeled classmates and, a year later, with her much less well-heeled but very determined-looking fellow revolutionaries in exile, end; the photographs of Soviet Russia begin. And the irony is, despite the fact that the world the photos from Soviet Russia depict entails the loss of everything lyrical and the unleashing of many of the basest of human instincts, these later photos are even more compelling. In these pictures, everyone is in the sweep of history in a way that is overwhelming, all-encompassing. Every photograph from the 1920s and 1930s shows people fully engaged, as if in some gigantic project—a sense of struggle, of commitment, of total engagement. As much as my grandmother lived in the tide of history when she was growing up, with the intense feeling of being part of her times, of needing to act, the feeling in the early Soviet photographs is that of lives being driven by their times even more intensely. This is a life that demands total attention. The clothes have changed—no one is wealthy anymore, no one has more money than anyone else, status has nothing do with material display; yet the serious, striving intellectuals and artists you see in these pictures have dressed themselves carefully, with a sense of dignity, with a need to show seriousness and propriety, in a way that is gripping.

Beyond which—and this is the part that astounds, that makes you reel with incomprehension, unable to fit all the pieces together—the background never changes. It all plays out on the same stage as Russia Part I, with the same props; and that stage and those props confer a quality that is so powerful, so defining, that the whole drama seems almost to depend on it. The heavy formality of Victorian and Edwardian architecture and decor surrounding these New People of the New World—it is like a surrealist double-exposure. Russia lived out its own drama; a place unlike any other in Europe, and for that reason nobody could be sure it really was Europe. It was raw, undeveloped, impoverished; yet its writers, its artists, its intellectuals, even its technical professionals, were in a class completely of their own.

Yes, Russia Part II was created out of Russia Part I. It had to be, because there was something in Russia that was unchanging. And it was largely that long-lingering, unchanging aspect of Russia that made my grandmother— and me, in my turn—want to go back.

Which legacy did my grandmother bequeath to me? Lovely, lyrical Pskov or threadbare, monumental Leningrad and Vladimirsky Prospekt? Which Russia was my grandmother trying to reclaim? She seemed to feel the two were compatible, perhaps even indivisible. Although, in reality, they were not.

CHAPTER 27. PRISON

Years later, playing back the tape and listening to my grandmother's voice recounting her great adventure, it struck me
that she had never said anything about how she felt when
she first realized that Rulia was in serious trouble and might
never return home. Was she scared? Did she feel guilty that her
young sister had been arrested instead of her? Had the feelings
receded, or been buried over the decades, overshadowed
perhaps by the far worse horrors of the actual Revolution that
came after? The Revolution that my grandmother longed for, so
she imagined, as a young idealist? It was as if Rulia's arrest, the
trip to the north, the time my grandmother spent with the other
exiles and the daring escape that followed remained forever
the ineradicable exploit of her youth, associated only with the
feeling that everything was still full of promise, unspoiled.

Nor did she ever confess to any sense of disappointment
or chagrin that Rulia had been the one to get arrested instead
of her. As things unfolded, with my grandmother taking
charge of the trip into exile and leading the escape, it slowly
transformed into *her* story. Being a revolutionary, arrest, exile,
escape—it all belonged to her; she became the protagonist.

And only she ever told the story, never Rulia. When I asked Rulia's grandchildren, my cousins in America, what she had told them about it, they answered, "Nothing. She never talked about it at all."

Armed with Levin's remarkably detailed list of "Information in print on the Bamuner family," Katya and I moved our base of operations from the main library on Nevsky Prospekt to the periodicals branch on the Fontanka River, a few hundred yards down the river's granite embankment from the Anichkov Bridge. With its four monumental bronze Horse Tamers (patterned after the marble originals on Rome's Quirinale Hill) towering above three graceful supporting arches, the Anichkov, which came into my view each morning as I turned the corner from Vladimirsky Prospekt onto the Nevsky, was the epitome of classical elegance in that city of stark contrasts (the seedy alleyways evoked in *Crime and Punishment* lay just a few hundred yards away; a plaque affixed to the inner wall of the bridge explained that the deep craters in the stonework were the result of Nazi shelling during the cataclysmic Siege of Leningrad in World War II—during which my grandmother's brother, the handsome, urbane, artistic photographer, Senya, perished; the only Bamuner sibling unable to find a place in one of the evacuation convoys before it was too late).

And just next door to the library stood the half-ruined, half-restored Sheremetevo Palace, where I couldn't help but think, passing by each morning, of the Oxford don, the ex-Russian Jew Isaiah Berlin, coming to visit Anna Akhmatova there in 1945; when the two of them sat up through the entire night talking about life and literature; the choices one makes in each, and the consequences that follow. The ruined palace, the talk existing at the highest level of art, philosophy, and emotion—purely, essentially Russian.

Each morning, Katya and I went into the library and took our place at one of the long tables, amidst the almost perfect silence, next to the rows of other researchers. I got the impression there, as I had in the library on Nevsky Prospekt and the archive in Arkhangelsk, that looking into the past—for knowledge, but above all, to make sense of what had happened—was a kind of national project in Russia.

Indeed I often wondered, during the weeks I spent in the library on the Fontanka: was I searching for the past by going to the library and reading the documents? Or simply by walking past the palace where Akhmatova and Berlin had sat up through the night; there, in that city which contained all of the history that came before Akhmatova, and all that came after—the time before the Revolution, still embodied almost perfectly by the physical presence of the city; and Soviet time, the extraordinary period of history that changed everything so vastly, for the worse as it turned out, but perhaps not absolutely, without any qualification. My daily visits to the library on the Fontanka were bathed in the strange tension between those two experiences, those two modes of seeking. Which was more immediate—immersion into the old texts, or being enveloped by the crumbling walls of the reading room with its balcony of shelves and the high ceiling above, the old-fashioned chandeliers, the rough parquet floor, the stone steps in front of the building; before which, when we came out each afternoon, the calm water of the Fontanka sparkled with the reflection of the evening sun, still high above the horizon during those late days of summer?

Levin's list had pointed us the way to the first article reporting Rulia's arrest, and the many that followed. We continued to leaf through the daily issues of the *Voice of Pskov*. We slowly turned over the fragile pages, Katya reading several columns ahead of me. I scanned the columns of Cyrillic print, rendered even more difficult to decipher because of the inclusion of the old letters that were discarded after the Revolution. Suddenly, Katya became animated.

"Chronicle!" she said. "Here it is!"

Here were the details that my grandmother had never told me.

The Voice of Pskov   May 2, 1908

Yesterday, at about ten o'clock in the morning, Eremin, former railroad conductor, was fatally wounded by a shot from the revolver of Anatolii Fallevich, former student of the Pskov Gymnasium. Fallevich had been following Eremin for a long period of time, waiting for the opportune moment to kill him. According to his neighbor, Eremin had started to notice that he was being followed since the beginning of the winter; more than once, he returned home and left again through the back fence. The assassin waited for Eremin outside the tavern across the way from his apartment, and as soon as he came out, to head into town, a shot rang out. Eremin tried to escape through the nearby kitchen gardens; eight more shots rang out behind him from what proved to be a Browning revolver. Eremin fell down, but after a short time got up and somehow managed to drag himself into the alley, where he fell again, unconscious. The killer ran in the opposite direction. The local constable ran out of his apartment in 'only my nightshirt,' revolver in hand, and gave chase. At the command, 'Hands up!' Fallevich threw down his revolver, turned, and declared, 'I don't shoot at innocent people.' The police chief came to the scene of the attempted murder, along with the city doctor, two witnesses, and the prosecutor. Having been determined that he had several serious wounds, including two shots through the lung, Eremin was taken to the field hospital of the Irkutsk Regiment, where normally those without hope of recovery are placed. Fallevich was arrested and taken to police headquarters.

Today, Fallevich was to have sat for his final examination for the baccalaureate certificate of the gymnasium.

The question as to which court Fallevich will be consigned—military or civilian—will be decided by the Ministry of Internal Affairs. In case that he is turned over to the military court, he will face a sentence of death.

And two days later, further details concerning the arrest of Rulia and the other young people:

May 4, 1908

Searches and Arrests

During the night of May 1 massive searches and arrests were carried out in the city. Those arrested, for the most part, were teenage students. We have been provided

*with information on the following arrestees: student
of the institute Mikhailov, students of the Gymnasium
Volyansky, Myutol, and Garlov, student of the trade
school Libman, students Andrushis and Lindenberg,
former student of the Gymnasium Kuzmin, students of
the Mariiinsky Women's Gymnasium Telp, Folkman,
Pal, Bamuner, Ioffe, and former student Gorlov.*

*On the same night ten railroad workers were arrested.
According to rumors, the arrests are all connected to the
attempt to kill Eremin. On the morning of May 2, the
student Svedzinski was arrested inside the gymnasium.*

During our taping session, I asked my grandmother what
happened after she got home and learned that Rulia had been
arrested the night before.

"Papa came the next day. He went to see all the important
people he knew, but he couldn't find anything out. The police
said they were waiting for instructions from St. Petersburg. It
seemed ridiculous at first, to arrest Rulia for being a revolutionary. Who could believe that? She was only fifteen years
old! We thought they would clear things up and let her go.
But slowly, we began to realize it was very serious."

"What did your father do then?" I asked.

"What could we do? We waited. Eventually Papa even
went back to Riga. I went to the jail to see Rulia as often as I
could, when they let me, to bring her things. By the fall she
began to get sick because it was very cold there. That's why
she developed such terrible arthritis later in life."

Levin's list contained one small item that likely would
have escaped our notice as we paged through the Pskov
newspapers for the year 1908.

The Voice of Pskov   July 1, 1908

In the Women's Prison

*Recently, a small dispute broke out between several
political detainees and the prison administration, as a
result of which the prisoners Bamuner and Kartysheva
were placed in solitary confinement for several days.
Following her release, Bamuner was permitted a meeting
with her brother, a student, but only in the presence of
an adjutant of the Gendarme Authority.*

The name of Rulia's visitor was not recorded, but this
would have been her older brother, Volya. My grandmother
had never told me that the stern elder brother—the one who
had opposed her revolutionary ideas and had chided her
later in life, saying that she was the one who should have
been arrested instead of poor Rulia—had come to see his frail
young sister, alone and isolated in prison.

I never met Volya—he died a few years before my grandmother and I came to Leningrad in 1963—but my grandmother
described him as having been conservative and studious, in
emulation of his father; later, in the Soviet Union, he became
a successful and well-known engineer, despite harboring
unreservedly hostile feelings toward the Communist regime.

His own son, my older cousin Alek whom I got to know
well when I spent time in Russia in 1998, was rather like
him—also an engineer and a thoroughly anti-Soviet conservative, even though he was born in 1924 and lived almost his
entire life under Soviet rule. Alek felt it was his duty to write a
memoir so that his descendants could understand what it had

been like. He finally found time in the 1990s, after the Soviet Union's demise. In his introduction, he laments that his main purpose—to expose the hypocrisy, folly, and monstrosity of Soviet life—has been preempted by the avalanche of material revealing those open secrets that appeared as soon as Soviet censorship evaporated. But he wrote it anyway.

The brief article caught me by surprise, suddenly evoking how traumatic it must have been for the whole family. Here perhaps was a true cultural, or generational, or historical gap: the article gave me a sense of the family pulling together under the strain of it all, something my grandmother had never talked about. Maybe she and the rest of the family simply accepted, even then, how easily history can throw people's lives into turmoil—as it was to do so many times again down the course of the twentieth century.

Eventually a sense of outrage began to appear in the press. I found this fascinating—that even under the autocratic regime, there were people with a sense of decency and compassion who felt compelled to speak out and, remarkably, were able to do so. In the end, the Revolution of 1905 had been suppressed; but the floodgates of resistance to the autocracy had opened, never to fully close again.

Pskov Life   September 27, 1908

Behind Prison Walls

On the first of May a shot rang out from the revolver of Fallevich and immediately afterwards the police authorities carried out massive arrests. Over the next several days 23 people were arrested.

*As is well-known, the case of Fallevich was settled
a long time ago; he was sentenced to prison with hard
labor in Orlov Province. And yet, those arrested in his
wake still languish in jail. In one year, our quiet and
happy city has suffered through two prison dramas.
One group of students was sent into exile not long ago.
Now, 13 young people who are only suspected languish
behind prison walls. Solomn Pal, Mikhail Mikhailov,
Modest and Vladimir Bradis, Aleksandr Kuzmin, Rakhil
Bamuner, Evgenii Volyanskii, Ivan Oinats, Vasilii
Suvorov, Vladimir Fallevich, Evgenii Garlov, Aleksandr
Lindenberg and Pavel Andrushis; almost all of them
youths from 17 to 22 years of age, but Rakhil Bamuner
is all of 15 years old.*

*And why do they languish? What crimes could
justify such prolonged and cruel imprisonment, the
severe privation they are subjected to behind prison
walls, and the irreparable damage to health that so
often affects the imprisoned: Lindenberg has developed
bleeding from his throat and Suvorov has been diagnosed
with rheumatism and severe liver disease.*

*What grounds permit the police authorities to act
so carelessly toward human life? None whatsoever. In
the searches preceding these arrests, nothing was found
except completely legal books and pamphlets.*

*We in no way underestimate the degree of political
perspicacity of the officers of our Gendarmerie, but
marvel nonetheless at the acumen of the officer who
spotted the subversive potential of 'Travels in Palestine'
of the archimandrite Methodius, found during the search
of the belongings of Suvorov.*

> *Pskov society is deeply concerned over the course of
> these events behind prison walls and waits with a pained
> heart to learn the fate of the young people. It is essential
> to calm the anxious state of public opinion and move
> swiftly to clarify this appalling affair.*
>   Z.

I savored above all the sarcastic passage in which the
journalist, signing only by initial, mocks the naivete of the
police—here, a guileless student, searching for exciting news
of the outside world, turns to an account by a pious monk of
the conservative Orthodox Church—hardly a rabble-rouser—
describing his tour of the Holy Land. But, the journalist insin-
uates, the authorities, in all likelihood unsure of where or
what Palestine might actually be, suspect the volume to be
a thinly veiled façade for radical political thought. This, in a
country where the tsarist censorship permitted the publication
and sale of Marx's *Das Kapital* when it first arrived in Russian
translation, misjudging it to be a purely scientific work on
the subject of political economy, as its subtitle announces.

But the protests were to no avail. A month later, when I
went to Pskov, I saw the document in the city archive that
foretold Rulia's fate:

December 28, 1908   SECRET

*From the Gendarme Authority to the Governor of
Pskov Province*

*Your Excellency, Given the fact that the Party
Committee of the SRs was infiltrated late last year*

*and suffered problems, when late last year many party
members were arrested; the remaining members formed
a new committee; they undertook the functions of the
armed committee and carried out the assassination
attempt. In light of which, I address your Excellency
with an appeal for administrative exile for Bamuner,
Oinats and the others, because the witnesses are afraid
of retribution and agree to testify only under the
condition that it not be given in court, in public.*

Here, finally, was the explanation of why there had been
so little clarity about a trial, a judicial proceeding, the "why"
of Rulia's arrest and sentencing—the questions that I kept
asking my grandmother. There simply hadn't been any. All
the proceedings had been carried out in secret, to protect
the "witnesses." In other words, according to the sinister
system that came into existence under the tsarist regime but
only flowered to its full ferocity during Soviet times: double
agents, informers, the police state. How chilling it was to read,
particularly since it concerned the fate of teenagers. One could
almost understand how the youthful Anatolii Fallevich had
decided to shoot a police spy.

The newspapers raised one last protest.

Voice of Pskov   February 2, 1909

Justice or Arbitrariness?

*16-year-old Rakhil Bamuner has now sat in the Pskov
Provincial Prison for almost seven months. She was
arrested on the first of May in Pskov. No interrogation*

*has been carried out, nor has any formal accusation
been made. To all entreaties for her release, or at least
some explanation by the Gendarme Authority for her
continued detention, not a single word is given in
answer. Confinement in prison has already severely
damaged Bamuner's health, the more so because
initially she was held in exceptionally harsh conditions,
namely in isolation in a punishment cell normally
reserved for criminals. For five months, the relatives of
Bamuner have been told, 'The matter will be resolved
very shortly, in the not distant future,' but this young
girl continues to be held in prison, without it being
considered necessary even to explain why.*

This is the question which accused persons everywhere are given an answer to, but which the Chief of Police Pokrozhinskii apparently does not consider it necessary to address, when someone is held under his authority.

What is this—justice or arbitrariness?

This latest expression of indignation, like the ones before it, went unanswered. News of the Ministry's decision arrived shortly thereafter.

Pskov Life   February 25, 1909

Concerning the Case of the Arrestees of May 1

*The case of those arrested on May 1, well known to our
readers, has been concluded by administrative decree.
On the 20th of February, the resolution of the Ministry
of Internal Affairs was received in Pskov.*

Vladimir Fallevich, Aleksandr Kuzmin, and Solomon Pal are deported to the Yakutsk territory for 5 years.

Vasilii Suvorov and Evgenii Volyanskii to a northern district of Tobolsk Province for 4 years.

Modest Bradis, Vladimir Bradis, and Evgenii Garlov also to a northern district of Tobolsk Province for 3 years.

Ivan Oinats and Rakhil Bamuner to Arkhangelsk Province for 3 years.

Aleksandr Lindenberg, Pavel Andrushis, Mikhail Mikhailov and Ivan Fedorov to Vologda Province for 2 years.

Altogether, 14 people are deported.

This time, the paper did not bother to editorialize its disdain for the authorities. It simply concluded, without comment:

"The gymnasium graduate Evgenii Garlov, having served for almost a year in connection with the Fallevich affair, is exiled as of March 1 to a settlement in faraway Tobolsk Province for another 3 years. His parents, living in the city of Ustuzhna, do not even have the opportunity to say goodbye to him, because his father is dying of cancer and his mother, accordingly, cannot leave home. Garlov himself shows all the signsof consumption."

CHAPTER 28. THE MOST WONDERFUL EXILE

I looked at the elegant, almost decorative Cyrillic letters running down the column of the newspaper and marveled at the bland bureaucratic language with which the fate of fourteen young people had been sealed. Rulia was to be sent a thousand miles away to live in a wooden hut in an isolated village where winter temperatures fell to twenty degrees below zero, with at best a small stove to keep warm. Vladimir Fallevich, the twin brother who had captivated her, was to be sent even farther, to the distant reaches of Siberia where the temperature sank to minus forty. He was all of seventeen years old when the sentence was handed down and likely had no connection whatsoever to the crime of his brother; only the misfortune to be related to him and to be a young idealist.

The order read as if the whole of Russia could be turned into a penal state, that somehow the march of time could be slowed, that the authorities believed that such actions could maintain the status quo and such displays would inspire citizens to come together in support of tradition, propriety, and parental authority—but it was too little, too late in a country of mostly illiterate, ill-treated peasants and workers at the turn of the twentieth century when the rest of Europe was industrializing and giving citizens the right to vote and elect governments, as much as the privileged classes there still controlled life. Fatally, the government had pushed people like my grandmother to want to become revolutionaries, which may have meant different things to different people, but which to almost everyone in the end meant the violent overthrow of the existing order. Reading the terms of the punishment ninety years later—understanding how an entire structure of power and authority was working to preserve itself above a mass of citizens, while millions were preparing to take violent action at the risk of their own safety and lives to end it—still had the power to shock.

"How did you and Rulia make the trip into exile?" I asked my grandmother.

"Well, let me see, I remember that we left from the train station in Pskov," my grandmother said, speaking into the tape, as if to solidify her memory one last time. It had been almost fifteen years since we had gone to Leningrad together and was to be another twenty until I went back to Russia myself to retrace her journey.

"My father got a special permit for Rulia because of her young age. Papa went to see the governor personally, of course he knew him, and the governor issued a special permit, a very exclusive permit, for her to travel with an older sister, to accompany her, and not be sent with a group of other exiles, because of her young age. She was allowed to go with me, on Papa's word that she would get to the place of exile and not escape along the way.

"Without a permit, she would have had to go with a group of arrested people, they would have to travel in a certain way where they would stop on the route in a town and stay in prison. In Russian it was called *po etapu*; well, that's a foreign word, that's not a Russian word; it means 'from one place to another.' Part of the time you rode in wagons, partly you went on foot. Papa was sure she would never get there, she would die before she got there, if she went by etapu.

"In any case, it was April. There was still snow everywhere, but it was starting to get warm, some of the trees had buds already. Oh, that only happens in Russia, that early springtime, you don't have that here, though sometimes when we went to Mohegan to open the house there would still be snow and a few flowers just opening on the trees. It always reminded me of Russia."

Exactly as it was when I first went back to Russia in April of 1996—snow still deep on the ground in the Summer Garden as the temperature warmed up to fifty degrees in the afternoon and the sun glinted off the spires of St. Petersburg. The beauty of the deep snow in the warming April afternoons was unearthly. One day my cousin Lyena and I took the train to Pavlovsk, a town not far from the city but already with the feel of being in the country, to a country palace that Tsar Paul had built at the end of the eighteenth century in the manner of an Italian villa set in an English-style park, a total artifice of nature in the English style, there in the northern Russian woods, snowbound in April. The palace had been destroyed by the Germans in World War II, but eventually the process of rebuilding had been undertaken. We went there just as the final touches were being put on, before the official opening, since Lyena worked for the museum authority in

St. Petersburg in the house-museum of the famous writer
Nekrasov (her mother, Tatiana Galushko, a well-known poet
in her own right, had worked in the Pushkin house-museum
before her) and had managed to arrange a private visit. We
were the only ones there, making fresh footprints in the April
snow, until we reached the palace and took a tour through the
newly redecorated, empty rooms of eighteenth-century finery.

"Well, how did you get to Arkhangelsk?" I asked my grandmother, but she couldn't recall many details of the train trip
north. She seemed more interested in what had happened
after she arrived, when she met the other revolutionary exiles,
including Kliment Voroshilov.

It was only through the documents I unearthed in Arkhangelsk that I was able to reconstruct the outlines of her journey.
Remarkably, I found the report documenting my great-grandfather's success in gaining permission for Rulia to travel
without police supervision, so long as she was accompanied
by my grandmother:

> *Order #1577*
>
> *From the Pskov Police Commissioner to his Excellency
> the Governor of Pskov Province*
>
> *April 16, 1909*
>
> *I inform your Excellency that from my side I see no
> obstacle to sending Bamuner to Arkhangelsk Province
> at her own expense.*

Following which, the dispatch announcing the beginning of the long journey:

> *Report #324*   SECRET
>
> *From the Pskov Police Commissioner to his Excellency the Governor of Pskov Province*
>
> *April 20, 1909*
>
> *Dossier of the exile under police guard, Rakhil, daughter of the Merchant Samuil Bamuner, sentenced for membership in the Pskov group of the Socialist Revolutionary Party:*
>
> *I inform Your Excellency that in accordance with your order of April 15, the merchant's daughter Rakhil Samuilovna Bamuner, held in the Pskov Provincial Prison, was released on April 19 and on the same date departed for Arkhangelsk with the transit permit I issued, to the disposition of the Governor of Arkhangelsk Province.*

And finally, the arrival in Arkhangelsk:

> *Report #157*   SECRET
>
> *From the Arkhangelsk Police Commissioner to his Excellency the Governor of Arkhangelsk Province*
>
> *May 2, 1909*

*I inform Your Excellency that on the first of May,
the political exile Rakhil Samuilovna Bamuner
arrived from the city of Pskov. Pending your further
instruction, she will reside under police surveillance in
the house of Professor Kostin in the first ward.*

My grandmother remembered their arrival in Arkhangelsk in vivid detail:

"When Rulia and I first came to Arkhangelsk, I don't know how people right away seemed to know about the exiles, about who was coming and who they were, but they had already arranged for us to live in the house of one of the exiles who was living there, an ex-professor. We stayed there for a few days until we went to Kholmogory. He was a lovely man, a real Russian man with a full reddish-blond beard, rather stocky and very jolly. And immediately he and his wife (she, on the other hand, was skinny and not very friendly, always looking like a kind of martyr, with a bunch of kids to take care of) insisted that we take their bedroom and sleep there. Although he was a heavy-set man, he and his wife gave away their beds to us, two young girls. That was the hospitality you found among the exiles.

"The next day, they took us down to another exile, to meet her. Her legs were paralyzed, she couldn't walk. She seemed to me to be very old, with white hair cut right up to her neck, very straight. Before she was sent into exile, she was in a jail and they held her overnight in one of the special punishment cells that they had. And it was filled with water, and very cold, and when they took her out her legs were paralyzed. She was supposed to be sent much further into exile, but after what happened she was allowed to stay in Arkhangelsk. She was like the mother of the exiles. She allocated the places where the exiles would live. Everyone looked up to her. She lived with a woman named Zhenya, who wore thick eyeglasses that magnified her eyes so that she seemed to be staring at everyone. But she had a heart made of gold. When the older lady was brought out from the dungeon, paralyzed, and they wouldn't send her any further, Zhenya gave up her room and found a place for the two of them together. Zhenya took care of her, hand and foot. It was an open house, the whole group of exiles centered in that woman's house, she was somehow the moral authority to everyone, a brilliant woman, a writer."

My grandmother never explained why it took them ten days to reach Arkhangelsk. In the summer of 1998, I traveled along the same railroad lines, surrounded by the same impenetrable forest, and reached Arkhangelsk in less than two days. The day after I arrived, I sat in the city archive reading the records of her visit, looking out at the same red brick factory buildings that had been there in April 1909, during my grandmother's stay. It was magical reading the contemporaneous accounts, as if the events they described had been captured, frozen, like the buildings across the courtyard—accounts which had been written at exactly the time the events they described were happening, when everything was still in place, when my grandmother was still nineteen years old, not knowing she would sit on a stone patio in Mohegan Colony one day telling the story to her grandson.

As I looked out at the Victorian buildings, Arkhangelsk seemed to conjure the world of my grandmother's youth—the old-fashioned trains, the horses, her father's elegant shop in Pskov, all spring-loaded in time and ready to move forward. But suddenly the story stopped, held in a freeze frame that would never again move; but also, never fade. In its place would come emigration, a journey by steamship with ocean air stinging the sisters' young faces, making them laugh; summers at the Riga seaside, where my great-grandfather spent the last twenty years of his life, shielded from the Revolution that had swept over Russia and changed irrevocably the life of the country my grandmother and her siblings had grown up in; and throwing those siblings together in the apartment on Vladimirsky Prospekt where they exchanged their fine suits with high collars for the shabby suits of the Communist century, no more servants, no more dance parties and theatrical evenings—well, there would still be theatrical evenings, but they became serious, diligent, meant to instruct and uplift, which had its own appeal and suggested a line of continuity to the cultural past, in that grave ceremonial style of Soviet cultural life. And though the world of my grandmother's youth ended that summer in Arkhangelsk, she retained it within herself no matter how old she got, in her memory, in the accent and lilt of her voice as she spoke into the tape.

The sisters' stay in Arkhangelsk among the cultivated group of exiles was short-lived. The governor's order announcing Rulia's final sentence was issued the next day.

Report #3458   *SECRET*

From the Chancellery of the Governor of Arkhangelsk Province to the Police Chief of Kholmogory

May 2, 1909

I direct that you permit the political exile Rakhil

Samuilovna Bamuner to stay in the city of Kholmogory
until the opening of navigation. Upon her arrival, I
propose that you place her under police surveillance,
and with the opening of navigation send her to the city
of Mezen, for disposition by the Mezen Chief of Police,
having forwarded all correspondence about her to him.
Until then, keep me informed of her actions and all
developments.

And so it was decreed by the governor's office in Arkhangelsk that in fulfillment of the sentence to live for three years in an outlying district of the Arkhangelsk Province, Rulia would be sent to the small settlement—barely worthy of the name "city" as it was officially designated—of Mezen, two hundred and fifty miles deeper into the wilderness from the admittedly remote, but at least relatively bustling port city of Arkhangelsk. To Mezen, "beyond the White Sea," as my grandmother invariably characterized it. And because the White Sea was still choked with sea ice, until the sea lane to Mezen reopened in early June the sisters were to stay in Kholmogory, twenty miles up the Severnaya Dvina from Arkhangelsk. Khomogory, which remained forever in my grandmother's recollection, "The most wonderful exile."

"What was so special about Kholmogory?" I asked.

"In Arkhangelsk we waited for only a few days before we could get a boat to go up the river to Kholmogory. Kholmogory wasn't far, just a few hours away on the Severnaya Dvina River. The river ice had already melted, so you could travel back and forth. One day, a political exile, Benny the shoemaker, came to meet us in the house where Zhenya lived, where she took care of the older, paralyzed woman, the mother of the exiles. Well, since this Ben was a shoemaker, he used to be allowed to go to Arkhangelsk to get his materials for work. He would come there, from Kholmogory, once a week or so, because the boats had only just begun to go. And he came that day, all excited—he had already heard that two young girls were going to be placed in Kholmogory before they went to Mezen. So, we were already expected in Kholmogory. They knew we were coming.

"Since there was such excitement that two beautiful young girls are coming, there was a whole to-do among the exiles, with everyone insisting that we should stay in their house. In Kholmogory, people would hire a peasant house, better than just a *khata* (a very modest peasant house, I later understood, when I listened to the tape), from a wealthier peasant who didn't live in their entire house, but rented rooms to the exiles, who lived in kind of communes. So everyone wanted us in their commune. How they decided I don't know, but when we came it was already decided where we would stay.

"We traveled by boat from Arkhangelsk overnight, and when we got to Kholmogory there was a whole community waiting there at dawn when we arrived. I still remember the first two people we met, one was a boy named Vasya and the other was a tall burly fellow who was a former teacher. Vasya was a student; he was the sweetest boy. He had a sweet nature, and he was very concerned about the two of us, he pitied Rulia. Vasya was charming, intelligent, and well-read, and the tall teacher was also very intelligent, an intellectual.

"In Kholomogory we lived in a house, a lovely house. Rulia and I had a room; we divided the work—I think we were five people in the house—cleaning, shopping, cooking the food. What did we eat? We mostly cooked fish. The peasants there were all fishermen; Rulia and I ate salmon lox all the time, once we ate half a fish and got dreadfully sick because back home it was a delicacy and we would only eat a little. Kasha, bread, sour cream, potatoes. We could go pick *schavel* (sorrel), it grew wild there. I once went to pick it, but I was unsuccessful. There was poison ivy that I picked by mistake.

"When we came to Kholmogory it was just the beginning of the White Nights. And really, one has to go up north to know what the White Nights are. We would have picnics, bonfires at night, singing, Vasya played the balalaika. Then we would sleep until one or two in the afternoon. We had wonderful times. Even Rulia enjoyed herself. Yes, Kholmogory, that was the most wonderful exile."

On the last morning of our stay in Arkhangelsk, after Katya and I had finished our work in the archive, my cousin Sasha's colleague Lyena came to pick us up for a trip to Kholmogory, as she had promised to do when we reached her by telephone earlier in the week. Lyena was a lively young woman in stylish jeans with an amused but observant air, a veterinarian by profession; intelligent, competent, and self-possessed—uncannily like a version of my grandmother a century later, the hip and casual clothing notwithstanding. Her boyfriend, a bluff Russian type in a flak jacket and laced-up boots, came along to drive their 4x4—it somehow went without saying that it was best to be prepared for rugged road conditions when driving in Russia.

We drove away through the quiet city, hugging the river's edge until we reached the outskirts and the forest abruptly sprang up around us. I was touched by the casual kindness, as if it were second nature, of Lyena and her boyfriend devoting their day to my pilgrimage to Kholmogory. This was a side of Russia, a country that could sometimes feel sinister, either from the after-effects of Soviet times or from something more intrinsic, that I associated from childhood with my grandmother and her Russian friends.

The road to Kholmogory ran through a dense pine forest, which opened from time to time to reveal a glimpse of the riverbank. As we neared Kholmogory the woods gave way to rolling countryside, wet and green—as if made of soft velvet. Low ridges, dotted with farmhouses and village churches, rose up alongside the broad curves of the river.

We continued on to Kholmogory, driving down the rutted road past occasional piles of discarded plastic bottles and other trash left behind by roadside picnickers. At the edge of town we passed a small church of gray stone with four small green domes surrounding a central dome covered in gold. Roadside garbage; an eighteenth-century church in the middle of the tundra. A scene of timeless, eternal Russia updated to the turn of the twenty-first century.

We drove into the town, which consisted of one main street and two small side streets, with a series of muddy lanes in between and a stretch of deserted waterfront along the river. Lyena's boyfriend maneuvered the 4x4 slowly down the muddy, pot-holed streets, carefully avoiding the ones that were several feet deep. "Tell people in America how wonderful our roads are," he said with rueful but good-natured humor.

The main street was lined with colored wooden houses bordered in front by a wooden sidewalk raised up above the muddy roadway. The street ended at a roundabout set above the riverbank. I asked Lyena to stop so that we could get out and have a look over the river. "There used to be a wharf over there, when the only way to get here from Arkhangelsk was by boat," she explained. I looked down to the spot where the remnants of the wharf, a few uncovered rotting pilings, stood at the edge of the water.

What had reduced Kholmogory to a ghost town of mud, goats, mosquitoes, and abandoned houses? Seventy years of Soviet life?

"Kholmogory was such a charming town," my grandmother had told me. "The waterfront especially was so pretty, because it was a fishing village. I, as a free person, was allowed to go to Arkhangelsk regularly; everyone used to give me all kinds of jobs, errands to run, to bring them books back from the libraries there. Yes, I made friends with everyone because I was allowed to move around."

I walked along the ridge for a few yards and looked out over the river. I could hear the names—Kholmogory, Severnaya Dvina—sounding in my mind as if spoken by my grandmother in her old-fashioned, musical Russian. The surface of the water was calm, but from time to time I could see the light swirls of the current, moving down the river to Arkhangelsk and the White Sea.

We left Kholmogory around eight o'clock. By now, at the end of August, it was almost sunset. A low, dense bank of soft gray clouds hung over the horizon. High above it, the sky was afire with streaks of red clouds. And in between the two banks of clouds the sky was clear, a limpid void of darkling blue, opening out into the distance.

By the end of May, the authorities began to press for Rulia to leave for Mezen. The most wonderful exile of Kholmogory was about to end.

Katya and I read through the series of files that we had managed to find with the help of Suprun's ingenious index. The arrival of the sisters in Arkhangelsk, the transfer to Kholmogory—the series of perfunctory orders from the governor's chancellery ordaining, one by one, the successive stages of Rulia's fate.

I turned over the next document. There, in an elegant handwriting unlike any I had yet seen, composed of thin, gracefully curving lines whose delicacy seemed to proclaim the culture of their author, I saw in front of me a letter written by Rulia herself, in May of 1909. The rest of the documents had been like cryptograms, full of indecipherable lettering that Katya and I had had to pore over. But as I looked at the new sheet front of me, my eye at once took in the immediately and unmistakably legible signature: "Rakhil Bamuner."

I looked at the ineffably elegant letter, unable to quite grasp that it had been written by the frail old woman I had known when I was a child.

To His Excellency, the Arkhangelsk Governor

> *In view of the fact that spending a year in jail has severely undermined my already weak nerves and very badly affected my health, which requires urgent medical treatment, I therefore request that Your Excellency leave me in Kholmogory. According to the examination of the district doctor, I am unable to travel.*

Rakhil Bamuner
16th of May, 1909

The file also contained the supporting, if ultimately noncommittal, report of the district physician:

Report of the District Doctor to the Kholmogory Police Chief

I have examined Rakhil Bamuner, held under police surveillance. She is ill with neurasthenia and blood loss from menstruation, and at the present time requires medical consultation.

District Doctor Brobov
14th of May, 1909

"Why couldn't you get permission for Rulia to stay in Kholmogory?" I asked my grandmother. "Your father got the special pass for you to take her from Pskov to Arkhangelsk. Why couldn't he do that again?"

"I already told you, I tried so many times, I went to the mayor to plead with him to let her stay because of her young age and poor health. I got a letter from Papa saying he had gone to the governor in Pskov to ask him to intervene, but by then it was up to the governor in Arkhangelsk, and nobody knew him. Rulia had written a letter, asking to see him, but she never got an answer. And I also went to the chief of police, many times. I used to plead with him, based on Rulia's age, to allow her to stay in Kholmogory, nearer to a big city; if she were to get sick, she could get help much faster. But he said, no, there will be no discussion, she is going to Mezen. And there was nothing that could help it."

As the next document confirmed:

Report #4313   SECRET

*From the Chancellery of the Governor of Arkhangelsk
Province to the Police Chief of Kholmogory*

June 2, 1909

*Further to my directive of May 2 # 3458, I propose that
you immediately send Rakhil Bamuner, under police
surveillance, to Mezen.*

The next dispatch, communicating that the governor's
order had been carried out, revealed that Rulia was sent
back to Arkhangelsk by transport—the harsh etap that her
father had feared she could not endure. Reading it came as
a shock. My grandmother never mentioned that Rulia had
been imprisoned again. And I had always understood that
the two sisters went to Mezen by boat. But here the report
said that Rulia was to be sent on to Mezen by etap as well:

Report #4912   SECRET

*From the Arkhangelsk Police Master to the Governor of
Arkhangelsk Province*

June 13, 1909

*I report to Your Excellency that the political exile
Rakhil Samuilovna Bamuner was conveyed to me by*

*etap transport from Kholmogory on June 12 and will be
held in the Arkhangelsk Prison until her transport by
etap to Mezen.*

But at the last minute—either because my great-grandfather's efforts finally succeeded, or simply through bureaucratic
caprice—it seems that my grandmother and Rulia received
permission to travel to Mezen by steamship under a transit
pass.

> *Report #4914   SECRET*
>
> *From the Arkhangelsk Police Master to the Governor of
> Arkhangelsk Province*
>
> *June 17, 1909*
>
> *I report to Your Excellency that on the 16th of June the
> political exile Rakhil Samuilovna Bamuner departed
> with a transit pass to Mezen, for disposition by the
> local Chief of Police.*

The decision on the nature of Rulia's transport had been
discussed earlier, in a series of dispatches between the police
chief in Kholmogory and the governor's office. On May 8,
1909, the police chief in Kholmogory wrote to the Chancellery
of the Governor's Office in Arkhangelsk:

> *You have told me to keep Bamuner here under surveil-
> lance until the opening of navigation; that is why I*

*request to know, how is she to go to Mezen? Through
Arkhangelsk by boat, or by etap transport on foot?*

The reply was scribbled in blue pencil on the side margin:

*Up to the police chief, but probably more convenient
by steamer.*

On May 17, the chancellery sent a more formal reply:

*In relation to your request dated May 8, the Chancellery
informs you that the means of sending Bamuner, under
police surveillance, to Mezen district is up to you, but it
would be more convenient by steamer.*

How bureaucratically, how casually the fate of people was
handled—shall we make her trudge across two hundred fifty
miles of swamp and marsh, or let her go in a boat? Well, it
depends on what mood you are in, it's up to you, Your Excellency. The Ministry has no particular preference.

This casual cruelty was doled out by obedient functionaries,
eager to please their imperial masters in a socially backward police
state at the beginning of the last century. And yet it resembles
so very closely the treatment human beings still receive in our
own time as they attempt to flee from danger and move across
borders. Shall we separate children from their families? Shall
we keep people in detention until their immigration hearing,
which might not come for months or perhaps years; or maybe
let them go free until then? Washington will review the matter.
We'll let you know.

Indeed was the final decision to send Rulia deeper into exile—instead of accepting the doctor's recommendation and granting her petition—inexorable or simply a result of bureaucratic whim? There really was no way to know. Once the papers were stamped, once the few strokes of elaborate handwriting were added (I sat in the archive, marveling at the elegance of the documents, their artistic and decorative design, all in the service of the bureaucratic disposition of human lives), that was the end of it. Another life adjudicated, to be sent off to the frozen wilds, to lose a few fingers or toes or part of a limb, perhaps, or one's eyesight, or to acquire a case of typhus or tuberculosis; or, on the other hand, to be set on the road to new adventures altogether. That was one possible outcome of exile during tsarist times, quite unlike anything that could happen under the vastly harsher Soviet version, the Gulag. Before the Revolution, people did manage to escape exile and go on to other adventures—people, for example, like Vladimir Lenin and Kliment Voroshilov. And my grandmother.

"From Arkhangelsk we went to Mezen by boat, first on the Severnaya Dvina, and then we entered the White Sea. I can't remember exactly how long it took," my grandmother said when I asked her how they had traveled to mysterious, mythical Mezen.

Katya and I combed through the archives for old almanacs with steamship schedules from the first decade of the century. We determined that my grandmother and Rulia would have left Arkhanglesk at midnight and set anchor around noon the next day, still several miles away from Mezen, as the Mezen River was too shallow for seagoing ships to dock in the town; only twice a day, when the tide swept in from the ocean, was the water level high enough for even small ferry boats to set sail for neighboring villages.

On my last morning in Arkhangelsk, I went out to have one last look at the harbor, trying to imagine the trip to Mezen, the one place I would never get to see. And as I walked out along the seafront, I suddenly experienced a moment of distilled intensity, a sense of events converging across time. Arkhangelsk in August, the wind with a hint of autumnal chill blowing in off the sea, just as it would have blown in August 1909, when my grandmother realized she had to find a way to smuggle Rulia out, for the two of them to flee, before the wind turned wintry and the harbor filled with ice. I could see them walking along the sea front, in their long skirts, capes, hats; earnest, young, happy despite the dire situation they found themselves in. They could do anything, go anywhere. Perhaps they already knew by then that they would go to America. What was there to stop them? What was 3,000 miles of open ocean to them? Nothing, then.

Their nighttime voyage would have taken place in twilight, since the summer solstice was approaching and they were sailing at the very edge of the Arctic Circle. On June 16, the sun would have risen a few minutes past midnight and not set again for ten days, hovering on the northern horizon as the partial dusk of each half-night turned to dawn. As my grandmother looked out into the twilight over the White Sea, sailing on the last leg of her journey away from everything she had known, everything that had made her, everything that was familiar and reassuring, did she know she was going to leave Russia to start a completely new life, to become someone else? Did she have a premonition, as they rode on the steamer from Arkhangelsk to Mezen, that half-night in June?

CHAPTER 29. MEZEN

"Mezen, beyond the White Sea," as my grandmother always described it. And so it was, at the tip of the northernmost peninsula before the frigid sea opens into the Arctic Ocean, a thousand miles from St. Petersburg, just below the Arctic Circle. It could be reached by boat for three months in the summer and overland for a few months in the winter by sledge. For the rest of the year the land route between Arkhangelsk and Mezen consisted of mud and swampland. Beyond it lay only frozen tundra, the Ural Mountains and Siberia. From the mid sixteenth century, it had been used a place of exile for enemies of the tsarist regime.

"In Mezen, Rulia became very moody, because it was so much further away, and she knew that at the end of the summer I would be leaving," my grandmother remembered. "It used to take ten days to get a letter from Papa in Riga, because it had to come by boat, and the boats only went once a week. In the winter it took six or seven weeks for a letter to come, because there was no navigation on the White Sea and the only way to get there was when the White Sea froze, and the mail would come on sledges. The people in exile told us about that when we got there. Well, that's all Rulia had to hear, that she wouldn't get a letter for six weeks. It was really very frightening. But she never had to submit to that, fortunately. Because we ran away.

"We arrived, and this time there was no one to meet us

the way they had done in Kholmogory. The police had been watching us on the boat, but once we landed there were no procedures. But somehow they had already found us a place to live. It was a new house—a kind of peasant house that they had there. It had two floors. On the first floor the fisherman lived with his family, and our commune had the entire top floor. I think there were six of us. There was Lyudmila, who was very attractive, tall and slim, with a beautiful figure. She had a few children by different men. I know she had an affair with Voroshilov before I came. She used to have fights with him, on a very familiar note. And then we two girls. The rest were men. One young man was a student, a very queer guy. When we prepared our communal meal, he used to eat everything from one plate, because everyone had to wash their own dishes after the meal. Yes, he was queer, but most of the people there were queer. They were far away from civilization, and the worst was that most of them were not intellectual. In Kholmogory, you had almost all intelligentsia, but not in Mezen. We even had a murderer, and eventually they sent him to Siberia. He was a very handsome, tall young man, with a black beard and a head of black hair. He always tried to show off his prowess, he could do all kinds of tricks, he was physically very powerful.

"We weren't friendly with the peasants. But we became very friendly with one family. The father was the chief of police, a member of the Okhrana, the secret police. That was the family who eventually helped Rulia to escape. We became friendly with them notwithstanding that the father was the head of the police, but he usually wasn't at home. The mother was a very interesting type, and such people you would only meet in Russia. She was a Tolstovka—she believed in Tolstoy's philosophy, his attitudes against authority and his belief in education and freedom for the peasants. And Tolstoy, you know, after he had thirteen children, began to talk against sex, which all the students made fun of. She had five or six children, with two older girls, and one was Rulia's age. Well, she felt very sorry for Rulia, poor Rulichka, as she called her, being sent alone into exile. We used to go to her house, sometimes she would invite us for dinner. The queer young man, the student, introduced us to her. She used to order books from Arkhangelsk and lend them to the intelligentsia among the exiles. So of course right away I met her, and she and I became friends."

Naturally my grandmother—the educated and attractive youngster from Pskov—immediately met and befriended the leading intellectual lady of tiny, remote Mezen. And then, she met Kliment Voroshilov.

The relationship was noted in a report from the local authorities:

SECRET

From the Mezen police constable to the Gendarme Department of Arkhangelsk Province

August 3, 1909

I report that the political exile Rakhil Bamuner, held under police supervision, has arrived in the city of Mezen and is residing with her sister, Eda Samuilovna Bamuner, who is known to be acquainted with several of the political exiles in the city.

How delicious it was to read the nearly hundred-year-old memorandum about my grandmother, an obviously dangerous visitor whose dealings with the exile community in Mezen were worthy of a surveillance report!

"Yes, very few of the exiles in Mezen were intelligentsia. I used to tell Voroshilov: 'You call this an exile?' Because it was so bad there, and I used to joke with him, 'You are all just here for stealing dirty laundry.' It was a very bad exile in Mezen, nothing like Kholmogory. Lots of the people there were criminals and drunkards."

"Did Voroshilov live in your commune?" I asked her.

"No, thank goodness, he didn't. He was quite crazy about me, you know, and why not? He was always visiting our commune; I wouldn't brag and say it was all on account of me, but he was pretty much gone on me, and I don't blame him for it. As I say, we were the only two decent, nice young girls there. A lot of the fellows had no use for us, because we were intelligentsia; they were afraid to shake our hands too strongly, as the saying goes. But you know, there's a different taste for everybody. My only real admirer in Mezen was Voroshilov.

"He was a short, very stocky man. He used to be an ironworker, and he had very powerful muscles and a powerful chest, and a cute, real Russian peasant face, with a nose a little turned up and high cheekbones. He had a marvelous spirit, always joking, always laughing, and a good character—he wasn't a cruel man, though he occupied a very big position for years in the Communist Party."

Perhaps the years had dimmed my grandmother's memory, or the enormity of what had happened in the Soviet Union had blurred for her in old age. I reminded her that he had been part of Stalin's inner circle, and she nodded silently.

Then again, the leaders of the Soviet Union, at least until the full breadth of Stalin's crimes became apparent in the late 1930s, were managing a project that had its own hypnotic power to captivate the world's attention and seemed to involve some movement toward the good, or at least the better, until everyone found out otherwise. In the early years of the Soviet Union, with the rise of fascism, the left-wing cause in the battles of ideology still seemed to make sense.

And without Voroshilov, the whole story of exile and escape might mostly have been forgotten or faded into a footnote to my grandmother's life. What were the chances that she would meet the man who was later to become one of the leaders of the Soviet Union, in the summer of 1909, in a remote village of political exiles, criminals, and fishermen? Without Voroshilov, my grandmother would never have gone back to Russia, and our family in all likelihood would not have survived the era of Soviet rule. No one would have been there to greet us in 1963, or in the next generation to greet me, in 1998.

Voroshilov was born in a rural settlement in what is now the city of Lysychansk, in eastern Ukraine. He grew up in a peasant family and worked from a young age but managed to enroll in a rural school and acquire an education. At the age of sixteen he began to work in an iron factory and joined the Russian Social-Democratic Labor Party, forerunner of the Bolsheviks and, eventually, the Russian Communist Party. He was arrested and sentenced to exile in Arkhangelsk Province but escaped; in early 1909 he was arrested again and exiled to Mezen. He first met the young Georgian Bolshevik Ioseb Jughashvili—or Joseph Stalin, as he later came to be known—in 1906 at the Social-Democratic Party Congress in Stockholm, where the two young revolutionaries shared a modest hotel room and began their lifelong relationship. He served alongside Stalin during the Red Army's successful defense of the city of Tsaritsyn (later renamed Stalingrad) during the Russian Civil War; in 1925, Stalin appointed him Commissar for Military and Naval Affairs. Demoted from the senior military leadership in the early forties because of Soviet battlefield reverses, he nonetheless remained one of the few so-called old Bolsheviks to survive Stalin's purges. He ended his career as ceremonial head of state of the Soviet Union in 1960 and spent the last years of his life in quiet retirement.

At first it might seem surprising that my grandmother and Voroshilov developed a close relationship. He was not the refined, intellectual type she was naturally drawn to. Part of what brought them together, no doubt, was simply youthful chemistry. The theme of attractive young men weaves through all my grandmother's accounts of life in exile. Voroshilov, in his own bluff way, was handsome, undoubtedly charismatic, and passionate about the Revolution. And he was the nearly the same age as my grandmother—they were both part of the remarkable generation born around 1880. No one was to see the world change as much as they would. Born into the era of the horse and carriage, they lived to see the atomic age. From entirely different backgrounds, they were nonetheless both part of the revolutionary movement that formed in Russia, cutting across class and ethnic lines, and that ultimately changed the world. So perhaps it was perfectly logical that they were captivated by one another, that my grandmother plunged into an affair with the future Political Commissar of the Red Cavalry, the revolutionary comrade of Joseph Stalin and hero of the defense of Tsaritsyn, the People's Commissar of Military and Naval Affairs and Marshal of the Soviet Union: Klim Voroshilov.

The stroke of one clerk's pen sending Rulia to Mezen, and of another's sending Kliment Voroshilov to the same place. Two nearly random acts that determined almost everything that was to follow. Though my grandmother, of course, could have stayed in Mezen. The escape might have failed. If she had, she probably would have married Voroshilov. In the end, he married a different Jewish girl, another exiled revolutionary—Golda Gorbman, sentenced to Arkhangelsk Province for three years for distributing revolutionary propaganda, beginning September 13, 1909.

CHAPTER 30. ESCAPE

My grandmother remembered the adventure of the escape in perfect detail.

"Rulia must have escaped sometime before August 20, because school usually started around then. Since Mezen was nothing but a small village, even though it was called 'city of Mezen,' there was nothing there for children's education, so the wife of the chief of police used to go on the last boat to Arkhangelsk, to settle there for the rest of the year so her children could go to school. And because we knew the family so well, Rulia got a special permit to come to the boat and see me off. I was supposed to leave on the last boat because I wasn't one of the exiles, officially. So that's how Rulia got onto the smaller boat that took us to the steamer for Arkhangelsk. The police were there, too, with the exiles who had finished their sentences and were going to Arkhangelsk, where they could continue on to different places in Russia by rail.

"There were about forty people that August who finished exile, among them was one of the exiles, Dyadya Trofim (meaning 'Uncle Trofim,' a term of affection and respect used by young people for older adults). Dyadya Trofim was a peasant, not an educated man, but he was politically educated.

He was a revolutionary, and eventually he was caught in his revolutionary work and exiled for three years. We met him in Mezen and we became very friendly with him. He always pitied Rulia: 'She will die here among the exiles; you don't know what the winter is like here,' he told me. And really, when the question came about the escape, without Dyadya Trofim it would never have happened.

"Well, the family of the police chief had a cabin. Almost no other passengers had a cabin; most of the people going to Arkhangelsk traveled on the *zwischendeck*, a place that was like the steerage for immigrants coming to America. It was the last boat before the sea freezes over, and suddenly, at the last moment, Rulia was able to come to see me off. And I realized, this was when she had to escape, it was her only chance to leave Mezen before the winter. When we got onto the boat, I immediately went to Dyadya Trofim and told him, this is the only chance for Rulia to escape. And I asked him, 'How should we do it?'

'Didn't you plan it before?' he asked me.

"And so, it was Dyadya Trofim's idea that Rulia should go into the cabin with the police chief's wife and stay there for the whole trip. He told me to open up to her and tell her about my plan. And remember, though she was a policeman's wife she was a Tolstovka, a dreamer, a peculiar woman but very wonderful, and she immediately agreed with me, 'Why of course, Rulia should spend the entire trip with me in my cabin. I will help get her off when we get to Arkhangelsk.'

"Dyadya Trofim had become acquainted with a stoker. A young fellow, I can see him in front of me now. And there were so many revolutionaries there, among the workers and the peasants; so the stoker immediately said, 'Oh it's wonderful, don't worry about it, we'll take care of it and make sure no one on the ship gives her away.' Trofim was a very sociable and kind man, and though he was a peasant, he looked like an aristocrat. I corresponded with him afterwards, and he would always write at the end of his letter, 'I kiss your hand.'

"I brought Rulia to the wife of the police chief and never saw her again for the rest of the trip. She was protected, there was no need to worry about Rulia anymore. I didn't even see her get off the boat. By the time I got off, she was already on the train in Arkhangelsk. She went on to Finland, to our cousin there. I didn't see her again until we met to cross the border into Germany."

In 1963, when my grandmother and I visited her cousin Abrasha at his seaside dacha in Finland, on our way to Leningrad, she never said a word about what had happened in 1909. Perhaps it all just seemed second nature to her, after so many years. Or perhaps the instinct to secrecy remained.

Katya and I read about the escape in a report from the same, now unfortunate, village policeman who had reported my grandmother's arrival a few weeks earlier.

SECRET

From the Mezen police constable to the Gendarme Department of Arkhangelsk Province

August 25, 1909, #163

I hereby report that the political exile under police supervision Rakhil Bamuner disappeared from Mezen on August 20, present whereabouts unknown. These facts have also been communicated by me to the constable in the neighboring village of Pechinin and the constable Zolotarev in Kholmogory.

Some of her things were left in her apartment. The following day, searches and measures to detain her were undertaken, but the efforts were unsuccessful. It is supposed that she may have left on the steamship of the Murmansk company for Arkhangelsk. On the 18th of August she traveled to said steamship to see off her sister, Eda Samuilovna Bamuner, who departed at 19:30 to return to her home and family. On the 19th of August Rakhil Bamuner returned to Mezen, and on the 20th she disappeared.

But Rulia, of course, had never returned to Mezen. My grandmother explained:

"What used to happen is this: in the house in Mezen, and Kholmogory too, all the doors were left open at night, you couldn't lock doors. Early in the morning, the local policeman would come into the house, and he knew how many people were supposed to be there, how many men, how many women. When we left, the people in the house put a dummy where Rulia was supposed to be and covered it up. By the time the police in Mezen realized what had happened and notified the authorities, Rulia was already in Finland. Of course when we arrived in Arkhangelsk, we didn't know what would happen; whether the police had been immediately notified that so many people escaped. But they weren't notified about Rulia until later."

Rulia was not the only one to escape that summer. Two students escaped as well. The village officer was obliged to file another dispatch later the same day:

SECRET

From the Mezen police constable to the Gendarme Department of Arkhangelsk Province

August 25, 1909, #166

I hereby report that the political exiles under police supervision Aleksandr Antipin, Aleksei Lemport, and Rakhil Bamuner disappeared from Mezen on August 20, present whereabouts unknown. Personal details: Antipin, 18 years old, height 1.8 meters, face somewhat pimpled, eyes hazel, hair, mustache and eyebrows light brown, nose ordinary; Lemport, 21 years old, height 1.75 meters, face clear, eyes gray, hair, mustache and eyebrows light brown, nose ordinary; Bamuner, 17 years old, height 1.4 meters, hair and eyebrows black, nose straight, face clear, eyes hazel.

The same hapless officer had already received a warning letter earlier in the month:

From the Arkhangelsk Gendarme to the Mezen police constable

August 15, 1909, #147

*You reported the political exile Koinats missing on
August 13, but he was already seen in Pechinin on
August 10. And you report that he had gone fishing!
You must check on the exiles every day, in person,
and not according to the word of the landlord. You are
hereby issued a strict reprimand. In case of repetition,
you will be sacked.*

My grandmother finished the story:

"Dyadya Trofim had already made all the arrangements for the escape down below, with the stoker. But then I confronted him with two additional escapees. These two students didn't live in Mezen itself, they lived in a village nearby, in another peasant house. One was a powerful big fellow, he looked like a blacksmith, though he was a student. The other was a typical Chekhov intelligentsia. You know, with a blond little beard, a slim face, tall, and very thin. They knew that I was leaving on the boat, and while we didn't see them too often, everyone knows everyone in exile, especially the intelligentsia; and even more rare, two girls. They came to say goodbye, because they knew I was leaving, and found out that Rulia had a permit to see me off. So, suddenly, they got the idea to escape as well, and of course I encouraged them. But the boat started a few miles away from Mezen, because it was too shallow there, you had to go way out for the boat. When the exiles were leaving with the police, they went on big rowboats until they reached the ocean steamer. So the students decided to escape, but how would they get to the boat?

"They lived with a fisherman, and they decided to get into one of the fisherman's rowboats and row to the steamer. They did it at night. I must have known about it, because I told that young stoker that there were two more exiles coming, and he promised to take care of them. I waited for them, with the stoker; everyone was asleep. We heard the splash of oars, and the boat arrived with the two guys. They were immediately taken over by that Russian stoker and placed on the lower deck. We had to change their appearance, because we didn't know whether the police in Arkhangelsk had been notified that people escaped.

"The strong, stocky guy dressed up as a peasant. People helped one another. People used to lug a bag made of heavy linen, which someone gave to him, and some kind of a hat. As for the other guy, the blond fellow, we got shoe polish and made his beard and mustache black. They left everything behind when they stole the rowboat. The main problem was to get them off the boat. We didn't know if we'd be met by a whole bunch of police. There were a lot of police there, uniformed men, but we didn't know if they'd been notified in advance about Rulia and the two guys. For Rulia, it wasn't such a problem, because she went off with a group of schoolteachers. When she left the boat, she had nothing to do anymore with the police chief's family. A group of teachers took Rulia off with entirely new clothes, they gave her a hat and a veil, completely different clothes from what she was wearing on the rowboat. I never saw her; I didn't know who she came off with, or when she came off. I didn't even see Dyadya Trofim anymore, because he went off with the whole group of exiles who were under police guard.

"I went off with the two guys, with the 'peasant' with the sack on his shoulders and his walking stick, and he wore the funniest hat. I walked with the other one, who was made up as a traveling salesman, very nicely dressed, and with the black mustache and little beard. And someone had given him a nice hat, too. When we got into the town, it was very late at night. We were walking through the silent dark street. The only people I knew were the exiles who were under police surveillance. Was it safe to take these guys there? I knew the way to the house where the old lady, the leader of the exiles we met before we went to Kholmogory, lived with Zhenya. I knew I had to get there, to their house, no matter what, and the old lady and Zhenya would take care of things.

"The door, as always, was open. They were asleep. So I woke up Zhenya. 'Where did you come from in the middle of the night!' she asked me. Everything she said or did was very emphatic, like a stick of dynamite going off. 'I have two men; you have to find lodging for them and get them out of Arkhangelsk as soon as possible.'

"They told me to bring the fellow with the shoe polish, which by then was soft and smeared all over him; the peasant remained outside. Zhenya took the peasant to a house somewhere, I never saw him again. The other fellow was taken care of, too, by someone through Zhenya, and I never saw him again either. Arkhangelsk was a port, full of boats going to places all over Russia, Europe, who knows where. They ended up in South America, though they traveled there separately. Later on, I got a few letters from them."

My grandmother made her way back to Riga, avoiding the police, and settled affairs with her father. It was clear she could no longer stay in Russia. At the end of the fall she met Rulia in the small city of Shavli—now Siauliai, in

Lithuania—where their father had made arrangements to have the sisters smuggled across the border.

My grandmother recounted the last of her youthful adventures in Russia:

"Papa arranged everything. We had to cross the German border near a little Jewish town in Lithuania called Shavli. And that town was right on the border of Lithuania and Germany. I can't remember how Rulia got there, all the way from Finland, but that's where we had to meet to go across. I also had to escape Russia. The police came to search the house in Riga, looking for me, because they knew that Rulia and I had escaped.

"There were special agents both among the Jews and the Germans who were paid and who did nothing but help people get across the border. We had to meet a certain man who arranged the time and place for us to go. And on the other side, just across, there was a German agent to receive us. Well, the fellow on the Russian side was a strapping man with big boots up over his knees, like a fisherman. We stayed in his place overnight, we had to sleep on the floor, he put down a lot of *soloma* (my grandmother used the Russian word for straw) for us to sleep. Very early, before dawn, a Jewish fellow came and told us that we had to go a certain spot. I can't remember if he took us there, or maybe we went there by horse. In any case, it was a narrow clearing in the woods, where we had to cross, and as soon as we got across, it would be Germany and we would be free. I suppose my father must have found out all about it, how to find the agent and arrange things. So we went there. I was a terrific adventurer, a revolutionary, it meant going to America to work in a factory like an ordinary worker. That's exactly what I believed in.

"Just before it got light, the agent told us, 'Run!' And we started to run, but then we heard shots being fired and people shouting! But we could see the men on the other side, so we just lifted up our skirts and kept running. And we got to the group of men and they grabbed us, and we were in Germany."

My grandmother never told me exactly how she and Rulia got to America. In the Ellis Island Archive, I found a facsimile of the passenger manifest for a transatlantic steamer of the German American Line, SS Pennsylvania, which contained the names of Eda and Rakhil Bamuner. The sisters arrived in New York on April 12, 1910, from Hamburg, Germany.

CHAPTER 31. LENINGRAD, 1932

My grandmother spoke little English when she arrived in New York, but she adapted to her new life with relative ease. Her background had prepared her well, coming as she did from the multilingual borderlands of Europe where Russia meets the West. As an assimilated Russian Jew, she instinctively knew how to operate across cultures. Functioning in more than one language was second nature to her. In the Baltic city of Riga, where her father had moved and where she lived for a time, people were as likely to speak German, Yiddish, Polish, or Latvian as Russian. There my grandmother spoke the German she had learned in the gymnasium as often as her native Russian. In New York, becoming literate, well-spoken, and well-read in English presented no great challenge.

Of course New York at that time was bursting with millions of new arrivals whose sheer numbers allowed them to acculturate and blend in rapidly. In New York at the beginning of the twentieth century, there was nothing terribly exotic about having been born abroad or speaking another language besides English. Rather like today.

Three years later, my grandmother met my grandfather, another assimilated Russian Jew who had recently arrived.

In 1913, they married, and their first son, my father, was born in 1915.

As much as my grandmother embraced her new life, she never really left Russia behind. Most of her family, with whom she corresponded regularly, was still there. Travel by steamship was relatively easy; with enough time and money, one could go back and forth and maintain ties. For Americans, Europe was remarkably inexpensive after the economic collapse of World War I (and remained that way, in different forms, until the 1960s; its bounty of history, culture and the diversity and charm of everyday life easily accessible to people with dollars—one of the features of the so-called American century, which still held sway when I was growing up, gone and forgotten though it is today).

In the early 1920s, travel to Russia, still in chaos after the Revolution and Civil War, was virtually impossible. But Latvia, where my great-grandfather lived, had become independent from Russia and was relatively stable. In 1922, my grand-mother, her husband, and seven-year-old son, my father, left for Riga to visit the family for several months. Her siblings who lived in Petrograd, as St. Petersburg had been renamed after the beginning of World War I, traveled to Latvia to meet her. Given my grandfather's lifelong lack of interest in working too hard, leaving his drugstore in the hands of an assistant who was tasked to forward a modest monthly stipend to support the family while they were abroad was an easy choice.

They returned home—to find the drugstore nearly run into the ground, but my grandfather managed to start another—and my uncle was born at the end of 1924. By then Rulia was married and gave birth to a child, Sonia, at nearly the same time. Within a few years Rulia and her husband divorced, and by then my grandparents had begun to go their separate ways as well. My grandmother, Rulia, and their two young children lived next door to one another and spoke only Russian at home. The family Russian brigade was born.

By the end of the 1920s, the Soviet Union had transformed dramatically. The postwar debates about how to revive the economy—whether to allow the existence of small private enterprise alongside state control of the major industries, whether farmers and peasants should be permitted to manage land independently and sell their produce—had been definitively resolved. Stalin decreed that Russia should fulfill the policy of "Socialism in One Country" with a "revolution from above." The state would exert full control; mass industrialization and the collectivization of agriculture were to be achieved rapidly.

The Soviet Union declared its first Five Year Plan in 1928. When it began, Russia was the world's fifth industrial power; by 1932, ahead of schedule, it had become the second, surpassed only by the U.S. Massive new factories were built to achieve the production quotas, many with the help of American material, expertise, and labor. As the Great Depression settled over the U.S. and Western Europe, the rapid growth of the Soviet Union seemed almost miraculous. There was even a movement among unemployed American workers to emigrate to Russia. The Soviet Union as it would come to be known to the world—the land of giant factories and dams, a huge armaments industry, collective farms, propaganda campaigns exhorting workers to build socialism and defeat "the imperialist wreckers"—came into being in those years. It would take much longer for the genocide in Ukraine that accompanied agricultural collectivization, the Holodomor, to become known. As it would for the horrors of Stalin's terror and the Gulag.

If ever there was a moment when people viewed the Soviet Union sympathetically, it was the early 1930s. Americans went there—Margaret Bourke White, the Reuther brothers, engineers, scientists, and laborers with leftist views. Europeans went—Le Corbusier, Gide, George Bernard Shaw. Many wrote glowingly of what they saw, though some left disillusioned. By the end of the thirties, the scales had fallen from most people's eyes.

Russia, after all, had always had that outsize scale, with its outsize pull. Before the Revolution, through the nineteenth century, there was a sense that Russia could change world culture and history. It seems hard to remember now, with the country so diminished materially, culturally, geopolitically, and morally over the decades following—and preceding—the dissolution of the Soviet Union. But in the early thirties, after twenty years of chaos and decline, Russia once again seemed poised to change the world. There was a great urge to go there, to see it, be part of it, to help it along if you believed in the ideals. Which my grandmother did. Until she learned better, like so many others.

For my grandmother, there were also the family ties, which were stronger in Russia than in America. The closeness, the engagement of people within the family was taken for granted. I inherited that two generations later; it was something I felt with my Russian cousins more than my American ones. And there was the quality of human relations in Russia in general—passionate, intense, engaged. My grandmother was attuned to that way of being with people. Not at all the same as in America.

And so, my grandmother—with her marriage failing, her older son preparing to leave home for college, her sister's marriage also ended; with both their children speaking Russian as well as English and all of them longing to see their Russian relatives and understand what life was like in the Soviet Union—decided to leave for Russia. For a year? Permanently? I never got the chance to ask her directly; but I'm not sure that when they left even she really knew.

The only problem was, how to get the necessary visas? Moving to Russia was not a simple matter. Soviet bureaucracy (proclivity for bureaucracy is a Russian national trait, noted from the time of Gogol on down) combined with a mindset of suspicion and paranoia, especially of foreigners, could make the process daunting. Alek—my older cousin (the son of my grandmother's brother Volya) who had been disappointed that by the time he decided to write his memoirs in the 1990s it was too late to reveal the horrors of life under Communism because others had already done so, but who wrote it anyway, recording in captivating style (in my copy, he placed a neat little insert at the front which reads, "To all my relations in America, knowing how to read Russian—Alek") his memories of life in Leningrad from the time he was a boy in the 1920s onwards—provides his recollection of the events leading up to the visit of his American relatives:

"When Eugene and Sonia were no longer infants, Eda and Rulia started to think about going with them to the Soviet Union for an extended stay. Not only to visit their brothers and sisters and to get to know their children, but to plunge into the life of the country where the Socialist Revolution had taken place—fulfilling, as it seemed to them from faraway America, the freedom-loving dreams of their youth."

Alek, like his father before him and my cousin Sergey after—three generations in succession—loathed the Soviet system with every fiber of his being his entire life, as he reminds the reader in the preface to his memoirs. He forgivingly mentions the difference in vantage point—"faraway America"—when describing the political inclinations of his American aunts; and emphasizes, with his light touch of sarcasm, the glaring mismatch between "freedom-loving" and "Socialist Revolution."

He continues:

"The required formalities, however, turned out to be very complicated, insofar as the 'Homeland of the Workers,' where the oppressed of the earth were supposed to be able to flow in through wide-open gates, in fact put up a fence with the rest of the world that grew higher every year.

"The Leningrad authorities were unwilling to take responsibility for such a serious matter—letting two American women with young children into the country. In the end, Arkady turned to Kliment Efremovich Voroshilov, People's Commissar of Military and Naval Affairs and Chairman of the Revolutionary Military Council of the USSR."

Sasha had shown me his copy of Arkady's letter, with Voroshilov's affirmative response, when I was in St. Petersburg. With Voroshilov's approval, the necessary documents were obtained.

At which point Alek concludes, "This letter with the instructions of Voroshilov, ratified with the official stamp of the People's Commissariat, not only allowed Eda and Rulia to receive long-term visas for themselves and the children, but also served as a safe conduct pass for the entire Bamuner clan over the course of several decades of Soviet totalitarianism. From the original, copy after copy was made; copies which Arkady, Senya, and my father repeatedly attached, when filling out various official forms and questionnaires, in connection with their positive response to the inevitable question, Do you have any relatives abroad?"

And so, twenty years after sailing into New York Harbor as refugees from the tsarist autocracy, as two idealistic youngsters, one twenty-one and the other seventeen years old—on their own, with no children, with the new life they had created for themselves still entirely ahead and unknown—now, twenty years later, the sisters with their two seven-year-old children sailed again under the Statue of Liberty, but this time in the opposite direction, toward the country they had left, now reinvented as the Union of Soviet Socialist Republics, as if full-born from the foreheads of Lenin, Trotsky, and Stalin, but in some profound way, still Russia as it had always been. When my grandmother left Russia, a soviet was a local council of workers, a raucous debating society of hundreds and, occasionally, no more than a few thousand individuals operating under their own direction, a self-governing collective. She was returning now to a vast new nation-state of Soviet Socialist Republics; the idea, the reality that the revolutionary mass meetings of her youth had been transformed into the official, power-wielding organs of a world-harrowing behemoth, that the soviets of old, now spelled with a capital S, were the ceremonial, official bodies of a great state, a great endeavor of workers striving to change human history, to change human beings themselves: this conferred a quality to the voyage that made it much more than a touristic family visit. She was on her way to visit her own past and, simultaneously, to witness the unfolding of a new future. The two somehow blended together into one tableau. Russia, it seemed, was managing to be both.

They disembarked at Cherbourg and traversed Europe by train, crossing the border from Germany into Lithuania and continuing on to Leningrad. A journey in reverse from the one they had taken twenty years earlier, into a world that had been shattered and remade by war, revolution, and the end of empire. The world my grandmother left had in many ways changed beyond recognition, but to her still looked and somehow felt the same.

They arrived in Leningrad in late June. For the first time they saw the large, still rather elegant (for its time and place) apartment that Volya had rented for himself in 1917; before being joined, during the twenties, by his brother Arkady and two sisters, Lilya and Lyosha. The gradual communalization of the apartment on Vladimirsky always reminded me of the scene in *Dr. Zhivago* when Zhivago returns to Moscow to find that his in-laws' luxurious two-floor apartment has been taken over by the Agricultural Academy and other new occupants, since a family no longer needs more than one room to live in. "Oh, and we don't call them 'rooms' anymore," his wife informs him. "It's called 'living space' now."

The Bamuners managed to create their own communal apartment—one family to a room—thereby protecting it from expropriation by the authorities. When my grandmother arrived, Volya and Nina were living in one bedroom with their two children; Arkady and Lyolya with their one child in another; and the two single sisters Lilya and Lyosha each in a small spare room. The arrival of the Americans raised the number of occupants to thirteen. Everyone shared the single toilet, bathroom, and kitchen. Just as they still did when we visited in 1963.

Alek recalls from his childhood that the apartment was furnished in rather grand style—apparently Volya and Arkady had managed to acquire and keep some elegant turn-of-the-century furniture and accessories. The large communal dining room, able to seat twenty-four when the table was opened out, had several buffets brimming with porcelain and glassware. According to Alek's recollections, most of it was traded or sold for food during the Siege of Leningrad. By the time we came in 1963, some remained, and the table could still be opened out; but there was only a faint echo of the by-then storied prewar comfort.

Arrangements were made to accommodate the newcomers. Arkady and Lyolya moved temporarily into the dining room, giving their bedroom to my grandmother and Rulia. The five children slept together in the little room, known as the nursery, next to the kitchen. But the Americans had arrived in late June. The primary order of business was not getting settled into the apartment on Vladimirsky Prospekt. It was time to move for the summer to the family dacha in Tarkhovka.

The little summer village of Tarkhovka sat on a narrow strip of land between the Gulf of Finland to the west, and the shore of a large inland lake to the east. Two unpaved streets ran its length, with a few small lanes between. On one side a steep slope ran down to the lakeshore. The slope was partly overgrown with pine trees and partly covered by open sand dunes. The village streets were lined with prerevolutionary wooden dachas, each with a veranda in front. The windows giving onto the verandas were filled with colored glass that sparkled and subtly changed color, according to the time of day, in the summer sun.

By the summer of 1932, Alek recalls, only a few dachas were still in private hands. The other owners had been washed away by the revolutionary wave, as he puts it—their houses passing to public ownership, with many falling into disrepair.

The trip to the dacha at Tarkhovka was a yearly affair. After a few days of preparation gathering linens, tableware, and bedding, a rented horse-drawn cart would appear in front of Vladimirsky, no. 8. The household belongings were loaded aboard, and the driver set out on the thirty-kilometer trip north. The family went to the Finland Station and boarded the train. When they arrived, a few hours later, the horse and cart stood waiting for them at the station.

They rented the dacha from a family named Bobrov, Alek recalled. It was a large two-story house with separate wings, each housing one family. In the summer of 1932, the Leningrad Bamuners made room for their sisters, nephew, and niece from America.

Playing on the seashore, boat trips along the lake—the serene dacha life that was carried on amidst the tumultuous atmosphere of Stalinist Russia was like a little cove of shelter in the reeds at the edge of a raging, torrential river. Hearing about the rich personal life of my relatives—summer games, picnics, theatricals, family photographs, love affairs, quarrels—I always felt a kind of wonderment at how they were able to live so privately, in such ordinary fashion, in the middle of the storm that was the political life, the history of their country.

My great-uncle Senya, the artistic photographer who perished in 1942 during the Siege, spent part of the summer with the family and left behind a trove of photographs. When Alek showed them to me, the scenes of the family by the seashore, in the woods, sitting on the veranda of the dacha, and gathered together in the evening for an amateur theatrical directed by Arkady, with the intense summer light captured in stark black and white, immediately reminded me of Bergman—*Wild Strawberries*, or *Smiles of a Summer Night*.

One morning in August 1998, when the Central Library was closed and Katya and I had a day off, I asked Alek if he could show me where the family had gone to spend the summer at the dacha in Tarkhovka. He thought for a moment in his methodical, engineer-like way, as if performing a calculation of pros and cons, then responded affirmatively. And added, in a somewhat melancholy tone, "I haven't been back since I was a child."

Alek, his son Volodya, grandson Sasha, and I climbed into Volodya's Renault—I was still getting used to the new, post-Soviet Russia where a professional like Volodya could actually earn a decent living and own a decent car, neither of which had been remotely possible in Soviet times—and set out on the drive north. The city slipped away, replaced by pine woods and glimpses of the morning sunshine glancing off the shallow water of the Gulf of Finland.

An hour later, we arrived. We drove along Sovietskaya Street. Nothing seemed familiar, Alek reported. He looked around, squinting in the sun, pondering the connection of the scene before him to anything he had known in the past.

At the end of the street, we reached the top of a sand dune falling away to the lakefront. The lake extended for miles; the surface of its blue-brown water, a mosaic of sunlight and shadow reflecting the cloud-flecked sky overhead, rippled in the light breeze. On the far shore, a sandbar extended from the water's edge into the woods. "Yes, that's where Uncle Senya took those pictures," Alek suddenly exclaimed.

"But where was our house? Where was the way we took down to the water?" he asked forlornly. The four of us climbed down the dune and walked along a path at the edge of the marsh, through the wet, green woods. "The house was up there, on the crest of the hill, I think. I'm not sure exactly where."

We started back up toward the street. A woman with her six- or seven-year-old daughter was walking in the woods, collecting mushrooms. Alek hailed her and walked over to see if she might be able to help. He described the street where he thought his house used to be. She said that she had been spending summers there since the 1950s; based on Alek's description, she replied, "Oh yes, it should still be up there. Over that way," she added, pointing.

We reached the upper street and stopped in front of a large new house under construction, surrounded by an ugly, high brick wall. "New Russians," Alek muttered, using the derisive term applied by cultured folk like himself to the post-Soviet nouveau riche.

Suddenly Alek's memory was triggered. Below us was a field with a summer camp where counselors were forming the children up in rows and organizing games. "That's where, on weekends, the local factory workers came, in big open trucks. A brass band played, and they all drank and danced and got drunk.

"And that's where we left for the picnic on the other shore," he continued, gazing at the lake shore below the field. When we got back to the city, he showed me the pictures, taken by Senya, of himself and my uncle as skinny seven-year-olds, smiling at the camera and covered in sand.

As we stood in front of the ugly new half-built house, Alek began to look intently at the house next door. "That was our house," he said suddenly.

"Yes, that's where father sat for the picture where he's holding me and Milochka." (The childhood name for my grandmother's beloved niece Mila.) Everything about the house had changed—there was a new roof, new windows, new siding—except for the porch and the entryway, where Volya had sat with his children for the picture. It was difficult to see the house clearly; it looked uninhabited and was surrounded by a thick, unkempt growth of bushes and trees. The new windows were made of clear glass with leaded latticework, seemingly intended to bring a touch of elegance but achieving the opposite effect. Alek looked disconsolately at the scene. So little remained of what he recalled from the days of his cherished childhood visits.

"There used to be more colored glass," he said, dispiritedly. And as we left the village, we drove past the local church. "Completely different appearance," he concluded, dismissively.

In September, my grandmother and Rulia went to Sochi on the Black Sea coast to enjoy the "autumn season" for a few weeks. (In Russian, "autumn season" in the south has its own adjective, translating not as "autumn" but as "velvety.") When they got back to Leningrad, my grandmother set about establishing a more permanent life for herself. She and my uncle could not live in the cramped quarters of Valdimirsky Prospekt indefinitely, and if she were to stay on in the Soviet Union, she would need to find work.

Despite months of effort, she could not find a place of her own. The chronic shortage of housing in the big cities combined with labyrinthine formalities and bureaucratic delays made it almost impossible, the difficulties only redoubling for a foreigner. Citing her bilingualism and skill as a translator, she applied for work at the Amtorg (short for "American Trade" in Russian, the organization that handled all the USSR's business dealings with the U.S.), but this attempt, too, was unsuccessful. (Interestingly—there was always a hint of intrigue surrounding my grandmother's dealings with Russia—after she returned home to New York she actually was hired by Amtorg.)

In April of 1933, my grandmother wrote to my father, already away at college in Wisconsin:

Dear Lenny boy,

To get living quarters is about the hardest thing possible here. I got a very special request sent from Moscow to the proper authorities; it has been here in Leningrad for over two months, but so far they can do nothing. Here one must develop an enormous amount of patience. There are such immense and very vital problems to be solved that the unhappiness or dissatisfaction of a mere individual can never be taken into account. And I am only a very minute, unimportant individual in this gigantic, struggling, aim-achieving mass of people.

> *Your pop writes to me that if I cannot get settled in the Soviet Union I should come back. Lyonchik (Russian endearment for Leonard), I cannot think about it! Russia is my home, to which I am tied with a million of invisible, but very strong, powerful attachments and strings.*
>
> *Eugene is very lonesome after you. I am sending you his letter; he wrote it all by himself [in Russian]. He is very much concerned about your Russian, and often asks me: "How will Lenny speak to people here, did he not forget his Russian? Can't he study Russian in college?"*
>
> *Please send me a photo of yourself. I am still waiting for my photograph to be made, and Eugene's, to send to you. But Senya is our photographer, and he is a real Russian, so there you are.*

By the end of the spring, my grandmother still had not found a job or a place of her own to live. After spending some time with their father at the family dacha on the Riga seashore, where they had spent their last summer before Rulia's arrest, the sisters decided to return home with their young children to New York.

Alek remembers:

"My mother told me, when I was an adult, how she used to look at Eugene and me as children and think, 'Here are two children playing together, first cousins, but how different their fates will be.'

"I mentioned this to Eugene when we were both already close to sixty-five. 'True,' Eugene answered, 'but my fate could have been completely different and certainly much worse. You may not be aware that my mom was seriously considering staying in the USSR permanently, and that it was only with great difficulty that she was finally convinced otherwise.'

"In fact, I had never heard that before. But one can only imagine, if they had stayed, what a tragic fate not only the Americans but the entire Bamuner clan would have met. I perfectly remember the spy mania of the late thirties. I believe that all the adults would have been turned to labor camp dust, and that the children would have been sent to specialized orphanages for enemies of the people."

"Timely," the Academician Ganelin had commented, when I told him my grandmother left in 1933.

CHAPTER 32. TIME PAST AND TIME PRESENT

Among the many things I discovered during the months I spent in Russia, there was one I did not uncover in a library, archive, or old newspaper. It was something I had sensed when I traveled to Leningrad with my grandmother in 1963 but could not yet put into words.

Only during my extended stay in Russia over the summer and fall of 1998, amidst a world that felt in many ways unchanged from 1963, and long before that, but was in reality changed completely, did I finally become conscious of the thing I had been looking for in the blank-slate world of suburbia when I was a child; the thing I had felt when I spent time with my grandmother in Mohegan and New York.

The simultaneity of time.

So much of what we experience in places that are precious to us is defined by the simultaneity of time. Our experience of those places is shaped as much by the beauty of the buildings and streets and trees as we look at them, by the weather that day, the color of the sky and the degree of whiteness of the clouds, as by what we know of the past, what we feel because of what happened there before; which makes the buildings and streets and trees more beautiful, and imbues them with meaning, making us feel we better understand where we are and how we got there.

During my trip to Russia in 1998, I experienced the past in two ways. One was by visiting the archives in St. Petersburg and Arkhangelsk, spending time in those cities looking at the places that had changed so little from the time of my grandmother's youth. And the other, by reading the documents describing the actual events that had occurred almost a century earlier, the things my grandmother had experienced and done, written at exactly the time they happened. It was like seeing my grandmother's story from two different vantage points simultaneously. Like looking out from one of the two moving trains of Relativity, watching the movement of the other, without quite being aware of one's own motion. Which can slow time, but not stop it.

A few months after my return to New York, one afternoon in the early spring, I passed by Lincoln Center. The faces on the posters in the glass cases out front had changed—no more Leonard Bernstein—but the stately travertine buildings and plaza looked the same as they had the day I came up from the subway to go visit my grandmother for my first Russian lesson. Looking up Broadway I could see the towers of the Ansonia Hotel where I used to go on Saturdays for my piano lessons.

I started to walk down 66th Street. The long, gradual slope of the block fell away to the shimmering expanse of the Hudson River beyond. At the corner of West End Avenue,

I looked at the bus shelter where my grandmother used to wait, elegantly dressed and holding her patent leather pocketbook, for the bus that took her to Lexington Avenue and 59th Street, to Bloomingdale's, that most European-style of her Manhattan outings, as if she were going to shop at the KaDeWe in Berlin or Galeries Lafayette in Paris.

I stood in front of her old building. The bright red color of the brick from the years after she moved in had faded to a burnished auburn; the original stripling trees were now several stories high, their long branches spreading out in front of the building's once-bare façade. The little balcony I used to look up to as I was leaving—where my grandmother usually came out to wave goodbye—had been enclosed to serve as an extra room, its shades drawn.

I looked toward the glassed-in lobby and caught a glimpse of my reflection, as I had that summer morning in 1963 when I came to meet my grandmother for our trip to Russia.

The two images in the glass, the image of my grandmother waiting at the bus shelter, of the two of us on the back terrace in Mohegan in the late afternoon as my grandmother painted; of us together in the hotel lobbies in Helsinki and Leningrad; of my grandmother's apartment on 66th Street with its Russian hutch; of the family apartment on Vladimirsky Prospekt—all of the images appeared before me in one form or another, fleeting but present, separate but simultaneous, evanescent but permanent.

The whole vast tapestry, with my grandmother's story the luminous golden thread at the center.

ACKNOWLEDGMENTS

My heartfelt gratitude to the academics in Russia who generously shared their time and expertise to help me explore the past. After courageously opening areas of previously forbidden research in the relatively free Russia of the 1990s, some later became victims of harassment and persecution by the Putin regime, committed as it is to rewriting history and suppressing any examination of the country's past misdeeds. Without such a reckoning, Russian society will never recover.

My gratitude also to my Russian cousins, who hosted me during my stays in St. Petersburg and Moscow and followed my research with enthusiasm. Thanks to those at Columbia University, especially Michael Stanislawski and the late Mark von Hagen, who advised me on accessing archival sources and provided introductions to Russian colleagues. I gratefully acknowledge invaluable background material drawn from Benjamin Nathans's remarkable study of the life of Jews in late nineteenth century Russia, *Beyond the Pale*, and Abraham Ascher's definitive history, *The Revolution of 1905*.

Special thanks to my dear friend and wise, patient editor and advisor, Leslie Daniels. And lastly, my thanks to all my Russian friends, people devoted to decency and to intellectual and artistic pursuits, the very best of the traditions of Russian culture, now under severe stress. I hope as ardently as they do for the restoration of those values to the center of Russian life.

Stephen Saletan was born in New York City and raised in the suburbs of Long Island. As a young child he was captivated by his Russian grandmother's stories of her youth in the old Russian city of Pskov and the revolutionary activities that led to her emigration to America. When he was thirteen he traveled with her to the Soviet city of Leningrad where he met his Russian relatives and learned more about the family's past.

After finishing his undergraduate work, he attended Harvard Medical School and completed his post-graduate training in oncology. He began his medical career at Cornell University Medical Center in New York and later served on the faculty of the State University of New York at Stony Brook. In the 1990s he earned a degree in journalism from Columbia University, studied Russian at Middlebury College, and returned to Russia to research his family's story.

He is the author and co-author of numerous medical research articles and reviews. *To the Midnight Sun* is his first book.

www.ingramcontent.com/pod-product-compliance
Lightning Source LLC
Chambersburg PA
CBHW050315160726
48002CB00001B/38